Canyon Country

Prehistoric
ROCK ART

by
F.A. Barnes

P9-CZV-216

An illustrated guide to viewing,
understanding and appreciating
the rock art of the
prehistoric Indian cultures
of Utah, the Great Basin and
the general Four Corners region

ANOTHER
CANYON COUNTRY
GUIDE BOOK

1982
Wasatch Publishers, Inc.

**This book is the FOURTEENTH in a series
of practical guides to travel and recreation
in the scenic Colorado Plateau region of
the Four Corner states.**

All written material, charts, maps and photographs in this book are by
F. A. Barnes unless otherwise credited.

Sketches by Terry Lan

CONTENTS

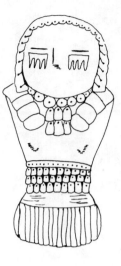

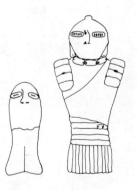

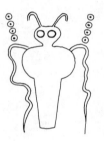

Cultural Calendar . . . . . **inside back cover**

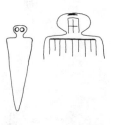

Horseshoe Canyon, Canyonlands National Park.

Indian Creek Canyon, Utah.

FOREWORD

An earlier Wasatch Publishers book, *Canyon Country Prehistoric Indians,* takes a broad look at the prehistoric occupants of Utah and the general Four Corners region, the Anasazi and Fremont cultures, and provides practical guidance to viewing the protected remnants of these cultures — their ruins, artifacts and rock art. For a once-over-lightly review of these subjects, readers are referred to this earlier book.

The subject of prehistoric rock art, however, proved to be so fascinating to a wide spectrum of historians, artists, anthropologists, scholars and the general public that Wasatch Publishers decided to produce a book entirely devoted to this challenging subject, a book large enough to permit the subject to be explored in more depth. Quite naturally, we asked Mr. F. A. (Fran) Barnes, the author and editor of our first very popular volume on Canyon Country prehistory, to write and edit this second book, too.

The author's intent in this book is to summarize the state of knowledge concerning the difficult study of the rock art of the prehistoric Anasazi and Fremont Indian cultures, to cover ground that could not be covered in the earlier book. To do this, he absorbed hundreds of scientific books and papers on the subject, scanned numerous popular books and articles and discussed the subject in depth with many specialists, by letter and in person.

In this book, the author tries to summarize for the average reader the hard knowledge, generally accepted theories, working hypotheses and analytical techniques that currently dominate serious rock art research. He also serves now and then as a "Devil's Advocate," criticizing research methods and trends from the viewpoint of his own considerable technical background and field experience in Four Corners region backcountry. Such criticism is, of course, intended to encourage improved scientific discipline in the study of rock art, something which has all too often been lacking in this particular field of research.

In addition to his literature research, personal communications and field observations, the author solicited direct written input from several leading researchers in the field of prehistoric rock art and from the various public authorities who are charged by law with protecting and studying rock art, such as certain federal and state land administration agencies, universities and museums.

Author Fran Barnes is well qualified to summarize the present state of knowledge about Anasazi and Fremont rock art. Prior to moving to the Four Corners region, he spent several decades in the aerospace industry as an engineer specializing in writing, editing and reviewing scientific and engineering documentation, and translating such technical literature into detailed procedures understandable to production and inspection personnel with limited technical backgrounds.

Since settling in Canyon Country in the mid 1960s, Fran Barnes has devoted full time to studying, exploring and photographing this unique and fascinating region and to sharing his enthusiasm for its myriad wonders with others by way of hundreds of magazine articles and the popular Canyon Country series of guide books and maps by Wasatch Publishers.

Melvin E. Davis
Wasatch Publishers, Inc.

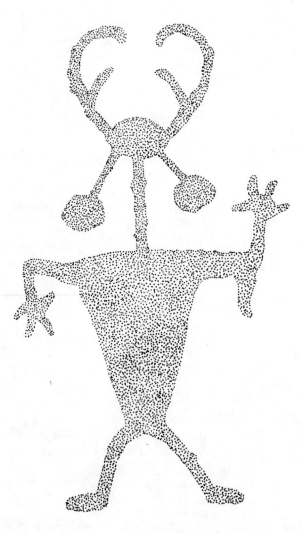

ACKNOWLEDGMENTS

While organizing the contents of this book, the publisher and I agreed that it would be appropriate for us to extend to the archaeologists of the many special areas within the Anasazi and Fremont cultural region the opportunity to contribute summaries concerning the rock art in their areas. Federal and state laws grant exclusive rights to the preservation and study of archaeological sites on public land to the land administration agencies and to academic organizations such as universities and museums. We thus felt it would be appropriate to give such specialists the chance to summarize the rock art situation in their special areas, especially since in most cases their knowledge has been acquired either directly or indirectly at public expense.

Most of the federal and state agencies contacted cooperated wholeheartedly, and we are taking this opportunity to thank them publicly. The summaries submitted by these field experts are printed in the photograph chapter of this book, each at the beginning of its own geographic section. In many cases, those who contributed summaries also loaned the use of representative photographs. A few dedicated contributors even took new photographs especially for this book. We offer a very special "thanks" for these very cooperative public employees.

We also wish to thank most sincerely the several amateur and professional rock art enthusiasts who agreed to write summaries for this book about certain areas or special subjects, in a few instances as substitutes for public land agencies that declined to cooperate. Our thanks, also, to the Rocky Mountain Regional Office of the National Park Service for encouraging the publication of this book, even though it declined to assist.

Of the public land administration agencies who did not provide information about the rock art in their special areas, a few could not because they simply had no one available who was knowledgeable, even though by law such agencies are required to inventory, study and protect the archaeological values on the land they administer. The failure to do this, by all too many public land administration agencies, is a major problem in the area of identifying, protecting and studying America's rapidly vanishing cultural heritage.

Other agencies who declined to honor our request did so out of a reluctance to publicly admit the existence of rock art within their areas. They declined out of the belief that the rock art sites could be protected by suppressing the knowledge of their existence in federal parks and on other public land. While we are happy to recognize and acknowledge the sincerity and concern of public officials who are trying to protect archaeological values on public land, we question both the effectiveness and legality of attempting to protect them by withholding information about them from the public.

As one who for more than a decade has observed and written about the impact of modern American culture upon the vanishing remnants of our historic and prehistoric cultures, I take the position that suppressing public knowledge of cultural remnants is not the best way to protect them, and that all attempts to do so will prove futile in the long run. It has been my observation, for example, that all too many rock art sites are already known to the principal forces of destruction — individual vandalism and development activities. It is rare to find a rock art site that has not already been vandalized by bullet pits or by the addition of modern names, dates and graffiti applied using paint or metal tools, and an appalling number of rock art sites have long since been totally destroyed by various industrial development activities. I believe that informing Americans who have a positive, protective interest in such sites will tend to balance such destructiveness with public concern, and thus increase the probability that the responsible land administration agencies will take effective action to protect the sites from further damage and loss.

Even though I believe that cultural heritage protection is better served by education than by the suppression of knowledge, this book does not give specific rock art site locations except where they are already protected and the responsible administrative agencies have provided for public visitation. In this book, I will strive to interest people in canyon country rock art who will help protect and preserve this endlessly fascinating aspect of the region's prehistory. Any serious rock art scholar who may need to visit the actual site of any rock art depicted in this book is welcome to contact me directly. My personal knowledge and extensive files of rock art photographs are always available for research purposes.

Fran Barnes

INTRODUCTION

THE LAND AND ITS PEOPLE

This book is about the prehistoric rock art of canyon country, a subject that is proving to be fascinating to a great many people for almost as many reasons. Rock art, both prehistoric and historic, is found throughout the West, and indeed throughout all of the Western Hemisphere, but for practical purposes this book has been limited to the two prehistoric American Indian cultures that occupied the least known and last explored region of North America, the canyon country of Utah and the general Four Corners region.

The geography and geology of this rugged, broken, high desert region is described in another Wasatch Publishers guidebook, *Canyon Country Geology*. Its wildlife, vegetation and special ecosystems are detailed in a companion guide book, *Canyon Country Hiking and Natural History*. Another book in this series, *Canyon Country Prehistoric Indians*, provides an overview of the region's two principal prehistoric cultures and contains sections about such surviving cultural remnants as ruins, artifacts and rock art. Following is a book length expansion upon that earlier rock art chapter.

It is appropriate in this book, however, to give a brief description of this unusual region and those who inhabited it during prehistoric times, and to define the cultural, geographical and temporal parameters that have been adopted in order to limit the size of the book.

For millennia, the present state of Utah, and a considerable region within the adjoining states of Arizona, Colorado, Nevada and New Mexico, was occupied by Amerind tribesmen in an early stage of cultural development that archaeologists called "Desert Archaic" or simply "Archaic." These primitive people lived at the subsistence level by collecting or hunting almost any kind of plant or animal that was edible. They had no agriculture. They were essentially nomadic and moved around seasonally, seeking edible plant products and game. Winter often brought malnutrition, starvation or even death for weaker individuals. This kind of life was hazardous and difficult for individuals but was ideally suited to species survival within the rugged country they occupied.

The land itself was unique in many ways and geographically isolated. It was defined on the east by the soaring Rocky Mountains, on the north and northwest by the Uinta Mountains, the Wasatch Range and the Great Salt Lake desert, on the west by the forbidding deserts of the Great Basin and on the south by the various mountain ranges that lie across central Arizona and extend on eastward into New Mexico. The mountains, plains and deserts that surrounded this vast high-desert region were all sparsely occupied or used by other tribes. Because of its generally inhospitable nature, these tribes had little reason to enter the region, at least not until the Anasazi and Fremont cultures had developed to a level that made trading and raiding worthwhile. Hunting and foraging was better elsewhere, so the early

Anasazis and Fremonts were largely left to themselves.

Fremont territory, mainly the region that is now Utah northwest of the Colorado River, was mountainous to the north but with many semi-arid valleys, canyon systems and basins. To the west, the mountains and high plateaus phased into the Great Basin, a vast, arid expanse of desert set with minor mountain ranges that lies between the Wasatch range in central Utah and the Sierra Nevada range in California and stretches from Oregon south into Mexico. The southeastern part of the Fremont territory was also rugged and semi-arid, or worse, except for the bordering mountains and such "island" ranges as the Henry Mountains.

Other than the mountains, the area was heavily eroded and deeply cut by the many tributaries of the Colorado River that penetrated the high desert plateau country. Long tributary rivers such as the Green, Price, San Rafael, Fremont, Dirty Devil, Escalante and Paria and their equally deep branches made any kind of long distance travel in the region difficult, even on foot.

The rugged, broken, generally arid nature of the non-mountainous terrain made living in their region difficult for the Fremonts. Once they gave up a nomadic life and adopted agriculture, they needed relatively level, arable land, reliable water sources and a reasonably long growing season for their developing agrarian lifestyle. This eliminated most of the mountainous areas. But within the lower terrain, suitable land and water were also rare, to be found only in small patches and strips along rivers and streams or near reliable springs. It was not a land or life to be envied by anyone, let alone the nomadic tribes that still surrounded them to the east, west and north. Yet the Fremonts persevered. If they did not thrive, at least they were better off than when they had tried to wrest a living from the same land by hunting and foraging. Now, at least they ate better and had time and energy for other pursuits. This is how agriculture supports the growth of civilization.

In many ways, the Fremonts seemed to emulate what they saw to the south, where the Anasazis were busily building a very desirable civilization within a land almost as inhospitable. Anasazi territory began at the south end of the Fremont region, at or not far north of the vast, complex gorge of

12

the Colorado River. From there, it extended on south into what is now northern Arizona and on east into the northwestern corner of New Mexico and the southwestern corner of Colorado. Virtually all of the Anasazi region was arid or semi-arid, broken by deep and complex canyon systems, set with forbidding plateaus and punctuated by a few "island" mountain ranges such as the Abajos, La Sals, the Kaibab Plateau and Navajo Mountain. As in the Fremont region to the north, arable land was scarce and widely scattered, and as the Anasazi culture took root and developed, its villages, pueblos and subcultural groups were also widely scattered.

The concept of agriculture with its attendant cultural changes was first introduced into the Anasazi and Fremont region around two thousand years ago. The idea probably came from the more advanced cultures to the south in what are now Mexico and Central America. As might be supposed, this major innovation took root at different times within the region, earlier in the south and later to the north. Archaeologists call this next cultural phase the "Formative," because it brings with it a series of interrelated stages of development.

The first of these steps was from a largely nomadic existence to one based within a fairly limited area of terrain, a patch of arable land plus the amount of surrounding land that could practically be used for hunting and gathering from a farm-village base. As the following centuries passed, the region's people developed better agricultural practices, phased from basketry into pottery, learned to build more sophisticated dwellings and other structures, created or adopted more complex religious beliefs and practices, developed trade and in general progressed down the road toward civilization.

Because of their geographic isolation from other tribes and from each other, the various cultural subgroups within the region did not all travel this "road" at the same speed, nor did they all even start at the same time. In general, the people who lived in the vicinity of the Colorado River and on to the south and east were the most progressive. Archaeologists have labeled this dynamic group of prehistoric Indians the "Anasazis," a Navajo term for "Ancient Ones." In their heyday, the Anasazis reached the highest state of civilization that was to be attained by any prehistoric North American Indian culture.

The vast region to the north of the Colorado River, now the state of Utah plus small adjoining areas of Nevada and Colorado, was occupied by a loose cultural grouping of tribesmen now called the "Fremonts" after the Fremont River in southcentral Utah, where their cultural remnants were first studied. The Fremonts were not, however, a unified culture. Rather, they consisted of several sub-groups that occupied fairly distinct geographic areas but not all at the same time, nor for the same length of time. See the cultural calendar on the inside back cover for more details. As with the Anasazis, the region's geography served to isolate the various Fremont subgroups from each other and surrounding cultures.

Beginning around AD 1200, for reasons still obscure, both the Anasazi and Fremont cultures began to retrench, retreat and regroup within the regions they occupied. Within a century, the various Fremont subcultural groups had vanished. Archaeologists still disagree as to why the culture died and what happened to its surviving remnants. The more advanced Anasazi culture retreated southward, with its remnants regrouping or joining other cultures that in turn vanished. The scattered survivors of that baffling cultural retreat were eventually given such modern tribal names as "Hopi," "Zuñi" and others. Collectively, the historic survivors of the Anasazi culture are sometimes called "Pueblo Indians."

Subsequent to the Anasazi cultural retreat and the Fremont disappearance, the vast region they had occupied was empty of humans, other than the few surviving enclaves of Anasazis in the south and some transient use by nearby nomadic tribes. It was still largely unoccupied when the first Spanish explorers entered the region in the mid-Sixteenth Century, thus beginning what is called the "historic" period of western America.

For practical purposes, then, this book will be confined to the Anasazi and Fremont cultures and their Archaic predecessors, to the geographic areas dominated by these cultures in their heyday and to the prehistoric period of time. While the advent of the Spanish penetration into what is now the American southwest did not change the prehistoric remnants already there, it did have an immediate effect upon the regressed Anasazi enclaves that were encountered. Thus, all rock art created by the historic Hopis, Zuñis and other Pueblo tribes must be considered culturally contaminated. Although the historic rock art in the former Anasazi and Fremont territories is a fascinating study in itself, it is not covered in this book except by an occasional example for comparison.

The limited purpose of this book, then, is to summarize the present state of knowledge and ongoing research concerning the prehistoric rock art found within the Anasazi and Fremont cultural territories. The cultural origin of some of the rock art found within this region is still in question, but since there is little doubt that it is prehistoric, it has been included in this book.

Anasazi petroglyph panel, San Juan River gorge, Utah.

14

THE HISTORY OF ROCK ART STUDY

Knowledge of the existence of primitive rock art in western North America first reached public attention in the early 1800s, as western explorers made reports to various eastern periodicals and academic institutions and to certain agencies of the federal government. Unfortunately, from the time such accounts first began to appear, the serious study of these enigmatic prehistoric remnants has been plagued by pseudoscientific researchers, extravagant hypotheses, questionable interpretations and unsupported conclusions. Then and today, the urge to delve into the "hidden meaning" of prehistoric American Indian petroglyphs and pictographs has proven to be irresistible to a wide spectrum of non-qualified but enthusiastic amateurs.

This dominance of the field of rock art study by non-scientists has created such an atmosphere of mysticism and irrationality about the subject that many qualified researchers have hesitated to enter the field for fear their professional reputations would be adversely affected. To an appalling degree, this situation continues today, with most of the published literature on American Indian rock art being authored by a wide assortment of people with backgrounds in such fields as art history, religion, medicine, philosophy, spiritualism and astrology. Solidly researched books and papers authored by qualified archaeological researchers well versed in scientific analytical methods are rare.

Despite their lack of basic qualifications, some enthusiastic amateur students of rock art have made valid contributions to the field, especially those with scientific educations in other fields who have limited themselves to collecting rock art images and to summarizing factual material, and who have refrained from making speculations about rock art meanings and purposes. These few talented amateurs and even fewer serious archaeological researchers have not, however, been able to offset all the damage done by the host of pseudo-scientists in the field.

Unfortunately, the more sensational, astounding and fantastic an idea about rock art may be, the more apt it is to become widely publicized in popular literature such as newspapers, magazines and other assorted periodicals. On the other hand, the more conservative, scientific studies and ideas get published only in scientific journals, the few serious science magazines and occasional books. Thus, the valid material becomes known to a relative few, while the sensational nonsense gets widely publicized. This has led to a great many public misconceptions about what America's prehistoric rock art is, who made it, what it means and how it was used by the prehistoric Americans who created it. One of the purposes of this book is to clear up some of these misconceptions.

Existing rock art literature commonly notes that research in this field is quite difficult and not nearly as rewarding as other facets of archaeological study and that this is why so few archaeologists enter the field. It is true that rock art study can be baffling, short on hard data and not very rewarding for a serious scientist, but it is doubtful that this is a major factor in keeping qualified researchers out of the field. After all, as elusive as this subject may be, it is certainly no more difficult than a great many other scientific riddles that have long since yielded to solid scientific logic and methodology. A more likely explanation for the lack of enthusiasm by trained archaeolgists for rock art study is that they prefer not to be associated with the historic and continuing aura of irrationality and sensationalism that surrounds the field. Or, perhaps they see too little promise of significant results at best. Doubtless, many archaeologists have already concluded that the total information potential in prehistoric rock art is far lower than most amateur enthusiasts are willing to admit.

While the general field of rock art study in America has been obscured by too many unqualified amateurs, or by people in other fields of study out to use rock art to prove a pet theory, the problem has been still further compounded with the rock art of Utah and the general Four Corners region — the Anasazi and Fremont territories. The rock art in this region is in many ways different, unique, because much of it was created in almost total isolation from prehistoric cultures elsewhere in America. As noted earlier, the land, itself, created and enforced this isolation. The prehistoric tribes that occupied the region had very limited contact with the sparse and often hostile Archaic level tribes that surrounded them on three sides until relatively late in their development, long after much of their rock art was already in place. All too many researchers who are studying Anasazi and Fremont rock art fail to consider this cultural isolation and thus tend to apply assumptions and use analytical approaches that may be useful elsewhere but which have very limited validity when applied to the rock art of Utah and the general Four Corners region. This failure to understand the unique nature of Anasazi and Fremont rock art has led to some highly questionable study methods, hypotheses and conclusions.

THIS BOOK

The first several chapters of this book will summarize the factual information that has been accumulated about Anasazi and Fremont rock art since early historic times. This information has been winnowed from hundreds of literature sources, such as books, periodicals, historical accounts and various kinds of scientific reports. Selected examples of these are listed in this book's bibliography. Additional information was gathered from extensive personal observations made while exploring these cultural regions over a fifteen-year period and from countless personal communications with both scientists and amateurs who have an interest in canyon country prehistoric rock art.

Following the factual material, three chapters are devoted to summarizing and discussing the more hypothetical, inferential aspects of rock art study, aspects such as the various analytic techniques, working hypotheses, interpretations and aesthetic considerations that appear in scientific and popular literature.

The next two chapters deal with rock art destruction, salvage, protection, restoration and recording techniques. These are followed by a listing of protected rock art sites that are accessible to the general public. The final section of the book contains photographs of representative rock art from various geographic areas within the Anasazi and Fremont territories, with brief introductions and some photographs by authorities who have specialized in the study of rock art in those areas. In each case, appropriate credit is given for such outside contributions of written material and photographs. It should be noted that the appearance of such material in this book does not necessarily mean that the contributors endorse the contents of this book.

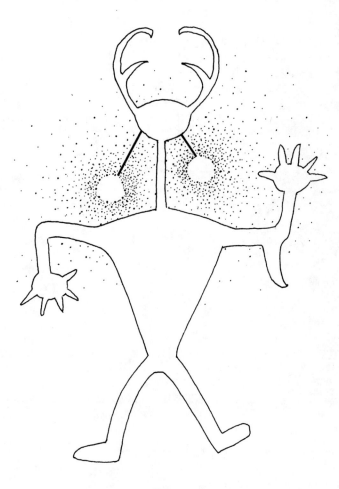

Thirteen Faces site, Horse Canyon, Canyonlands National Park.

ROCK ART LITERATURE

EARLY REPORTS

The story of the discovery, reporting and study of prehistoric rock art in Utah and the general Four Corners region is as strange as the rock art itself. The story began more than four hundred years ago, has made only erratic and limited progress since then, and has not ended yet — nor is any end in sight.

The story began in AD 1540, with the penetration of the region that is now Arizona and New Mexico by the Spanish explorer Coronado and the later establishment of permanent settlements in what is now northcentral New Mexico. Other Spanish expeditions, some sponsored by the Spanish church-state, others by commercial interests, then set out exploring in several directions, using Santa Fe as a base.

One such group, heading west in AD 1583, reported camping by "El Estanque del Peño," a large, perennial pool of spring water at the base of a gigantic sandstone monolith that dominates a high, rolling region near the present Arizona-New Mexico border. This huge bluff, later to be dubbed "El Morro," had prehistoric Anasazi pueblo ruins on its top and numerous petroglyphs around its base, but the 1583 exploring party did not report them. Nor did others who visited the welcome pool, by then called "El Agua de la Peña," or "Water by the Rock," including one Juan de Oñate, then governor of the Spanish-owned territory of New Mexico, who first visited El Morro in 1599, then inscribed his own name on its base in 1605. This inscription was the earliest historic date among the numerous prehistoric petroglyphs, yet little if any written notice was taken of the glyphs by the Spaniards who camped at the El Morro water source over the next two centuries, although many did add their names to the monolith, which is now protected within El Morro National Monument. Doubtless, other Spanish explorers during this period, such as the Dominguez-Escalante expedition of 1776, also saw prehistoric rock art other places within Utah and the general Four Corners region. But again, written reports of that rock art were only notable by their absence.

In the early 1800s, Utah and the Four Corners region was penetrated many times by such unofficial explorers as trappers, herders and prospectors, some with now-famous names, but none left written accounts of the rock art they must have seen, although a few did leave their own names inscribed on rock here and there.

Thus, the earliest discoverers of Anasazi and Fremont rock art saw no value to these mysterious remnants and made little if any note of them, even though some of the Spanish explorers wrote voluminous and detailed reports about their travels, observations and adventures.

In 1821, Mexico declared itself to be a nation, free of Spain, and the

New Mexico territory, plus other regions of the Southwest, became part of the new independent nation of Mexico. From then until after the war in which the United States took it from Mexico by treaty in 1848, not much was reported out of the remote and little known general Four Corners region. The new government of Mexico took little interest in it but actively discouraged American intrusions of any sort.

Adjacent historic and prehistoric rock graphics at El Morro National Monument.

Despite this, a few Europeans and Americans did penetrate the area during this period. One was young Christopher "Kit" Carson, who is believed to have visited El Morro with a party of traders on their way to California in 1829. He did not inscribe his name on the rock then, however, probably to avoid incriminating himself with the Mexican authorities who would have forbidden the trip had they known about it.

In the mid-1840s, a German national named J. Gregg also did a bit of exploring in what is now western New Mexico. His 1845 report contained the first account of the Anasazi pueblo ruins in Chaco Canyon, although it failed to mention the considerable rock art there, some of it quite close to the ruins.

In the years 1846 and '47, Lt. Colonel W. H. Emory led a military reconnaissance between Fort Leavenworth, Kansas and San Diego, California. In his report, made to the Thirteenth U. S. Congress in 1848,

Emory described a number of prehistoric ruins and rock art sites along his route west, which followed the Gila River for some distance. These sites were from pueblo cultures to the south of the Anasazis.

In 1847, Mormon leader Brigham Young brought the first settlers into what is now Utah. Within a few years there were Mormon settlements many places within the erstwhile Anasazi and Fremont territory, but these hard-pressed pioneers were evidently too busy with other affairs to report the prehistoric rock art they must have seen, although brief mention of one site was made in the diary of Ethan Petit, one of the group that settled Moab Valley in 1855.

The year after the Mexican-American war ended in 1848, a Lt. J. H. Simpson of the U. S. Topographical Engineers led a military reconnaissance party from Santa Fe into what is now eastern Arizona. His report described a number of prehistoric Anasazi ruins sites, such as Chaco Canyon, Zuñi, El Morro and Canyon de Chelly, and made the first recorded comments about the rock art seen there. Lt. Simpson's account of their approach to El Morro first noted the many inscriptions on the "stupendous mass of rock," then indicated that "The greater portion of the inscriptions are in Spanish — and the remainder in hieroglyphics, doubtless of Indian origin." Simpson, and the party's artist, a Mr. R. H. Kern, then set about making the first known copies of the historic "inscriptions of interest" but neglected the more enigmatic prehistoric rock art.

In 1851, Captain L. Sitgreaves of the U. S. Topographical Engineers was sent to check out a proposed route west that would follow the Rio Grande and Colorado Rivers. This was still eighteen years before anyone but a few hardy trappers knew anything at all about the Colorado River gorge between eastern Utah and the lower end of the river. Sitgreaves headed west along the Zuñi River only to find that this river joined the Little Colorado, not the Colorado. Further, the Little Colorado could not be followed all the way to the Colorado. Sitgreaves did, however, report many abandoned pueblo ruins along his route, one so extensive that buildings "occurred at intervals for an extent of eight or nine miles." He did not note the rock art that must also have been seen.

In 1852, a Lt. J. W. Gunnison, also of the U. S. Topographical Engineers and better known for his later railroad route survey across the center of the western states, published a report on the Utah Mormons. In it he included references to some rock art found in central Utah near the town of Manti. Sketches of the rock art were also included.

During the years 1850 to '53, a Mr. J. R. Bartlett, Boundary Commissioner in charge of surveying a new boundary between Mexico and the United States as required by the treaty that ended the Mexican-American War, explored, surveyed and documented a wide swath of the land between Yuma and El Paso. His bulky narrative, published in 1854, noted and described numerous prehistoric pueblo ruins and even depicted several petroglyph sites along the Gila River but, again, this rock art was the product of pueblo neighbors to the south of the Anasazis.

In 1853 and '54, a Lt. A. W. Whipple, surveying a railroad route closely parallel to Sitgreaves' route of 1851, noted a lot of rock art in New

Mexico, some in the vicinity of the Canadian River in the eastern part of the state, still more at Zuñi and other sites in the west. Some of the western sites were probably prehistoric and Anasazi.

In 1857, an ex-naval lieutenant, Edward (Ned) F. Beale, set out from Albuquerque in charge of a party assigned to establish a wagon route from Fort Defiance, on the present Arizona-New Mexico border about 25 miles northwest of Gallup, on west to the Colorado River in the vicinity of the present Davis Dam. Along the way, his party camped at El Morro, added a few names and dates, then continued westward through the heart of Anasazi country. But Beale's report makes no significant mention of the rock art that must have been seen along the way. The first group of settlers to follow "Beale's Road" in 1858 ran into serious Indian trouble at "Beale's Crossing" on the Colorado and the survivors had to turn back. This disaster led to the establishment of Fort Mojave at Beale's Crossing.

In 1859, an exploring group led by Captain J. N. Macomb of the U. S. Topographical Engineers traveled from Santa Fe into the terra incognita of canyon country, now the southeastern corner of Utah, mapping and searching for mineral deposits. The group's ultimate goal was the fabled but as yet unseen confluence of the Green and Grand Rivers. At that time, the "Colorado River" began at this confluence and ran on to the Sea of Cortez. Professor J. S. Newberry, a medical doctor who was also serving as the expedition's geologist and biologist, wrote a report of the exploration. While that report described in detail the large number of ruined prehistoric pueblos encountered near the Animas, Dolores and San Juan Rivers and in "Labyrinth Canyon" (lower Indian Creek Canyon), it made no mention of the rock art that must have been seen at or near these ruins. Newberry wrote in great detail about the geology of the region.

Ten years later, in 1869, Major John Wesley Powell led his first expedition down the Green and Colorado Rivers. In upper Glen Canyon, near a ruin, he reported that ". . . on the face of the cliff, under the building and along down the river for 200 or 300 yards, there are many etchings." F. S. Dellenbaugh, who documented Powell's second journey down these rivers in 1871, also made mention of "picture writings" in Desolation Canyon of the Green River. In his account published in 1895, Powell also described pueblo ruins in the upper Gila River drainage system, in the same region then occupied by the "Pimas, Maricopas and Papagos." After remarking about the prehistoric pueblo architecture, pottery, weaving and irrigation system, Powell said, of the puebloans:

"They were deft artists in picture-writings, which they etched on
the rocks. Many interesting vestiges of their ancient art remain,
testifying to their skill as savage artisans. It seems probable that
the Pimas, Maricopas and Papagos are the same people who
built the pueblos and constructed the irrigation works; so their
traditions state. It is also handed down that the pueblos were
destroyed in wars with the Apaches."

Throughout the 1870s, there were various reports from "official" explorers and local citizens about rock art in the Nevada region of the Great Basin. One enthusiast, a Mr. R. L. Fulton of Reno, in a lengthy and detailed letter in which he described many sites, stated that he personally had seen Great Basin rock art "which extends in broken lines from Arizona far into Oregon."

In the years 1874, '75, and '77, W. H. Jackson, representing F. V. Hayden's U. S. Geological and Geographical Survey of the Territories, explored Anasazi ruins in southwestern Colorado but made no contribution to the scant literature on the rock art of the region, nor did other probes of the famed Hayden Survey on into the Four Corners region, or the equally famed Wheeler Survey that explored the Great Basin region north of the Grand Canyon, both prime Anasazi cultural areas, although plenty of ruins were described.

Another member of the Hayden Survey, however, a W. H. Holmes of the Bureau of Ethnology who studied a number of the prehistoric ruins in the Four Corners region in 1875 and '76, described, discussed and sketched many rock art panels there, along the Mancos and San Juan Rivers. His report, made in 1879, was perhaps the first to take serious notice of the region's prehistoric rock art and to make more than passing mention of it. Others followed shortly.

In 1875 and again in 1878 and 1883, a Mr. G. K. Gilbert of the U. S. Geological Survey described and made sketches of the petroglyphs and pictographs at several sites within Utah and Arizona. In one area in Arizona, Gilbert reported that "so many localities of petroglyphs were seen that I regard it as probable that a large number could be found by search." Other U. S. G. S. field workers also contributed descriptions and sketches of Utah rock art, beginning in the 1870s.

In the mid-1870s, F. S. Dellenbaugh wrote a lengthy report on "The Shinumos, A Prehistoric People of the Rocky Mountain Region," which described and sketched many of the rock art panels found in Glen Canyon during the earlier Colorado River expeditions led by Powell, plus others in the region. According to Dellenbaugh, "Shinumos" was the Paiute term for the vanished pueblo people of the Colorado River gorge region of Arizona and Utah, the "Anasazis" of the Navajos.

In 1876, a Mr. E. A. Barber authored an article in a respected scientific journal entitled "Rock Inscriptions of the Ancient Pueblos of Colorado, Utah, New Mexico and Arizona."

In 1877, Lt. A. G. Tassin of the Twelfth U. S. Infantry made a report on the Mojave Indians in southern Nevada in which he included sketches of petroglyphs in the vicinity of Dead Mountain, the abode of "dead bad Indians," according to Mojave folk tales. A contemporary rock art researcher indicated that "the whole of this series of petroglyphs is regarded as being Shinumo or Moki," on the basis of "resemblance to drawings in Arizona known to have been made by the Moki Indians." The term "Moki" was at that time applied specifically to the Hopi pueblo Indians and somewhat loosely to the other historic pueblo Indians of Arizona and New Mexico as well as their vanished prehistoric predecessors. "Moki" or "Moqui" still appears in modern literature but is obsolete and still poorly defined.

In 1879, a Professor E. D. Cope, a member of the Wheeler Survey noted earlier, published an independent report on the Indian populations in northwestern New Mexico. In it he included sketches of some of the rock art in that region.

In 1883, an H. H. Bancroft published a report on "The Native Races" which contained illustrations of several "rock inscriptions" in Utah. In 1884, Mr. A. F. Bandelier reported making sketches of prehistoric rock art in northwestern New Mexico.

In the late 1880s, a major breakthrough was made in the study of the rock art of American Indians by a "paper" accompanying the "Tenth Annual Report of the Bureau of Ethnology" made by J. W. Powell, Director. The "paper," entitled "Picture Writing of the American Indians," written by Garrick Mallery with a foreword by Powell, was a compilation of virtually all that was then known about this heretofore largely neglected subject. It was printed in book form by the U. S. Government Printing Office in 1893. In its modern reprinted version it fills more than 800 pages in two thick volumes and contains many hundreds of illustrations. Among other things, it contains a state by state summary of reports of rock art, both official and from contemporary private citizens. One such citizen report, from a Mr. Edwin A. Hill of Indianapolis, noted his observation of petroglyphs in New Mexico along the right-of-way of the Denver and Rio Grande Railroad and that beside a road in the same area there were "rude sculptures, lining the valley on both sides of the road for a long distance, at least several miles." Mallery's monumental work is still a basic reference for all serious rock art scholars.

Although other explorers of the Four Corners region in the early 1890s did not follow Mallery's good example, a Dr. J. W. Fewkes did discuss and illustrate rock art in the Four Corners region in several reports published during this period. These bore such titles as "A Few Tusayan Pictographs," "Reconaissance of Ruins in or near the Zuñi Reservation," "Archaeological Expedition to Arizona in 1895" and "Two Summers' Work in Pueblo Ruins." Fewkes wrote extensively on many aspects of the prehistoric and historic pueblo cultures well into the Twentieth Century.

Baron Gustaf Nordenskiold, a wealthy Swedish explorer and amateur archaeologist, carried on the serious treatment of canyon country rock art by publishing in 1893 a book entitled "The Cliff Dwellers of the Mesa

Verde" (translated from the Swedish in which it was written). The book, now a classic, contained a summary of existing information about this fascinating Anasazi occupation site, but also detailed the first attempt at scientific collection and excavation there. The book also had chapters on the artifacts found in the vicinity, the nearby rock art, and other chapters summarizing existing information on other southwest ruins, the "Moki" Indians and the region's other historic pueblo tribes.

Even during the last decades of the 1800s, not all researchers took rock art seriously. Two brothers, Victor and Cosmos Mindeleff, did extensive field work for the Bureau of Ethnology in Arizona and New Mexico in the 1880s. Victor left the Bureau in the late 1880s, but Cosmos continued, making detailed studies and even restorations of Arizona pueblo ruins. His lengthy study of Canyon de Chelly archaeological sites was published in 1897 but contained only casual mention of the extensive rock art found there.

THE TWENTIETH CENTURY

The first quarter of the Twentieth Century saw a continued preoccupation with the more rewarding study of canyon country ruins, to the neglect of the more enigmatic rock art to be found near many of the pueblo ruins being studied. Rock art was mentioned in a few reports but only in passing. In the late 1920s, however, a few serious researchers began to show an interest in the rock art of Utah and the general Four Corners region.

In 1927, archaeological field research began in southeastern Utah, supported by the Claflin-Emerson Fund and sponsored by the Peabody Museum of American Archaeology and Ethnology at Harvard University. W. H. Claflin was at that time Curator of one section of the Museum. Work was continued in 1928, '29 and '30 by a Mr. Noel Morss, who wrote a report dated 1931, and by a Mr. Henry B. Roberts. Morss' report covered collections and excavations made at several sites, depicted some of the rock art in the area and became the basis for establishing the "Fremont" culture as distinct from the prehistoric pueblo culture farther south, now known as the Anasazi.

In 1928, a Mr. Donald Scott, soon to be Assistant Director at the Peabody Museum, took a trip into southeastern Utah. There, he promptly contracted a fascination with the region's rock art that lasted until he died in 1967. During that period, Scott made numerous field trips to Utah and produced an endless stream of photographs, sketches and rubbings of the rock art there. The "Scott Collection" is still a prime source of information and inspiration for serious rock art scholars.

These promising starts into serious rock art research were not, however, to lead to any general interest in the field among archaeologists. In 1929, a Mr. Julian H. Steward authored a report for the University of California entitled "Petroglyphs of California and Adjoining States." The "adjoining states" included Baja California, Nevada, Utah and Arizona. He wrote another report in 1936 for the Smithsonian Institution entitled "Petroglyphs of the United States," in which he decried the abundance of "amateur speculation" and the dearth of scientific research in this fascinating but neglected branch of archaeology.

From 1931 through 1934, a Mr. Albert B. Reagan wrote a number of archaeological reports about several prehistoric sites in eastern Utah. These were published in various respected scientific journals. Some of the reports concentrated on rock art panels in that region.

But these two writers turned out to be anomalies. In his 1936 report, Steward summarized the situation quite succinctly. His summary is almost as valid today as it was when written:

"But there was one class of American antiquities to which the blessings of scientific method came but slowly—the carved and painted petroglyphs which are found on rocks in all parts of the United States. Here amateur speculation retained its hold and, zealous in its last stand, even today stoutly resists the threats of science. Popular fancy musters petroglyphs in support of theories abandoned by science half a century ago. It offers them as proof that Egyptians, Scythians, Chinese, and a host of other Old World peoples, including the Ten Lost Tribes of Israel, whose fate continues to have absorbing interest to many persons, invaded America in ancient days. It claims them to be markers of buried treasure, signs of ancient astrology, records of vanished races, symbols of diabolical cults, works of the hand of God, and a hundred other things conceived by feverish brains. Devotees of the subject have written voluminously, argued bitterly, and even fought duels.

"Owing largely to methodological difficulties in the study of petroglyphs, archeologists have unduly neglected them. It was not until 1886 that petroglyphs were accorded their first comprehensive and genuinely scientific treatment. Garrick Mallery, interested in the primitive pictographic writing used by certain North American Indians, included many petroglyphs in a large volume, Pictographs of the American Indians, published in the Fourth Annual Report of the Bureau of American Ethnology. In a subsequent and more extensive treatment of the same subject, Picture-writing of the American Indians, Tenth Annual Report of the Bureau of American Ethnology, 1893, he published further material on petroglyphs. Although Mallery drew attention to the many similarities between petroglyphs and pictographic writing, he warned against any interpretations of the former which could not meet rigid scientific standards. Unscientific speculation continued rife, however, and is still unabated today."

It should be noted that Steward called all Western rock graphics "petroglyphs," whether pecked or painted, while "pictographic writing" to him meant the actual picture writing developed during historic times by Plains and Great Lakes Indian tribes, as described by Mallery.

SERIOUS STUDY

According to some sources, the serious scientific study of America's prehistoric rock graphics did not truly begin until the 1960s, even though information, photographs and other types of recordings of them did continue slowly to accumulate in the files of academic institutions, museums, various branches of the government and private citizens. After a slow start, the rock art of Utah and the general Four Corners region came into its own as a prime source of relatively unspoiled rock graphics, especially once certain major development projects in the region got underway, projects that were to totally destroy great quantities of rock art. Much of the archaeological study that has been performed in the region during the last two decades has been stimulated and funded by such development projects, rather than by any concerted effort or interest on the part of academic institutions or government land administration agencies. "Salvage archaeology" is discussed further in a later chapter.

Other literature published about the prehistory of the region during the last two decades continued to reflect a mixed attitude toward rock art study. Popular articles written by enthusiastic amateurs and full of startling nonsense kept the public fascinated but uninformed, and continued to scare off competent professionals. Massive archaeological reports, purporting to summarize everything known about the Anasazis and Fremonts, slighted or studiously ignored the critically important fundamental efforts at graphics made by these prehistoric Formative cultures.

On the positive side, a few professionals and a lot of serious, dedicated amateurs began to band together in efforts to call attention to the neglected field of rock art study and to do something about that neglect. Some of the more competent individuals within such groups have generated a growing list of publications on the subject. Certain private publishing concerns have also helped by issuing scientific works on Western rock art that otherwise might not have seen print.

Thus, even now, the bulk of rock art literature is still generated by a few sincere amateurs, rather than competent professionals who are trained to handle all aspects of the subject.

And despite all such earnest efforts by a few, it could safely be said that the serious scientific study of canyon country rock art has still not begun. The all too limited academic funding for archaeological field work must, of course, be spent where it can be the most productive. This rarely includes the detailed study of rock art, which can be maddeningly frustrating and unproductive. Federal land administration agencies have been charged by law with "inventorying" public land under their control for archaeological values, but have been given little funding for the massive effort this would actually take. No effort is underway by any organization to even make a comprehensive inventory of canyon country rock art, or any geographic area within the immense region. Even worse, the information gathered during some earlier detailed individual surveys has never been published.

It has been noted that conventional archaeological training and procedures are not very appropriate for truly scientific rock art research. This is another factor that has caused the field to be neglected.

What kind of background would be needed for the serious study of canyon country rock art? Well, certainly a firm basis of education and experience in scientific logic and methodology would be essential, as would detailed knowledge, however acquired, about the several prehistoric cultures involved and the lands they occupied. Other highly desirable working tools would be general knowledge in the fields of anthropology, ethnology, psychology, biology, geology and the fundamental laws of probability, plus detailed knowledge in the special branches of psychology and biology that deal with human visual perception and learning processes. Knowledge of primitive art might be useful in the study of graphic concept sophistication but could also be misleading because, as discussed earlier and in the later chapter on interpretation, there is little likelihood that Anasazi and Fremont rock art had anything to do with "art" in the usual sense of the word.

There are, of course, two other factors absolutely essential to any serious study of canyon country prehistoric rock art. One is a thorough understanding of the principles behind "Ockham's Razor," which is discussed further in a later chapter. The other is called "common sense." In rock art study, common sense means the rare but necessary ability to wade through fogs of misleading assumptions and clouds of verbal fantasy, without becoming contaminated, without losing all sense of direction and all ability to think rationally, without completely losing sight of the real world.

Does Anasazi and Fremont rock art actually contain any untapped scientific value that careful study can reach? Yes, but not as commonly supposed. Rock art research can be a highly rewarding field for those who wish to use its scant and ambiguous information to support some preconceived notion, some pet theory. Such "researchers" have little trouble finding whatever they wish to find in the crude scratchings of prehistoric cultures barely sophisticated enough in graphics concepts to make recognizable two-dimensional images by banging rocks together.

But truly qualified scholars, trained in the rigors of the scientific method, will find rock art research baffling and not very rewarding at best. If they are adequately educated in other aspects of the region's prehistoric and historic Indian cultures, they will find occasional support in rock art for inferences and assumptions made in the main field of study. Such support may in the long run prove to be about all that rock art has to offer. But rock art cannot be a separate subject, isolated from other aspects of the originating culture and isolated from other aspects of human history, psychology and behavior.

Is there any place for amateurs in serious rock art study? Of course, but largely as gatherers of data — recording locations, taking photographs, etc. — under the guidance of experienced professionals. Such amateurs can make significant contributions to the collection of information because in the study of archaeology, willing and enthusiastic field labor is always in short supply, and skilled amateurs have made many contributions with their field work. As Julian Steward of the Bureau of American Ethnology noted in his report on American rock art in 1936:

"... thanks largely to the enthusiastic cooperation of many nonprofessional observers who have painstakingly sketched and photographed petroglyphs, material has continued to accumulate in scientific institutions. Little has been published, but when competent archeologists can be enticed to set aside their spades long enough to ponder petroglyphs, we may expect a much better understanding of this interesting subject."

Perceptive amateurs can even suggest ideas that should be considered, but should leave the actual consideration to those trained and experienced in scientific analysis. Otherwise, they may further obscure an issue already badly clouded by unscientific thinking.

Serious rock art scholars who set out to acquire background from existing rock art literature, especially amateurs who lack a broad scientific education, will find most of that literature written in the pedantic, opaque prose of the professional archaeologist, even though most such writers are not, in fact, archaeologists. Unfortunately, there is an all too human tendency, even among scientists, to use and to be overly impressed and influenced by such complicated and stilted linguistics, even to the extent of losing sight of how rational or irrational its author was, or how soundly his inferences, assumptions, hypotheses, conjectures and extrapolations were based upon solid evidence.

Thus, the serious rock art scholar must be prepared to wade through an enormous amount of fairly recent literature that is ponderous, scholarly-seeming and couched in an astonishing assortment of ill-defined, semantically-misleading but impressive-sounding words, many of which have little meaning in science or the real world. Because of this, those who study existing rock art literature should do so with healthy scientific skepticism. They should be prepared to pare everything they read down to its unassailable hard data by discarding all inferences, then doing their own thinking, without being influenced by the author's questionable assumptions and semantic confusion.

As Steward noted in his 1936 report, "It is the unhappy lot of science that it must clear the ground of flimsy and fanciful structures built upon false premises and errors of fact before it can build anew." There has always been a lot of such ground-clearing to do in the field of serious rock art study, even within its most scholarly scientific books and papers, and today there is even more clearing to be done than there was in 1936.

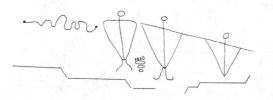

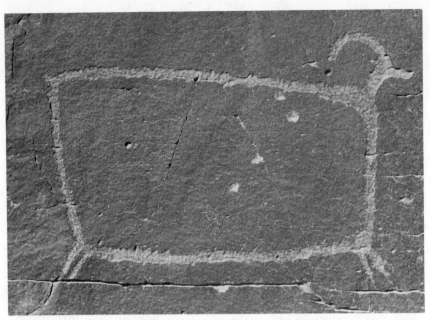

Typical petroglyph, Sevenmile Canyon, Utah.

Typical pictograph, Salt Creek Canyon, Canyonlands National Park.

DEFINITIONS

DEFINING BASIC TERMS

A basic task to be performed when setting out to study a subject is to define the more commonly used terms. In recent years some progress has been made in establishing uniform terminology within the field of rock art research, but there are still weaknesses, and some of these weaknesses are actually inhibiting the study process.

After a considerable amount of earlier confusion, which is still visible in all but the most recent literature, two terms have by common agreement come into almost universal use. The composite word "petroglyph" or "rock marking," means an image of any sort cut into a rock surface by one method or another. The resulting image might be shallow or deep, made of scratched lines or rubbed grooves or drilled pits or chipped out lines or areas, and might be made by any of several techniques, but is still defined as a "petroglyph," an "image in rock." The contraction "glyph" is sometimes used for the word "petroglyph."

The second basic term is "pictograph," meaning "painted image." As the word is generally used, a "pictograph" may be created by any number of application techniques, using a wide variety of pigments, but is essentially an image painted on a rock surface. The term is also applied by some writers to images painted onto the mud-plastered walls of native structures, but this is a questionable use of the term as commonly defined. This illustrates that the term "pictograph" is weak in that its application to rock is not implicit in the word. The contraction "picto" is sometimes used for the word "pictograph."

In practice, those who created canyon country rock art generally either painted an image onto a rock surface or cut it into rock, but at a few sites petroglyphs were also painted. In most such figures, centuries of weathering have left only faint traces of the original paint.

Other terms for petroglyphs and pictographs appear in older literature on the subject, such as hieroglyphs, rock paintings, rock drawings, rock carvings, petrographs, paintings on stone, engravings on stone, rock markings, Indian writing, ideographs and iconographs, but most such terms are either non-definitive, incorrectly used, confusing or awkward to use.

Most modern writers use the standardized terms for the two basic types of prehistoric graphics, but there is still no generally accepted and scientifically accurate generic term for all types of prehistoric graphics on rock. The most commonly used general terms are "rock art" or "picture writing," yet both have serious flaws. "Picture writing" is the worst. The term implies that the images are a primitive form of writing with pictures for the purpose of communicating. This may be true of Mayan glyphs and even some of the graphics of historic North American Indians but is almost certainly not true

31

of the great majority of rock images made by the Anasazis, Fremonts and their predecessors.

The term "rock art" is closer to being a valid generic term but is still flawed and semantically misleading because the word "art" lends highly questionable implications. One writer has suggested that one definition of the phrase "monumental stone art" might fit the apparent contents, intent and use of Anasazi and Fremont rock art, but a scientifically accurate term should avoid semantic implications, and it is doubtful that such a lengthy phrase would ever be adopted for common use.

A more accurate generic phrase might be "rock graphics," which is descriptive without adding implications as to use, intent and meaning which have yet to be indisputably established. Since the generic phrase "rock art" is currently in wide use, however, it is used in this book to mean rock graphics in general, while the words "petroglyph" and "pictograph" are used for specific images as appropriate. The more accurate general phrase "rock graphics" is also used where semantic accuracy is important.

Although it is not the prime subject of this book, the term "kiva art" is applied to the paintings found on late Anasazi kiva walls. In this application, some valid argument could be made for the applicability of the word "art," although it is well established that kiva art had religious significance and ceremonial use and was not simply created for decorative purposes. It should be noted that the term "pictograph" does not apply in any way to the images or decorative patterns found on prehistoric pottery, although some researchers claim to have seen a possible relationship between particular rock art images and certain non-pottery ceramics.

At some earlier occupation sites, pictographs similar to those commonly found on rock walls have also been observed on the mud-plastered stone walls of dwellings. These are not the same thing as late Anasazi kiva art but are true pictographs placed on artificial rather than natural walls for reasons known only to the persons who painted them. On a very few rock dwelling structures, petroglyphs have been found on individual rocks within a constructed wall. Possible explanations for these "misplaced" pictographs and petroglyphs are discussed in a later chapter.

PROBLEMS WITH SEMANTICS

Within the field of rock art study and analysis it is easy to become semantically confused and thus led into misunderstandings and highly improbable lines of conjecture. Such terms as "art," "abstract," "writing" and others are commonly used in rock graphics literature, both popular and scientific, yet such words bear meanings to modern Americans that simply did not exist in the minds of those who created prehistoric rock graphics. When such words are used in documenting, analyzing and discussing these graphics, the modern mind is thus led astray all too often by the automatic, subconscious application of concepts totally alien to the subject in the real prehistoric world of Stone-Age primitives.

For example, as noted earlier, the word "art" is semantically misleading. To modern Americans, one major meaning of the word "art" infers an original, individualistic creation of some form of beauty, using any of an almost limitless variety of techniques, materials and subjects, with the main purpose being freedom of expression and personal originality in the creation of aesthetic beauty — art for art's sake — with no "true meaning" necessary in the end product. Every aspect of this concept or definition of "art" is virtually the opposite of the situation with prehistoric rock graphics. Because of this, the use of the word "art" in relation to the rock graphics of the Anasazi and Fremont cultures can, and does, lead to misconceptions about its originators, their purposes and the meanings of their graphics.

Typical "abstract" petroglyph, Behind the Rocks, Utah.

The common use of the word "abstract" by rock graphics researchers also leads to confused thinking. To users of American English, when the word "abstract" is used in connection with graphics, it implies considerable knowledge and sophistication on the part of the artist, who applies this understanding to reducing the complexities of a particular subject to its essentials, then producing this "abstract" in a graphic form that retains all of the primary elements of the original subject, without all of its details and complexities.

There is an immense and very important difference between such a knowledgeable abstraction process and what actually happened when a nomadic, half starved Archaic-level Indian stood scratching straight or curved lines into a cliff, or simple stick-man figures onto a boulder or hand-held rock. That native's knowledge of graphics was far less sophisticated than that of a modern child just a few months old, a child that has been surrounded by diverse and complex graphic images from its birth on.

That prehistoric man did not create stick-men rock figures as an end product of an "abstraction" process. He produced them for the same reason

33

that a one-year old modern child produces them as a first attempt at creating graphic images — that was all he knew how to do. He simply could not conceive of any other way to produce a man-image with the very limited knowledge, tools and techniques he had. Nor did he even imagine that there might be other, better ways to do the job. He definitely was not surrounded by examples of higher order graphic imagery of any sort. The stick-figures he was creating were, themselves, the highest order of graphics in his entire world and were thus something quite marvelous to him and his contemporaries.

But for a modern researcher to apply the word "abstract" to such stick-figures is to imply an understanding, a mental process, a purpose, that simply did not exist when the figures were made, and this is misleading and semantically confusing, both to those who use the term in their research and to those who later read the term.

Two words commonly used in rock graphics literature, "art" and "abstract," have been used to illustrate the serious problem with semantics that exists within this field of study. Similar problems with other terms, such as "writing" are discussed in later chapters. Problems with the misuse of words might seem minor to the casual observer, yet rock graphics literature is full of examples of where "minor" problems with semantics have led otherwise capable and sincere researchers into unsupported and even ridiculous lines of investigation.

Serious students of Anasazi and Fremont rock graphics should fully understand, then, that the use of semantically inaccurate terms that are viewer-interpretative and at odds with creator-intent, can and do lead to the making of unsupported assumptions, faulty analyses, weak hypotheses and highly questionable conclusions. An understanding of the principles of semantics is important in any scientific field, especially a field in which humanity is involved, and most especially in the field of rock art study, where researchers must deal largely with inferences rather than solid, factual evidence.

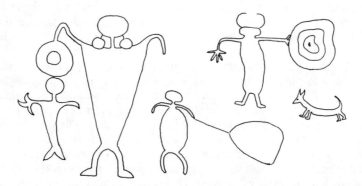

LOCATIONS

WHY ROCK AS A MEDIUM?

Virtually all objective, indisputable scientific data about Anasazi and Fremont rock art that exists is limited to two categories, its actual physical location and its actual graphic shape. Almost everything else that is "known" or assumed about such rock art is either pure speculation or based upon semantic confusion, questionable conjectures or inferences made from circumstantial evidence. There are other factual clues to be found by the careful examination of petroglyphs and pictographs in the field, but for the most part these do not lead directly to unchallengeable conclusions, even though they are useful in building inferences or supporting working hypotheses.

Study of the many aspects of where rock art is actually located can yield many clues as to its possible uses and meanings, as can consideration of the graphic medium itself.

The concept of "rock" or "stone" is a basic part of both types of Anasazi and Fremont graphics, even though it is not implicit in the composite word "pictograph." Painted and even carved graphics did appear on structure walls late in the existence of these cultures. Such exceptions, however, are but minor variations on the dominating theme of this region's prehistoric graphics on natural rock in its natural condition and location.

To the casual observer it might seem strange that prehistoric Indians chose to place their graphic images on rock, which is a difficult medium. The answer to this puzzle is twofold. First, there are many indications that most rock art was created for long-range, repeated use, that the images were not intended for casual, one-time use. Durability seemed to be a factor, and creating images on rock provided this durability.

Second, the isolated prehistoric cultures of canyon country had no knowledge or tradition of semi-permanent or temporary graphic media such as markings on paper, parchment, animal hides or tree bark, or tatoos on living human skin. Some of these innovations appeared in other prehistoric North American Indian cultures, but within the Anasazi and Fremont cultures they came late, if at all.

Thus, while it is interesting to assume that these isolated native Americans considered all the available artistic media that sophisticated modern Americans could devise from a primitive, natural environment, and that they then deliberately chose rock, it is far more probable that they used rock as a base for their imagery simply because it was so readily available. In fact, raw, bare rock absolutely dominated the region in which they lived.

Exposed rock is a relative rarity in most of North America, except above timberline in the highest and youngest mountain ranges and in the great southwestern desert areas. But in these arid reaches, bare rock suitable for making visible and durable markings is so plentiful that it is unlikely that the thought of or need for other graphic media even occurred to the region's inhabitants. If an individual got the urge to make a mark or an image of some sort, for one reason or another, it was very easy to just pick up one rock and use it to scratch or chip another handy rock surface, and that is substantially all there is to most of the older rock art in western America. Later, of course, more thought was given to the choice of location for petroglyphs and pictographs.

In sum, why did the Anasazis and Fremonts develop their traditions of placing graphics on rock, rather than other media? Because it was handy, durable and plentiful — so plentiful that little else was even considered until fairly late in the development of these cultures. The few exceptions, certain ceramic figurines and pottery decorations, simply serve to emphasize the dominant pattern of using natural rock in the creation of serious graphic images. These exceptions are discussed further in later chapters.

GENERAL LOCATIONS

Variations in the land itself imposed limitations on where rock art could be created. In the mountains, exposed rock was plentiful, but little rock art was put there, probably for a variety of reasons, among them the simple fact that places suitable for agriculture and permanent habitation were generally far removed from the higher mountainous areas. Further, the kinds of rock that dominate the mountains of this region are not as amenable to the cutting of petroglyphs as the sandstone in the lower elevations, and the mountain rock does not erode as well into the caves, alcoves and overhanging ledges that are needed for the protection of pictographs from the elements.

At the other elevation extreme, in the arid, sprawling deserts of the Great Basin, there is plenty of rock but largely in the form of exposed and eroded gravels, stones, small boulders and rock outcroppings. While some early rock art does appear on such surfaces, most of it in this region is found associated with the small, somewhat less arid "island" mountain ranges that occur throughout the Great Basin.

Between the two elevation extremes of high mountains and arid desert is the high-desert canyon-plateau region that dominates the heartland of the Anasazi and Fremont cultures. There, sandstone occurs everywhere. In the Great Basin region, igneous and metamorphic rock predominate, neither a very good medium for rock art. But most of the various kinds of sandstone found in canyon country are ideal, neither too hard to work nor too soft for durability.

Within the canyon-plateau region there are two general types of sandstone, "aeolian" or wind-deposited, and "sedimentary" or water-deposited. A few sandstones are mixtures of the two. The best sandstones for rock art are the thick aeolian deposits, such as Navajo, Wingate and

Entrada, and the several thick, uniform coastal sedimentary deposits such as Cedar Mesa, White Rim, Dakota and others. These tend to erode in a manner that creates near-vertical surfaces, such as cliffs and canyon walls, and to contain the minerals necessary for the formation of desert varnish. Water erosion of some geologic formations even tends to create caves, huge, relatively shallow alcoves and overhanging ledges. Thus, due to the amount and nature of the sandstone exposed there, the high-desert canyon country was an ideal place for the development of a rock art cultural tradition.

In general, prehistoric rock art in this region is found along the base of cliffs, on large detached boulders, in large overhung alcoves and beneath protruding ledges. Most is found on near-vertical surfaces, but a few petroglyphs have been found on the relatively level surfaces of exposed masses of sandstone or on the horizontal undersides of overhanging ledges. In general, there seems to have been little discernible preference for what direction the near-vertical surfaces faced, although researchers have noticed that various types of "astronomical" images tend to be oriented certain ways. In contrast, at many locations, all sides of a giant boulder may contain ordinary petroglyphs.

Those who created canyon country rock art had to be more careful in choosing a location for producing pictographs than for petroglyphs. Petroglyphs, being essentially gouges, grooves, scratches or pits in fairly hard, erosion-resistant rock, could be put almost anywhere without concern about wind and water erosion, although given time, all rock erodes away, even in arid desert country. Pictographs, however, being painted images, were quite sensitive to rain erosion and to abrasion by wind-borne sand and dust.

This was apparently well known to those who made them, because almost all pictographs are found in well sheltered locations such as in caves and spring-seep alcoves and under overhanging ledges of rock. Some pictograph painters were better than others at choosing locations, however, because the images at some sites are badly weathered.

Another factor has also tended to defeat efforts to protect pictographs by situating them away from direct water erosion, a factor that continues today. Most of the caves, alcoves and undercut ledges where pictographs were placed were formed to begin with by the slow, indirect water erosion process of seeping moisture, by sporadic heavy rain runoff or flashflooding, or by gradual undercutting that caused intermittent massive rock wall collapse. These natural processes are still active, although the region's climate is somewhat drier now than it was a few centuries ago, during the heyday of the Anasazi and Fremont cultures.

Thus, even while sheltering their more delicate painted imagery from immediate attack by the elements, canyon country pictograph "artists" doomed their creations to eventual obliteration by less obvious forms of natural erosion, the exfoliation of moist sandstone and the catastrophic collapse of undermined sandstone walls and ledges. Many pictographs have already been destroyed by such continuing natural processes.

Weathered pictograph in shallow alcove, near Hellroaring Canyon, Utah.

SPECIFIC LOCATIONS

From the purely physical viewpoint, the best places to make petroglyphs are on near-vertical stretches of sandstone along the bases of cliffs or on large detached boulders, with the sandstone surface hard, fairly free of irregularities and well coated with "desert varnish."

Desert varnish is a dark brown or black coating that slowly accumulates on sandstone and other kinds of rock with long exposure. The coating is composed of various manganese and iron compounds and is created by a process that is not thoroughly understood. It is known, however, that mineralization, moisture, air and sunlight all play a part in the slow process of building up desert varnish on sandstone and other suitable rock. The right conditions for the process are largely limited to arid and semi-arid regions.

Desert varnish is the mineral end-product of an inorganic chemical process and is distinct from other coatings which sometimes appear on exposed rock surfaces, such as mosses, lichens and the whitish crusts that may build up on rocks exposed to highly mineralized water. Sandstone well coated with dark desert varnish is desirable for petroglyphs because removing the varnish in the desired pattern exposes the light-hued sandstone beneath, thus producing a glyph with pleasing contrast. Petroglyphs produced in areas where the sandstone does not become coated with desert varnish must be cut much deeper in order to produce an acceptable visual effect.

It soon becomes apparent to field researchers in the Anasazi and Fremont regions that an ideal physical location was not the only prerequisite considered by those who created rock art. It doesn't take long for a serious searcher for rock art in the myriad sandstone gorges of canyon country to discover that the region has literally millions of apparently ideal sites for petroglyphs, where smooth, well varnished expanses of hard sandstone stretch enticingly along the bases of cliffs or cover the faces of gigantic boulders standing like sentinels on great talus slopes or along canyon bottoms, with these eminently suitable sites totally bare of petroglyphs, even in areas known to have seen centuries of prehistoric human use. Among canyon country rock art searchers, the disappointment of finding ideal sites completely innocent of rock art is so common that some have adopted a trite comment which is muttered disgustedly at each seemingly perfect but blank site — "Well, they sure missed a good chance THERE!" or something similar but unprintable.

Many rock art field researchers have observed apparent factors in the location of petroglyphs other than suitable physical conditions. With far fewer suitable locations available for pictographs, it is more difficult to draw inferences about other factors in site selection. Not even all sites protected from rain are suitable for pictographs. The rock surface must be fairly smooth, hard and light colored for paints to adhere and be visually apparent, yet the walls of many caves and alcoves and the vertical surfaces under overhanging rock ledges, are soft, flaky, powdery or even moist from seepage, making them unsatisfactory for pictographs. This relative scarcity of good pictograph sites resulted in petroglyphs becoming the predominant rock art mode in canyon country, and providing almost all clues as to

Typical petroglyphs cut into sandstone lacking desert varnish, Chaco Canyon, New Mexico.

secondary factors in the location of rock art sites by those who chose the sites.

Various researchers have noticed apparent correlations between rock art sites and other cultural activities, with some relationships being seen so many places that they become highly probable in spite of the fact that all the evidence is inferential. Rock art is often found near flowing water, such as springs, streams and rivers, near game trails or human trails or migration routes, near transient hunting, gathering and farming camps or isolated food storage sites, and near canyon confluences. In a few places, rock art has been found near the remnants of prehistoric game blinds and traps.

Within the Great Basin desert, rock art seems to occur more commonly on hilltops, hill bases, ridges or saddles in ridges, near lithic chipping sites and on canyon walls, where these exist, but not near habitation sites. Within the Anasazi subgroup that occupied the area that is now southern Nevada, virtually all rock art was located away from dwelling sites, in the vicinity of areas of transient use. This may have been dictated by a scarcity of suitable rock surfaces near their riverbank villages or may have had other significance.

PUZZLING LOCATIONS

The occurrence of rock art in the vicinity of places of permanent habitation is an enigma and varies from area to area and even site to site. There seems to be no pattern, yet there could be. At some dwelling sites, rock art is plentiful at the site or nearby. At other sites, even some that were occupied for hundreds of years, there is no trace of rock art at or near the dwellings. In some areas, all rock art was located near dwellings but not all dwellings had rock art near them. In one occupied canyon, all rock art sites were near habitations, yet only twenty percent of the dwellings had rock art nearby.

As noted earlier, in a few places rock art was actually placed on the dwelling structures, rather than on natural rock surfaces. At one major complex of late-Anasazi dwellings, all pictographs were found on the dwelling structures themselves, while virtually all petroglyphs were on natural rock walls. Some researchers have even noticed what may have been area "ownership" markers, large rocks set in a perimeter around a dwelling site, with petroglyphs on their outward-facing surfaces. It was assumed that the glyph figures on these boundary markers were warnings understandable to contemporary trespassers, or perhaps were clan symbols which had implied territorial meaning.

As yet, no researcher has discovered a consistent, meaningful pattern of relationship between Anasazi and Fremont dwelling sites and rock art sites.

Other anomalies in the location of rock art have also been observed. One canyon that was occupied and used by the Fremonts had a geologic setting that created terraced rather than sheer canyon walls, with numerous suitable rock art locations on each terrace. Yet in that canyon, researchers noted that the plentiful rock art in the canyon diminished in density and complexity in relation to its height above the canyon floor. This may or may not have been due to any "laziness" on the part of those who created the rock art. Within another Fremont area, rock art density remained essentially the same at various distances above the Green River, and there were about equal proportions of petroglyphs and pictographs altogether, but the ratio of pictographs to petroglyphs increased noticeably with elevation. This may have been due to improving opportunities for sheltering pictos but could also have other significance or perhaps none at all.

A common puzzle is why a single large rock art panel will have on it rock art by several different artists, done at different times or even by different cultures, even though there were plenty of suitable rock surfaces nearby where fresh, clean starts could have been made by each new craftsman. Why this impulse to put new rock art close to, or even superimposed over, older rock art? Was there a cultural rationalization for this? If so, it must have been a strong one because such culturally and temporally mixed rock art panels are fairly common in canyon country. Was the cause for such crowding and mixing of rock art simply a holdover of some human territorial instinct, a subconscious male need to put a personal mark where other males have already marked, like male bears claw the same trees, male cats spray the same bushes, or male dogs urinate on the same fireplugs? If so, this instinct is still with us, because all too many prehistoric rock art panels also contain historic and modern names, dates and assorted graffiti, even in locations where unblemished rock is plentiful nearby.

Typical crowded petroglyph panel, Sand Island, San Juan River, Utah.

41

So far, no serious researcher has proposed an explanation for the crowding of rock art that is so apparent many places in canyon country, or even recognized the strangeness of the phenomenon.

Another location anomaly that has been noticed, although rarely subjected to scientific analysis, is the odd fact that quite a bit of rock art is found in caves, alcoves and on cliff surfaces at heights that are presently well above normal human reach. In some cases, the answer is obvious — the craftsman stood on a dwelling structure roof or wall that has since collapsed, or on slabs of rock that have since settled or fallen. At some locations, however, there are no easy answers to out-of-reach rock art — no rock slabs and no earlier structures.

One possible answer to above-reach rock art is that the craftsman either climbed up using the narrow cracks and ledges that are common in sandstone, or he used a kind of tree-pole ladder that was in common use in prehistoric times. These obvious possibilities are often overlooked by researchers who speculate only that the ground level must have lowered due to wind or water erosion.

As an example of this, one respected archaeologist reached the totally indefensible conclusion that "where evidence exists of soil erosion beneath a panel of petroglyphs, those petroglyphs which are higher on the vertical cliff and are of a different style antedate the petroglyphs positioned below."

It is a fact that in canyon country caves and alcoves, and at the bases of cliffs, the ground level does fluctuate, but not always in the down direction. Changing wind patterns repeatedly build up, then remove, huge amounts of sand and dust within caves and along cliff bases, thus changing the ground level in either direction and within a relatively short span of time. This wildly variable process is still further complicated by water erosion cycles that remove sediments from canyon bottoms during one climatic phase, then build them back up during the next. To illustrate this, rock art has actually been found below the existing natural ground level at some archaeological excavation sites.

Because of these natural variables and other possible answers to the puzzle of above-reach rock art, only a trained scientist familiar with canyon country archaeology, geology, weather, paleoclimate and erosional modes could determine the prehistoric ground level at a particular site and then only after a detailed and complex analysis.

In the final analysis, the answer to this rock art location puzzle may not be important, but the numerous offhanded inferences based upon "lower ground level" that appear in rock art literature are indicative of the kind of unscientific thinking that has so far dominated the field of rock art research, a factor that is very important. For example, one widely respected researcher, upon observing some rock art fifteen feet above the bottom of a sheer-walled canyon, wrote that "such height might suggest considerable antiquity" without even considering the much simpler explanation that the rock art craftsman has used a common pole-ladder.

IMPLICATIONS FROM LOCATIONS

There is virtually no limit to the number of inferences, or educated guesses, that could be drawn from the unchallengeable facts of rock art locations. A great many appear in rock art literature, some weak and poorly supported, some reinforced by evidence or inferences from other areas of archaeological study. A few examples of the kinds of inferences that could be drawn from rock art locations are noted in the following paragraphs:

Inference from rock art concentration at some sites, none at equally good nearby sites, none near many heavily used dwelling sites, choice of protected sites: much rock art was serious business, with the craftsmen being a select few who chose their locations for repeated use and to fit special conditions in addition to practicality.

Inference from "boundary marker" type petroglyphs: some rock art had territorial or clan-related uses.

Inference from numerous rock art locations near special use areas such as dwellings, game trails, water, travel routes, foraging areas: some uses of rock art were related to the daily lives of the people within the cultures that created it.

Inference from many major rock art panels being located far from dwelling sites: the ceremonial uses of some rock art sites were important enough to warrant considerable travel and sacrifice of time, energy and resources by those who used them.

Inference from location of some rock art very near ground level: it was made by children. One researcher made this ridiculous assumption without considering that in canyon country ground levels change, and despite plentiful evidence that children were strictly forbidden to make rock graphics.

Inference from location of rock art near game trails, watering holes, hunting blinds and traps: hunting magic was a part of the prehistoric cultural heritage of the region.

Inference from the total lack of rock art near sites occupied over long periods of time: there was a very strong cultural taboo against the creation of rock markings by anyone not specially designated for this, a taboo so powerful and consistently enforced that hundreds of children over hundreds of years of occupancy did not make a single glyph of any sort on handy rock walls that simply begged for graphic displays. An alternate to this "taboo" inference might be that at some occupancy sites not one person ever conceived of the idea of graphics on rock and that the idea was never introduced by contact with other settlements. Of the two, the "taboo" inference is by far the stronger.

Inference from the relative scarcity of rock art within a region that was occupied and used by hundreds of thousands of prehistoric Indians of several cultures over a period of several thousand years: the creation and use of rock graphics was not all that important to most individuals in relation to other cultural activities.

Some researchers automatically assume that if a panel of rock art is within the known use area of a particular prehistoric culture, then it was probably created by members of that culture. They then construct additional inferences upon this one, such as attempting to date the rock art on the basis of the assumed cultural affiliation. This kind of multi-level inference building is another major flaw that appears all too often in existing rock art literature. While this kind of conjectural extrapolation is a valid analytical tool if properly used, and in rock art study may sometimes be the only tool available, serious rock art students should bear in mind that the probable validity of an idea goes down rapidly with each added level of inference.

It should be borne in mind that all of the foregoing inferences are simply ideas that might be true. They should not be considered "fact." Many other inferences could also be made from the bare facts of where rock art is located, and where it is not located, within the Anasazi and Fremont cultural areas. Some of these inferences are discussed in later chapters, as are others based upon rock art techniques, materials, graphic styles and apparent subject matter and age.

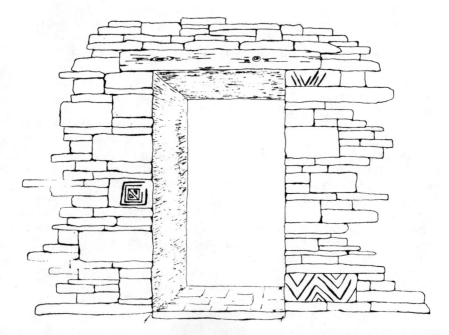

SUBJECT MATTER

WHAT ARE THEY?

As noted in the previous chapter on rock art locations, virtually all of the indisputable factual evidence concerning Anasazi and Fremont rock art falls into two categories — its actual location and its actual graphic shape. It is important to note that this observation states "graphic shape" not "subject matter," which is not factual but a matter of inference, another example of "viewer interpretation" versus "creator intent."

In fact, with rock art subject matter, the philosophical axiom "nothing is what it seems to be" is quite appropriate. There is bound to be an enormous, unbridgeable gap between what a highly educated person of the late Twentieth Century sees in a rock graphic and what its Stone-Age creator had in mind while producing that graphic many hundreds, perhaps thousands, of years ago. Modern adults have a miserable record of determining the subject matter of even their own children's early attempts at graphic representation. A crudely scrawled crayon figure that looks like "doggy?" may instead be an "airplane" or "da-da!" And the graphic concept gap between the modern adult and a prehistoric rock art craftsman is infinitely greater than with a modern child who has been surrounded by graphic examples and conceptual sophistication from birth on.

Thus, the identification of actual rock art subject matter is in many cases much like cloud-watching — no two people will see the same shapes in the same cloud mass. There are many examples of this kind of subjective thinking in rock art literature. For example, one honest researcher noted that while the large "ear loops" on a particular petroglyph figure were assumed by others to be big whorls of hair similar to those affected by historic Hopi girls, the loops "might as readily represent ears, or the horns of curly-horned mountain sheep."

Another researcher, who was trying to count the numbers of "anthropomorphs" and "zoomorphs" on a big rock art panel for the purpose of making a statistical style analysis, became so befuddled over trying to tell stick-figure men with oversized phalluses from stick-figure lizards with tails that he finally made an arbitrary decision — if the phallus/tail was longer than the rear legs, it was a tail, and the figure was a lizard. Otherwise, it was a man. It would be difficult to imagine a more scientifically meaningless exercise than the resulting style analysis, yet all too many "scientific" rock art analyses and reports are based upon just such subjective assumptions about the subject matter of rock art.

In every analysis of rock art that involves the subject matter and meaning of rock art figures, if the purpose is to make valid inferences about those who created the figures and their cultures, then it is imperative that the analyst know exactly what the rock art craftsman had in mind as to subject matter, rather than what it looks like to the analyst. A certain figure may appear to represent a human, for example, but that is inferential, subjective judgment, not objective fact. A researcher who labels certain rock art figures "headhunters" or "ghost figures" is making unfounded assumptions. For certain analytical purposes it is valid to make assumptions, but in no case can the result of that analysis be any more valid than the facts and assumptions upon which it was based. This is simply another way of stating the old homily, "a chain is only as strong as its weakest link." In scientific analysis, the chain links are facts and assumptions, and the conclusion based on these is the chain's net strength. There are a great many weak links in the chains of logic found in most rock art literature, and serious students of that literature should maintain a healthy scientific skepticism while reading it.

Typical "anthropomorphs," or human-like figures, Ninemile Canyon, Utah. Did the figures represent humans? Shamans? Spirits? Dieties? Kachinas? Only the person who created them could be certain.

In the real world, on actual rock art panels, no modern human can know with certainty what a prehistoric Anasazi or Fremont rock art craftsman had in mind when he made a particular figure, not even a modern American Indian in the same cultural lineage. If researchers see a great many rock art figures that appear to be humans, then it is fairly safe to assume that at least some of those that look like humans were intended to be humans. But even then it is not very safe to conclude that any specific figure represents a human, because it has also been well established that prehistoric craftsmen depicted gods and other supernatural beings in human form.

Thus, while fairly good general assumptions about the actual subject matter depicted by rock art figures can be made from a large number of observations, the use of such general assumptions for detailed analyses is very bad science and can only lead to highly questionable conclusions.

Those who choose to study Anasazi and Fremont rock art solely for its charm, craftsmanship, sense of antiquity and aesthetic beauty need not be too concerned over what subjects are actually depicted, but serious researchers who wish to study rock art as one facet of a complex prehistoric culture, and to use it as a key to other aspects of that culture, must be coldly factual and objective about rock art subject matter, age, meaning and use. The principal hard facts about canyon country rock art are its actual location and actual graphic shape. Ideas concerning what those shapes represented to their creators are simply conjectures, guesses, assumptions, with varying degrees of probability of being correct.

SOME ASSUMPTIONS

A number of attempts have been made to classify rock art on the basis of its apparent subject matter. The most basic of such systems divides all rock art into two groups of subjects, representational and non-representational, that is, images that appear to represent something in the real world and those that do not. This is basically a simple and unambiguous classification, but serves little purpose beyond providing important-sounding labels for verbal descriptions of rock art images.

The "representational" group of rock art subject matter can be further broken down into groups such as "anthropomorphs" or human-like figures, "zoomorphs" or animal-like figures, supernatural beings, vegetation and "who knows?" Several writers have even compiled lengthy glossaries of terms for various rock art subjects. Some of their terms are quite subjective. Again, however, such classifications are largely useful only as descriptive labels, although some highly questionable attempts have been made to perform statistical analyses based upon such arbitrary groupings.

At present, after several decades of field work and study by a few professionals and many dedicated amateurs, enough Anasazi and Fremont rock art has actually been seen and photographed to make some pretty good general assumptions as to what subject matter is depicted, even though care must be exercised in applying these general assumptions to specific images. From this cautious viewpoint, then, it is possible to say that certain kinds of natural or "representational" subjects are depicted in canyon country prehistoric rock art. Among these kinds of images are humans, both male and female but predominantly male; large animals such as deer, desert sheep, bison, elk, cougar and antelope; small animals such as foxes, skunks, coyotes, wildcats and bats; birds such as geese, ducks, eagles, turkeys, macaws, cranes, herons and other species less easy to identify; reptiles such as lizards and snakes; insects, centipedes, spiders and scorpions; human weapons such as atlatls and darts, spears, stone knives and axes, clubs, bows and arrows; flutes, pottery, and astronomical objects such as the sun, moon, planets, stars and the occasional supernova.

The "dragon" of Black Dragon Canyon, Utah. With the original pictograph image very faint, the chalked outline is highly questionable.

Other subjects of less certain identity are human children, dogs, certain hand tools, shields, rattles, rain clouds, lightning, tadpoles, a few plants, and such supernatural entities as gods and spirits. In the "extremely improbable" class there are prehistoric creatures such as "mastodons" and "dinosaurs" and mythical creatures such as "dragons." There are rock art images that look like these creatures, but their appearances are most likely a matter of poor artistry, mistaken identity or incorrect age determination for the image. The "dragon" pictograph in Black Dragon Canyon, Utah, was extremely faint until some helpful person outlined with chalk what he thought was shown. Before that, the shape could have been almost anything. The "dinosaur" image in White Canyon, Utah, could be some prehistoric or historic craftsman's flight of fancy, but is certainly not a sketch of a brontosaurus made from life. The two "mastodon" petroglyphs near Moab and Monticello in Utah are obviously too recent to have been made before these creatures went extinct in North America many thousands of years ago. Steward, writing in his 1936 report about claims that some rock art depicted extinct animals, said that:

". . . none of these claims is wholly convincing, for careless and unskilled drawing produced such distortions of the humbler species that they might easily be mistaken for anything under the sun and for many things that never existed. It is very often impossible to know whether the artist intended a now extinct species, or a purely imaginary creature or whether he simply could not draw any better. As well suppose that the blundering scrawls of modern children are prehistoric monsters."

Within the category of "human" images there are many variations. They may be simple stick-man figures such as a very young child might draw, or their bodies might be round, oval, triangular, rectangular, trapezoidal, hourglass shaped, or combinations of these. Rarely do the bodies even come close to true human proportions. The bodies may have heads of many shapes or no heads at all. Isolated human heads and faces are common. Facial features are always simplistic or missing entirely. Legs and arms may be simple or complex, or there might be arms only or neither arms nor legs. Feet and hands are generally missing or rudimentary.

Human frontal and side views both occur, but frontal is more common. Angled views are virtually nonexistent. Male genitals are fairly common. Female breasts and genitals occur but are relatively rare. Clothing is either rare or not indisputably clothing. Body and head ornaments are common, weapons less so. Human coition is depicted in several ways, as is bestiality or human-animal coition. Human and animal pregnancy and human birth are occasionally depicted, either in realistic or symbolic form. Hunting scenes appear many places, as do human handprints, a few with missing thumbs or odd numbers of fingers, and both human and animal footprints. Sandal prints are not uncommon.

Typical petroglyph panel depicting animals, Behind the Rocks, Utah.

In a few hunting scenes, humans disguised as animals are depicted, usually wearing what appears to be the head and skin of the animal being stalked and carrying a hunting weapon such as spear or bow. At some sites anthropomorphic figures appear to be dancing or running or performing ceremonies. Other human figures apparently represent special cultural personages, such as chiefs or shamans, and some seem to be holding captive birds on leashes. Some birds are depicted perched on the heads of human figures, a practice believed to have religious significance.

One particular human-seeming figure appears almost universally throughout the Anasazi-Fremont region, even though some researchers have concluded that the image was introduced into these cultures from Mexico fairly late. The figure varies from place to place but generally depicts a humped-back human in profile, blowing a flute and with an exaggerated, tumescent phallus. The figure has been labeled "Kokopelli" after a Hopi "kachina" which it resembles, although it is not certain that there is a direct cultural connection.

"Kokopelli" figures may be simple stick-men or more complex. They may be standing, walking or lying on their backs. Most but not all have flutes to their mouths. Some are accompanied by what seem to be dogs, and a few carry bows and arrows. A few look insectile in shape, but that may simply be a subjective interpretation of a poorly drawn figure. Not all Kokopelli figures have exaggerated, erect phalluses, nor do all have humps on their backs. There are two schools of thought about these "humps." One asserts that they are actual or symbolic deformaties. The other holds that they are backpacks full of certain practical and ceremonial items.

Typical "Kokopelli," with flute and tumescent phallus, La Cieneguilla area, New Mexico. R. A. Williamson photo.

Whatever the details and meanings associated with the "Kokopelli" images, there are many of these images, especially within the Anasazi region. Some large petroglyph panels there depict dozens of these distinctive anthropomorphs. Kokopelli, or the flute-man, is discussed more fully in the chapter on rock art interpretation.

Certain kinds of images are conspicuous by their absence from canyon country rock art. Determining why they are absent or rare could lead to valuable knowledge about the cultures that produced the graphics. Among specific items common to the real world of the Anasazi and Fremont cultures, yet extremely rare in their rock art, are fish and plants. Also quite rare are depictions of such basic human characteristics and activities as slavery, brutality, aggression, war, personal combat and death, all quite common in the graphics of other prehistoric cultures.

50

While some researchers claim to see "decapitated heads" on some rock art panels, the "heads" could just as easily be ceremonial masks. The "shields" that appear late may also be ceremonial or something else entirely, and the few man-to-man "fighting" scenes could be ritual or symbolic rather than actual combat. Similarly, most of the few reported "fish" and "plant" graphics could as well be something else when the actual images are examined. Certainly fish were known to the Anasazis and Fremonts. Pioneers found the region's rivers teeming with several species of large fish, and Coronado, the first Spanish explorer through the Arizona-New Mexico area, reported that the pueblo tribes there, when asked to draw pictures of all the animals known to them, "quickly painted two for us, one of the animals and the other of the birds and fishes." Either way, the scarcity in Anasazi and Fremont rock art of such ordinary subjects and basic human activities and characteristics is highly significant and should be systematically studied.

Another whole category missing entirely from the spectrum of canyon country rock art subject matter is that of items that were an intimate part of Anasazi and Fremont daily lives and should thus have been depicted in their graphic lexicon. Among these are pottery, cooking utensils, hand tools, dwellings, foods, clothing, blankets and other textiles, footwear, games and musical instruments, however crude. Only Kokopelli's "flute" appears. Harvesting, a very important activity in an agrarian culture, is also not shown. The "Harvest Scene" in The Maze at Canyonlands National Park could easily be some other activity. It has been conjectured that such items and activities were not depicted because they were women's things, while the rock art craftsmen were men, depicting men's things. These ideas are discussed further in the next chapter.

Non-representational rock art shapes are endless in their variety but include some that occur many places and often several times on the same rock art panel. Whether this repetitive use of certain figures is meaningful or not is unclear, although some researchers have built elaborate hypotheses upon statistical analyses of such repeated occurrences of rock art figures. The value of such hypotheses is debatable.

Fairly common geometric or non-representational figures or patterns include circles, spirals, concentric circles, parallel lines, zigzag lines, rows of dots, squares, rectangles, trapezoids, diamonds, triangles, cross-hatching, chevrons and stippling, plus endless combinations of these forms and others that defy description or labeling. A few researchers claim that some geometric shapes and patterns of lines represent things or have meanings. A squiggle of curving, connected lines is supposed to be a "map" of a canyon system. A series of short lines is a counting system, or other combinations of lines may be "ladders" or "plants" or "animal tracks" or "rainbows" or "wheels." While a few such conjectures may, of course, be true, most are like cloud-watching — very subjective.

In summary, while the apparent variety of Anasazi and Fremont rock art subject matter is quite broad, when its diversity and quantity are considered from the viewpoint of the total geographic area, the large numbers of people and great length of time involved, there is amazingly little total rock art, and what does exist is startingly limited in variety of subject matter. Whole broad categories of items and activities known to have existed within the cultures, or known to have been common in other prehistoric cultures, are either very rare or missing entirely from the region's rock art. It could be said that what is not found depicted in canyon country rock art is just as significant and interesting as what is found, and even more difficult to study.

A FEW INFERENCES

In the previous chapter some sample inferences were drawn to illustrate how the hard facts of rock art location can be used to hypothesize about other aspects of the culture that created the graphics. Similar extrapolations can be made from the "facts" of rock art subject matter, although since the actual identity of so many rock art figures is uncertain, any inferences made on the basis of such identity assumptions will be equally uncertain. To give two examples, if an inference is based upon the fairly solid assumption that a great many human figures are depicted in canyon country rock art, then that inference will be fairly valid. However, if an inference is based upon the assumption that the anthropomorphs on a particular rock art panel were intended by their creators to be humans, an assumption very poorly supported by indisputable fact, then that inference and all analyses and hypotheses based upon it will be equally weak and unsupported.

Following are some examples of the kinds of inferences that could be, or have been, drawn from subject matter apparently depicted by Anasazi and Fremont rock art:

Inference from predominantly male-interest subject matter: most if not all rock art craftsmen were adult males.

Inference from the frequent occurrence of obviously non-human anthropomorphs, and ceremonial-type apparel, decorations and gear on human figures: many rock art sites had religious significance and were used repeatedly for ceremonial purposes.

Inference from the general lack of graphics showing war, combat, captivity, slavery, torture, mutilation, execution and other similar common human activities: the Anasazi and Fremont cultures were peaceful, and prosperous and had little contact with other cultures. They were apparently so non-aggressive and non-violent that their cultures were singular anomalies among prehistoric, historic and contemporary human cultures. This inference alone is deserving of considerable study.

Inference from the general lack of figures depicting such "higher personages" as kings, chiefs, nobles and members of a religious hierarchy: the Anasazi and Fremont cultures were remarkably democratic and lacked a highly developed class system. Coronado first formulated this inference when he encountered the Anasazi remnant enclave at Zuñi in 1540. While trying to make peace with a particular Zuñi pueblo, he asked to see their "lord" but remarked, "by what I can find out and observe, none of these towns has any lord, for I have not seen any principal house by which any superiority over others might be manifested."

Inference from the relative scarcity of rock art and scenes depicting objects and ceremonies related to the basic functions of living: canyon country prehistoric agrarian cultures were largely so successful that they were not preoccupied with bare subsistence and could spend time and effort on more esoteric religious ideas and practices.

Inference from the widespread existence of apparent celestial rock art subject matter: the cultures had knowledge of and an interest in astronomical affairs, and used their knowledge for practical purposes. This is discussed further in a later chapter.

Inference from the appearance in Anasazi and Fremont rock art of figures similar to those found in the graphics of other prehistoric American Indian cultures: the ideas for the similar figures must have migrated into the canyon country cultures from those other cultures. With such subjects as Kokopelli and parrots, this inference is fairly well warranted, but with "shields," astronomical images and certain geometric designs, the inference has considerably less validity. It ignores something that has occurred countless times throughout human history and that is basic to human nature — parallel but independent invention.

Within current rock art literature, many relatively weak inferences, hypotheses and "facts" are based upon apparent, but not indisputable, rock art subject matter. Some examples:

Inference: valid information about such cultural attributes as clothing worn, tools used, animals domesticated, ornaments worn, foods eaten, colonization programs, etc., might be derived from rock art subject matter.

Inference: the very limited scope of rock art subject matter was due to "tradition." This inference ignores many other vital factors that could affect the variety of graphic designs.

Inference: the fairly common appearance of "crosses" in canyon country rock art is somehow related to the cross of Christianity, or the occasional appearance of a swastika is somehow linked to a prehistoric form of fascism. Such inferences ignore the facts that "crosses" and "swastikas" of various types are common throughout the graphics of most Western Hemisphere prehistoric cultures and that two crossing lines, whether straight or bent-armed, simple or decorated, are such an elementary graphic design that it could hardly fail to be invented in any graphics-oriented culture.

Inference: there is a temporal relationship between certain rock art geometric designs and similar-appearing designs on prehistoric pottery. Such a relationship may exist, but it has not to date been demonstrated and is unlikely for several reasons. Efforts to date rock art images by comparing their designs with similar ones on datable pottery are highly questionable.

Many other inferences could be and have been made from apparent Anasazi and Fremont rock art subject matter, some more reasonable than others. In a field of study so lacking in hard evidence, inference-making is a valid scientific tool. That tool must be used, however, very carefully and with knowledge of its inherent limitations in use and with equal consideration given all alternate explanations for the same basic hard data.

Readers should bear in mind that all of the preceding inferences are simply possibilities, not facts, with each possibility having its own probability of being correct. Some of the noted ideas have a good chance of being substantiated by further research, while others will doubtless prove to be errant nonsense. The biggest single variable in making inferences from rock art subject matter is determining exactly what each image was intended to be by its creator. Still other variables in the study of rock art are discussed in following chapters.

Canyon de Chelly National Monument. NPS photo by David P. Fletcher.

THE ARTISTS

ARTISTS OR CRAFTSMEN?

It is difficult to stand before a panel of canyon country rock art without wondering what kind of people, what kind of individuals put it there, yet most serious literature on the subject studiously skirts this important question or makes a carefully hedged guess, then goes quickly on to other matters. A few researchers make casual assumptions, while others avoid any mention of the subject. The field of study does not even have a word or phrase for those who create rock graphics, let alone one that is suitable, unambiguous and generally accepted. That is why none was noted in the earlier chapter on definitions.

It is logical, of course, to say that those who created the "rock art" were "artists." The semantic hazards inherent in the use of the word "art" were discussed earlier and are explored further in the chapter on interpretation. By extension, use of the word "artist" is equally unsuitable for serious applications.

The word "craftsman" is used in this book since it is more appropriate than "artist," yet "craftsman" is also less than perfect. The word contains implications that the creation of Anasazi and Fremont rock graphics was a craft, and only a craft, which is far from true. In fact, the crafting process seems to have been largely incidental to other more serious purposes and of little importance in itself. Certainly, an enormous amount of rock art was created with little attention to detail, technique or quality of image, with the end result hardly the kind of product that a skilled, conscientious craftsman would be proud to display. For lack of a better, standard archaeological term, however, the word "craftsman" is used in this book for the individuals who made rock graphic images. Where the word "artist" is occasionally used, it is used with the full understanding that it is not semantically correct.

WHICH CULTURE?

While very few serious rock art books or reports even try to analyze in depth the questions of who created the graphics — which culture and what individuals within that culture — many of them do make the usually unspoken assumption that if the rock graphics were within the known usage area of a particular culture, then that culture created them. This assumption may, in some cases, be fairly valid, but in others it is not sound enough to serve as a basis for still further assumptions and inferences.

Even within the relatively isolated canyon country heartland of the Anasazi and Fremont cultures, the land usage pattern was rarely simple, especially if consideration is given to the entire span of time during which some form or another of rock art was being produced in the general region. Most archaeologists agree that the oldest rock graphics in this region date well back into the Desert Archaic era, long before the official beginnings of the Formative stage Anasazis and Fremonts. This makes it necessary to consider a time span of several thousand years when assigning specific rock graphics to specific cultures. That even the approximate age of rock art is not always apparent is illustrated by the fact that with one controversial panel of pictographs in Canyonlands National Park, various experts assign it to cultures more than one thousand years apart in age.

It is quite probable that some limited areas within the general region were used only by one particular sub-group of one specific and well defined prehistoric culture, thus making it fairly safe to assume a direct relationship between that cultural group and any rock art found in its usage area. In most of the region, however, occupancy and use patterns were not so simple, nor for that matter have these tangled usage patterns even been determined. While it is known that most of the region did get multicultural use during the last several thousand years, little is known about the details of such uses, their geographic and temporal boundaries and possible periods of coexistence and cross influence. It is also well established that many major dwelling areas saw several periods of usage, some of them separated by decades, even centuries of non-occupancy. As a further complication, the nomadic tribes that roamed the mountains, prairies and deserts to the north, east and west of the region did occasionally venture into the region, despite its isolation and forbidding nature. These tribes also had rock graphics traditions, and no doubt left samples of their work in canyon country.

With so much of the Anasazi and Fremont region having a mixed cultural background, one could reasonably conclude that serious researchers would be very careful about assuming the cultural origin of any particular panel of rock art, yet such caution is rarely apparent in contemporary literature on the subject. As with rock art subject matter, it is sometimes desirable and relatively safe to make certain general assumptions for the sake of scientific analysis, but only on the basis of statistically large amounts of information. Conversely, it is not safe to make more detailed, specific assumptions about rock art cultural identity, or to apply the general assumptions to the study of specific individual rock art sites. Even so, these analytical errors occur frequently within existing rock art literature and cast doubt upon their scientific validity.

To illustrate how difficult it is to assign cultural affiliation to a specific rock art panel, take two typical examples, one at or very near to a dwelling site, the other remote from any occupancy site.

With the first example it is easy and very tempting to assume that the pictographs on the alcove wall above the dwelling ruins were painted by those who built the dwelling, but this ignores a number of questions and other possibilities. Was the site occupied and used by more than one culture or subcultural group? If so, which one, or ones, made the pictos? Or were the images there even before the occupation of the alcove? If so, what culture put them there? Could they have been painted long after the last

Typical rock art associated with dwelling ruins, Salt Creek Canyon, Canyonlands National Park.

occupation period? If so, by whom? Even if the site saw only one occupancy, couldn't some nomadic culture, or some hunting or foraging party of a nearby dwelling area, have made the pictos while camping out one night in the alcove, either before or after that occupancy?

Difficulties in dating rock art make it almost impossible to answer such questions, even after a dwelling site may have been excavated, dated and thoroughly studied. But, until a rock art researcher has positive, factual answers to these and other such questions, it is simply poor scientific discipline to assume that rock graphics and ruins found at one site were both created by the same group of people. Even apparent evidence may not be conclusive. A government explorer reported in the 1820s that pictographs found near some cliff dwellings in southwestern Colorado "were certainly done by the cliff-dwellers and probably while the houses were in process of construction, since the material used is identical with the plaster of the houses." The "identical" conclusion was based only upon a casual visual comparison, not chemical analysis, and is hence questionable. Nor does the explorer even consider the possibility that some later visitor to the deserted pueblo could have used its plaster to make the pictograph paint.

With rock art sites remote from dwelling areas, cultural association is even less certain. With no way to date the rock art, it could conceivably fall anywhere within a span of several thousand years, although by now enough information has been accumulated about rock art aging, application techniques and subject matter to narrow the time frame down to several centuries with many sites. Even so, that leaves the matter of cultural affiliation in question many places. Still other factors that complicate cultural identification are discussed later in this chapter.

In determining the cultural affiliation of an isolated rock art site, many questions should be considered. Was the rock art made by the culture that occupied the nearest permanent dwelling site, wherever that may be, or was it made by an intruding group that was trying to avoid the local people for practical reasons? Was the rock art even contemporary with the local culture? If the area had seen multicultural use, which one, if any of them, created the rock art? Or was it the work of a hunting-foraging party from some nearby nomadic tribe?

If two or more groups of rock art on a remote panel exhibit distinct differences in technique, subject matter, graphic design or age, does each group represent a different cultural origin, the same culture at different times or simply several individual craftsmen, each with his own approach to rock graphics? Was the site near some obvious usage area, such as a hunting-foraging camp or a summer camp for a remote field under cultivation? Was it near a game trail, a source of water or a seasonal migration route for humans or local herbivores? Was the site used repeatedly for ceremonial purposes? All of these questions and many more bear upon the association of a specific remote rock art site with a specific culture, yet rarely are such analyses made in most literature on the subject before a cultural assignment is made, then used throughout subsequent analyses.

To summarize, while it is possible to assign some canyon country rock art to particular prehistoric cultures with reasonable certainty, and it is possible to draw certain generalities about the region's rock art and its cultural affiliations, a considerable percentage of the rock art within the general Anasazi and Fremont cultural regions cannot be assigned with certainty to those cultures. It is even difficult at times to distinguish historic from prehistoric rock art, unless obviously historic subject matter is depicted, such as horses or firearms.

It can be generalized that most of the rock graphics within the Fremont territory were created by the Fremonts or their Desert Archaic predecessors, and that much of the rock art found in Anasazi territory originated from that culture. But each of these regions experienced cultural intrusions before, during and after their principal occupation periods, and there was even considerable variation within the two main cultures. These and other factors make cultural identification of most canyon country rock graphics a matter of inference, or educated guessing, with very few such identifications being based upon indisputable scientific evidence.

WHAT INDIVIDUALS?

With rock art cultural identification so difficult, is anything known about what kinds of individuals made rock graphics? As noted earlier, the locations, limited subject matter and relative scarcity of rock art in canyon country indicate that not just everyone went around pecking, rubbing, scratching or smearing images on rock wherever they found a handy or suitable place, and whenever they felt a creative or communicative impulse.

If not anyone and everyone, then what particular individuals made rock graphics? This question is, of course, inseparable from questions about rock art use and meaning and other cultural matters. For example, consider the probable interest of the general Anasazi or Fremont population in rock art, and try then to decide who within that population might have a positive, creative interest in the subject and who had the time to pursue that interest.

In making this analysis it must be borne in mind that even with the help of crude agriculture, it was not so easy to make a living in canyon country that three-fourths or more of the population could turn its attention to more civilized, creative matters as happens in more modern agrarian cultures. The Anasazi and Fremont cultures did find the time and energy to make steady advances in such aspects of early civilization as architecture, religion, ceramics, communications and trade. However, both cultures, even in their heyday, were balanced precariously on the brink of disaster at all times, totally vulnerable to the slightest variations in the high-desert weather and climate upon which their agriculture depended. Ultimately, one such variation contributed toward the extinction of these thriving cultures.

Thus, it is fairly safe to conclude that even as the two major canyon country cultures progressed into their Formative stages, they could afford to support very few if any non-working individuals. This leads to a tentative conclusion that the creation and use of rock art was not a major function of the population but rather was delegated to a very few specialists who also had other duties.

Who could these specialists be, and were they given "exclusive rights" to create rock art? If so, why? Did the average pueblo dweller have any urge or reason or ability to make marks on rocks? Did children get into the act? If not, as seems highly probable, why not? How do you keep generations of kids from imitating things they see adults doing at special times and places, often quite near their dwellings? These and many other questions still plague serious rock art researchers, although most have so far managed to ignore the subject. Yet, with the question of "who made rock art" so intimately linked with its uses and meanings, neither of these aspects can be studied scientifically without also addressing the problem of who created these first graphics within these primitive cultures.

Some early American explorers took a simple approach to solving this question when they first began to encounter prehistoric rock art. They asked the local Indians and were told quite firmly, "supernatural beings." This simplistic answer to the puzzle is still with us, among some

Sego Canyon, Utah.

contemporary Indians.

Some modern researchers seek answers to the riddle by extrapolating back through time from the present and historic Indian customs of tribes believed to be descendents of the Anasazi culture. One archaeologist notes that historic Hopis made periodic pilgrimages to remote sites for various alleged reasons and made clan-symbol petroglyphs at the site each time, with the glyphs supposedly made by the clan leaders or medicine men. Prehistoric rock art panels, however, do not commonly exhibit such repeated, stylized images, so this hypothesis concerning the creation and use of such rock art does not seem to be supported by the evidence.

Another writer has noted that at certain Rio Grande area pueblos, it is the custom for certain tribal members to fast for a time, then make petroglyphs of their "visions." This would imply that the having of a light-headed "vision" was the main, or only, prerequisite for being a rock artist. While this concept may have some merit, especially if the use of certain available natural hallucinogens is considered in addition to fasting, the relatively narrow scope of apparent rock art subject matter does not seem consistent with the wide scope of human "visions" from either source.

Thus, as with cultural identification of rock art, if enough basic data is accumulated, it is possible to generalize about the individuals who created rock graphics with some fair chance of being correct. It is not, however, possible to look at any particular prehistoric rock art panel and say with any great assurance that it was created by one particular kind of individual and not another.

SOME GENERALIZATIONS

As noted already, it is quite unlikely that rock art could be created by just anyone in the Anasazi and Fremont cultures. The hard facts of rock art locations and apparent subject matter seem to preclude women and children as rock artists, although a cartoon that appeared recently in a popular magazine showed several primitive women painting pictographs in a cave and commenting — "Isn't it strange that all artists are women!?"

There is considerable local evidence to support the idea that prehistoric canyon country rock art was male business, and male subject matter, and its creation was protected by a powerful taboo that kept women confined to decorative graphics, as with basketry, pottery and wearing apparel, and children out of the act entirely, except perhaps for an occasional boy who was being trained as an apprentice. This view is strongly supported by ethnographic studies in other parts of the world.

There is further evidence, primarily in rock art subject matter, that relatively few adult males produced rock art and that those who did only did so as a necessary but not major aspect of their total duties. They were apparently not highly skilled and practiced craftsmen-specialists who took pride in their work, but rather men who out of duty took the time to produce images barely suitable for their purposes, with little thought or concern for image quality or skill improvement.

Again, a study of the raw information about rock art locations and subject matter seems to indicate that the principal purpose for most of it was sacred, ceremonial, sympathetic or protective magic, and hence firmly within the province of the local religious leader, whether he was called "shaman," "medicine man" or something else.

The exception to this is rock art that may not be religion-based, such as some that appears to be counting or record-keeping, decorative, boundary-marking, astronomical, story-telling or just plain doodling of one sort or another. In such cases, the craftsmen could have been almost anyone, including women or children, although with diminishing likelihood for the latter two.

Further, even though it is safe to generalize that most Anasazi and Fremont rock art was created by a select few and very special men, with some occasional other uses and craftsmen, even in those bygone days people were people, and there must have been within these cultures over the centuries a few defiant individuals or aspiring artists who simply couldn't resist making their own petroglyphs or pictographs off in some remote location away from those who enforced the tribal taboos. No doubt, most of these "amateurs" found the effort to be too great, or the end results disappointing, and soon gave up their heretical activities, but not before leaving their enduring legacies of rock graphics to bemuse and confuse modern researchers.

Also, beyond doubt, a few of these unorthodox individuals must have persisted and developed their own techniques, subject matter and graphic styles. Thus, many anomalous rock art panels could be nothing more than the products of prehistoric individuals doing their prehistoric "thing," rather than mysterious "cultural intrusions." Such rock art would not, of course, be culturally significant in any way. It would merely illustrate the basic diversity among human individuals. In the case of canyon country rock art provably made by intruding cultures, only a careful study of those cultures could indicate who within them was allowed to create rock graphics.

Some generalities about rock artists can also be inferred from rock art that can be roughly dated with some fair assurance of accuracy. There is a distinct possibility that has yet to be explored properly, that as the creation and use of rock art developed within the prehistoric cultures of Utah and the general Four Corners region, from late Desert Archaic through early Formative, then backward a big step, there was a general pattern of change in who created the rock graphics and in the cultural importance of the graphics.

Several researchers have noted pieces of this pattern, but no one seems to have brought it all together into one working hypothesis. The apparent general pattern is this, although it varies with each culture and sub-cultural group:

The earliest canyon country and Great Basin rock art appears to have been the first halting efforts by a very primitive people at making graphics of any kind. Their graphics were largely crude scratchings, drillings or chippings on handy, loose rocks or small boulders, with the subject matter either non-representational lines and patterns or simple figures of the sort a very young modern child might make on first attempt. The implication, then, from the medium, technique and subject matter, is that these were largely isolated and random first experiments with a brand new concept — graphics — and that at this early stage there were no particular restrictions or taboos on who did the experimenting. It could be almost anyone with the urge, curiosity and time.

As the isolated cultural groups developed and phased into the Formative stage, the creation of graphics — largely rock art — became a special thing, restricted to a special few, and used for special purposes. This phase represents the main body of this region's prehistoric rock art, and with the Fremonts seems to have persisted until their mysterious and rapid disappearance. With some if not all of the Anasazis, however, a third phase seems to have begun about the time the kiva came into its ultimate use as the primary site for important ceremonies. This third phase of Anasazi rock art appeared during the late Pueblo III stage of the culture or between A.D. 1200 and 1300.

One researcher notes that at about this time all of the datable petroglyphs within a major area of the Glen Canyon region seemed to regress in application technique, design quality and subject matter. All petroglyphs made from then, until the Anasazis finally withdrew completely from the region, were made by hammerstone alone, with no use of the more sophisticated hammerstone-and-chisel technique that had been in use for hundreds of years by the same culture, within the same area. Certainly, some of the petroglyph dating, which was done by association with datable pottery fragments nearby, may have been questionable, and the regression in technique may not have been so universal as reported. Still, the pattern of a change in the creation and use of rock art was strongly indicated, and a similar regression has also been noted by another researcher in Canyon de Chelly, a major Anasazi occupation area to the southeast of Glen Canyon. There, the subject matter depicted in the cruder rock art was also less restricted, with more subjects taken from daily life.

What could have caused this change? There is a good possibility that the change was related to the parallel increase in the use and importance of the kiva as a prime ceremonial place. This hypothesis would hold that as use of the kiva and kiva-wall art for religious functions increased, the use of near or remote special outdoor sites and rock art for these purposes would decrease, as would the importance of rock art in general and taboos against its creation in particular.

Thus, gradually, or in some cases fairly quickly, most or all cultural interest in and control over the creation and use of rock art would cease, reverting back to the aboriginal situation in which just about anyone with the impulse, ability and time could make petroglyphs, and to a lesser extent even pictographs. This drastic change in who was making rock art once the kiva-phase was well underway could easily explain the obvious fact of a deterioration in quality of rock art late within the Anasazi culture.

To date, no other explanations for this trend have been proposed. The most difficult fact to accommodate while considering alternate ideas is the virtually complete reversion to the archaic hammerstone-only petroglyph-making technique. What could induce a whole region's experienced petroglyph makers to go back to using a crude, relatively ineffectual technique that had been abandoned centuries earlier? Or if the late Pueblo III petroglyphs were not made by experienced men, why not, and who did make them? Why had they not been carefully trained in the hammer-and-chisel technique that had been passed on within "shaman" circles for many generations? Did all of the skilled, traditional rock craftsmen suddenly leave the region in the great cultural retreat that was in progress about then, and without training anyone to make rock art for the few people who chose to stay behind?

Whatever the reason for the transition, the concept of untrained, unskilled amateurs taking over the rock art field seems to be the only likely explanation for the strange decline in late-Anasazi rock art quality.

APPLICATION TECHNIQUES

INTRODUCTION

The prehistoric rock graphics of the Anasazis, Fremonts and their predecessors can vary from the simple scratches of one rock on another or smears of natural minerals on a rock made with a wetted finger, to elaborate panels of well designed, elaborately decorated human figures cut into desert varnish, or great murals of complex images painted onto light-hued sandstone cliff faces with durable, multicolored mixtures of mineral pigments.

In between these two extremes of technique sophistication there are several distinct stages and combinations of technique, yet there are factors common throughout the entire range of techniques used to produce prehistoric canyon country rock art. And, as with rock art locations and subject matter, negative factors can be as interesting and important as the positive.

One such negative factor is the virtual lack of pattern or uniformity of technique in relation to originating culture and each culture's steady development in other facets of civilization. Difficulties in dating rock art with any degree of certainty further confuse the study of this problem. Stages of sophistication in application technique can be seen, but fitting these stages in any logical sequence on a cultural development calendar is simply not possible with any acceptable degree of certainty. Generalities can be drawn, but these generalities cannot be used to make useful inferences. For example, the oldest known rock art in the region is some incised pebbles from the Great Basin. These are from an Archaic culture thousands of years in the past, but it is not safe to infer from this that all such primitive-technique incised rocks are that old. In fact, one researcher claims many are from the Fremont period, because some of the rock images somewhat resemble mid-to-late Fremont clay figurines.

It can be shown that, in general, technique sophistication varied between the Anasazi and Fremont cultures, but for some reason the more highly developed Anasazis were somewhat behind the Fremonts in rock graphics technique. Thus, technique sophistication cannot be used as a basis for extrapolations about the using culture.

In general, petroglyph-making techniques developed from the simple scratching of one handheld rock with another, to scratching or chipping a big boulder or cliff face with a harder rock, to a more precise hammer and chisel method with a variety of pits, lines and chipped areas produced. Pictograph painting developed from simple finger smears with native minerals and clays to the use of various kinds of brushes and compounded paints. A few painted petroglyphs were made, and it is known that at a few sites the designs were first sketched out with charcoal or light scratches. But within a cultural area these various stages of development did not march along in lockstep with the general trend of cultural sophistication, nor did each stage appear in any logical sequence as might be expected had prehistoric craftsmen devoted serious thought and time to the subject of rock art techniques. Further, while the simplest and probably the first form of rock graphics was scratched rock, and the most complex was pictographs made from compounded paints, there are no signs of smooth, step-by-step progress between these two technique extremes, even within small cultural groups.

It can thus be inferred that technique was not very important, even to those who made rock art, and that it was left to develop more or less at random, an individual rather than cultural process.

Another factor common to all application techniques was the restraint imposed by the rock medium itself. How this affected rock art locations was discussed in an earlier chapter. The medium also imposed restraints upon application techniques. Using naturally occurring materials, there are very few ways to make lasting marks on rock. From the study of petroglyphs throughout the West, it seems that every one of those techniques was tried, somewhere or another, by someone or another, at some time or another, with no noticeable order, system or sequence. But, again negative data, little effort seems to have been made to pass along and share "new" skills, new methods, even within the narrow scope of those methods. There apparently was no "great rock artists craft union" whose goal was sharing innovations or producing uniform craft quality or technique. One rock art craftsman might be quite skilled and show considerable graphic sophistication, while his contemporary across the canyon system was still pounding away at stick figures or making colored-mud pictographs with his fingers. It was every man for himself, perhaps even with each man's skills and techniques jealously guarded from others.

It can thus be inferred from the almost random mix of rock art application techniques used within the Anasazi and Fremont cultural areas that there was little if any relationship between culture and technique, and that most if not all variations were based upon the individuality of the craftsmen. In sum, the evidence supports the idea that in the development of rock art application technique, parallel but independent development was the rule rather than the exception.

One possible exception to the individuality concept is that in some Anasazi areas, some researchers have noticed a general trend toward technique innovation beginning around A.D. 900 or at the start of the Pueblo II phase. A possible degradation of petroglyph-making technique in certain Anasazi areas was discussed in the previous chapter.

Another uniformity of technique only partly related to the mechanics of making rock art — graphic design concept sophistication — is discussed in the chapter on dating, but this, too, is more closely related to general cultural level than to local variations in development.

PETROGLYPHS

Petroglyphs, by definition, are images cut into rock surfaces. The cuts may be shallow or deep, depending on the intent of the glyph maker, the condition of the rock being cut and the technique used in the cutting.

There are three general types of prehistoric petroglyphs found in the Anasazi and Fremont territories. One type is the shallow scratches found on small, fairly hard rocks and pebbles that have already been shaped and smoothed by river or stream tumbling. The second type is glyphs cut into sandstone that is coated with desert varnish. Such glyphs need not be very deep to produce visual contrast but are usually deeper than the first type because of the way they are produced and the somewhat softer rock into which they are cut. The third type is cut into sandstone, or occasionally some other kind of rock that has no coating of desert varnish, so the glyphs must be cut quite deeply in order to make them visually apparent.

It is highly probable that the earliest petroglyphs produced were the kind found on small rocks. These were made by the simple expedient of scratching one hard rock with another, with one held in each hand. Natural circumstances would have offered many opportunities for this to occur among primitive people. Has anyone ever sat down by a stream without picking up one water-polished rock and marking on it with another? About the only variations in technique possible were to twist a tip of the "tool" stone on the work surface to produce a round spot or to rock the tool stone slightly while holding it firmly against the work surface, thus "walking" it along and producing a tight zigzag line. All three techniques — scratch, twist and walk — were used, although the commonest was simply repeated scratching. Most of the older Archaic-age inscribed pebbles have simple straight or curved lines and non-representational patterns on them, but some, thought to be more recent, depict anthropomorphs. The designs of these seem too sophisticated to be Archaic.

With the other two types of petroglyphs, the images are cut more deeply. Usually, a harder "hammerstone" is used to cut into a softer working surface of sandstone or other rock. If the rock surface being cut has a coating of some sort that has a color different from the native rock beneath, then the glyph need only be deep enough to cut through the coating and reveal the basic rock, thus producing a glyph with suitable visual contrast. With most canyon country glyphs such surface coatings are the very thin, dark desert varnish that builds up on many exposed sandstone surfaces. But other coatings have been used to produce petroglyphs, such as the whitish encrustations often found on rock exposed to mineral-laden water, dark colored lichens, and even the soot on the walls and ceilings of caves. Petroglyphs cut into desert varnish need not be very deep and will endure for centuries with little change, but glyphs cut into minerals, lichens or soot are generally short lived unless cut deeply enough to penetrate the basic rock.

On sandstone and other rock that has no contrasting surface coating, a petroglyph would not be very visible unless special measures were taken. At some such locations, the glyph lines were simply cut more deeply so as to produce visual contrast by shadowing. At a very few sites, the desired contrast was produced by painting the glyph grooves, painting enclosed areas, or both.

In addition to the coating variable, the hardness of the rock being inscribed can also affect the depth of the glyph and, of course, its durability. The sandstones in canyon country vary in hardness from quite hard to so soft that a stick can easily make grooves, although even at its hardest, sandstone does not approach the hardness of granitic rocks. These have dense, crystalline structures that have been hardened by heat, pressure and time, while sandstones are largely sand and other small particles held together by various forms of chemical cementing and bonding.

Petroglyphs cut into rock lacking desert varnish must be deeper in order to provide visual contrast. Chaco Canyon, New Mexico.

Thus at least two factors affected how deeply a petroglyph was cut — the hardness of the work surface and the need to produce an image with suitable visual contrast. Did other human factors also affect petroglyph depth? Did a deeper than necessary glyph mean a more dedicated craftsman? Or one with more brawn than brains? Did it mean the craftsman had a personal style or a touch of creative vanity? Or was it simply a matter of macho overkill, or time to kill? A deeper glyph meant more hard work, more than may have been needed, but when has human behavior ever been strictly logical at any cultural stage?

However deep this type of petroglyph impression, and for whatever reason, it was normally produced using another "hammerstone" rock held in the hand, a rock that was harder than the sandstone being incised. The hammerstone was used in one of two ways, either to impact directly upon the surface being cut, or to hit a second "chisel" rock. The chisel also had to be quite hard in order to cut the work surface and to withstand repeated impact from the hammerstone.

The material removed by each direct blow of a hammerstone was not precise in size or location. This made hammerstone-only petroglyphs look far cruder than those produced using a chisel and hammer. A chisel stone could be held in the proper position, then struck, making much smoother lines. The working edges or points of such chisel stones were fairly sharp, as were those on hammerstones used for direct impact. The occasional drilled petroglyph holes were made using small pointed shards of hard rock fastened to a short wooden shaft. This shaft was spun between the craftsman's hands while the drill tip was held against the work surface.

In addition to harder stones, such as agate, chert, jasper and flint, other fairly durable materials were occasionally used as tools for making petroglyphs, if the work surface was not too hard. Antler, bone and even hardwood sticks were practical on some sandstone, but with rock that soft, the petroglyphs were not very resistant to wind and water erosion.

As noted in the previous chapter, there was a general regional trend of sophistication in making petroglyphs that went from scratched pebbles to hammerstone-only to hammerstone-chisel, with many exceptions at the local level. With the Anasazis, however, at least with certain subcultural groups, there was a distinct step backward in technique late in their cultural existence, back to the hammerstone-only, poorer quality glyphs and a change toward more mundane subject matter. This giant step backward in application technique deserves full investigation, but to date has only been noted in passing by serious researchers.

Also as noted earlier, there is ample evidence upon which to base an inference that in the making of petroglyphs, technique was far less important to these prehistoric image makers than site location and perhaps other unknowable human factors. A modern artist, or even a conscientious craftsman, might consider all the variables of rock hardness, coatings, tools, locations, exposure to erosion, visibility and anticipated use, then choose a site that would be optimum. But each Anasazi and Fremont craftsman apparently had his own priorities, with technique and product quality usually far down the list. He would pick his site, sometimes a poor one, then simply proceed to make petroglyphs by scratching, rubbing, pecking, drilling, chipping, chiseling, gouging, scraping or whatever, until a crude version of the mysterious image in his mind's eye was produced.

PICTOGRAPHS

As noted in the chapter on canyon country rock art locations, pictographs were generally located in protected sites such as in caves or alcoves or beneath overhanging ledges, even though the erosional forces that formed such shelters were still active. At most locations suitable for pictographs a stretch or patch of sandstone wall was used that was fairly firm, smooth, dry and uncoated. Light-hued, uncoated sandstone produced suitable visual contrast with almost any color of pictograph paint, even white. At a few locations, powdery or uneven rock surfaces were smoothed off before the pictographs were applied. This was done by vigorously scrubbing the surface with a handheld chunk of sandstone. Most sites, however, show no signs of surface preparation.

The rock surface was smoothed in preparation for painting the faces of these pictograph figures in Davis Canyon, Canyonlands National Park.

The simplest form of pictograph painting, and probably the first used, was a wetted finger rubbed in a vein of soft, powdery mineral, then smeared on a nearby rock surface. There are many pictos within canyon country that were made this way, whatever their purpose. Quite commonly, thin layers of chalky, colorful minerals are sandwiched between harder layers of sandstone or mudstone. And often, nearby, simple pictographic images are found that are the same color as the layered mineral, with painted lines that are finger-wide. The ready availability of colored clays in some areas has also no doubt contributed to the early creation of pictographs using finger techniques.

There may be other distinct developmental phases in pictographic techniques, but to date little serious research has been done on the subject. When it is, however, it is likely that as with petroglyph-making skills, little pattern will be seen that can be related to other cultural factors or trends. Quite probably, as with petroglyph makers, the biggest variables in pictograph painting techniques were the individuals, perhaps because they were the same individuals.

70

Here, again, is a question that may never be resolved: did one individual in a clan or pueblo make both kinds of rock art, or were there specialists for each type of graphic? The skills were not the same, nor are there many sites that have both petroglyphs and pictographs where it can be proven that the craftsmen were even contemporary, let alone the same individual. Many areas do not even have both kinds of graphics. Most evidence, then, tends to indicate that rock art craftsmen made either petroglyphs or pictographs but rarely if ever both. The question is far from settled, however, and there are interesting cultural inferences involved either way.

Simple wipe-and-smear pictograph painting with handy muds, clays and minerals seldom produced superior, long-lasting images unless by chance the substance used happened to be naturally compounded for endurance and a suitably protected site was chosen. Prehistoric pictograph paints were basically like modern paints in that if they were to last long, they had to contain three basic ingredients, although in some cases a single ingredient could serve two purposes.

The indispensible ingredient was a pigment of some sort. Most but not all compounded picto paints were made using native ores or mineral clays that naturally retained their color and were relatively insoluble in water. These inorganic pigments lasted, they endured the centuries very well, so long as they were protected from the mechanical forces of wind and water erosion and rock surface scaling.

The vegetable pigments or dyes sometimes used were organic and did not last. This has had two major effects on pictograph durability. If vegetable colors were used entirely, the pictographs simply disappeared in time, or parts of images made with such pigments did. A number of pictograph sites in Utah have "headless" animals or humans. Some researchers think these may once have been complete, but painted with purely organic-based paints. If the paint used was a mixture of mineral and organic colors, then the original colors would change with time, as the organic color decomposed, leaving only the mineral color. Thus it is rarely safe to assume that an existing pictograph has always looked the same except for the obvious scaling or erosion. It might once have been other colors entirely, perhaps with some parts long since faded to invisibility.

The second basic ingredient in compounded pictograph paints was a "binder," a material that would serve to bind the pigment particles together and the paint to the rock, once it dried. The third ingredient was a "vehicle," a fluid that would make the paint liquid enough for practical application with whatever technique was to be used.

Chemical and spectrographic analyses of pictograph paints have shown that a variety of natural and readily available materials were used by canyon country prehistoric Indians to make paint binders, although some are considerably better than others. Among the substances used were blood, egg white, egg yolk, seed oils, plant resins, certain plant juices, milk and honey. Certain minerals, such as hematite, gypsum and aragonite served as both pigments and binders.

Vehicles, or diluents, commonly used in pictograph paints were plant

71

juices, water, animal oils and urine, which was always available, even in a remote, bone-dry canyon. Some of the fluid binders noted could also serve as vehicles, thus doing double duty. Also, certain minerals used as pigments such as hematite, could bond very well using water for both binder and vehicle. Hematite is a dark red iron oxide mineral that is common to canyon country. It is the predominant colored pigment used there and makes a durable pictograph paint with water only, which explains why so many of the region's pictos exhibit the characteristic maroon-red.

Although dark red and white dominate Anasazi and Fremont pictograph paints, at least those with mineral bases, many other colors also occur, some based upon specific minerals, others a mixture of minerals. Colors found are reds, rose, pink, browns, grays, greens, yellows, lavender, purple, blues, orange, black and shades of white, plus many other exotic hues. Minerals commonly used for specific types of colors are listed below. Mineral clays such as ocher were also used.

reds, browns	hematite
greens	malachite, other cuprous-copper minerals
yellows	lemonite, goethite
whites	gypsum, lime, chalk
black	charcoal, graphite, manganese ores
blues	turquoise, azurite, other cupric-copper minerals

Of the various colors found in pictographs, greens are found only a few places, and black is rare. Hues such as pink, rose and lavender are usually darker colors mixed with a white mineral. Grays can be any number of minerals, not mixes of black with white.

Some minerals could be used as found. Others needed to be ground. Grinding tools with remnants of mineral pigment on them have been excavated from several ruins, as have paint palettes, "paint pots" and cakes of prepared pigment, indicating that at least some pictograph craftsmen did not depend solely upon available sources when they made excursions to remote sites.

As noted earlier, the first pictograph painting tools were probably fingers. Although more sophisticated techniques were developed, such as brushes made of animal hair, plant fibers, yucca spines and frayed fibrous twigs, direct "hand" techniques were apparently never given up. In addition to the usual variety of brush-on approaches, paint was also applied with the fingers, by painting a hand then slapping it onto the rock surface, by throwing gobs of pigment, usually against a cave ceiling, and by blowing a mouthful of diluted paint against a wall, perhaps through a hollow reed. This spraygun technique was often used with a hand held flat against the wall, thus making a negative hand image. Some positive hand-slap images were not solid paint but crude patterns painted first on the hand. Other slap images were subsequently enhanced with additional paint to make longer or extra fingers. Some pictographic hands were entirely painted by brush or finger. A few pictographs were simply charcoal drawings, although these are rare, possibly because they were not very durable.

Typical negative and positive pictograph hand prints, plus two footprints and other assorted images. Needles district, Canyonlands National Park.

TECHNIQUE STUDY

Serious researchers who wish to keep in touch with the real world, and to understand some of the practical problems that prehistoric rock graphics craftsmen faced, should make a series of field experiments. The few scientists who have actually done this have accumulated a considerable body of new and useful information.

To acquire a basic understanding of each type of rock art — scratched pebbles, incised stone and pictographs — an attempt should be made to produce each type using only tools and materials that were available to the prehistoric craftsmen.

To try the scratched pebble type, first go to almost any stream or drywash and select a clean, hard, water-smoothed rock of almost any size, but preferably one fairly dark in color. Then pick up another rock small enough to hold that has a sharp edge and start scratching out a figure or design on the larger rock. It may be necessary to break a rock in order to get a sharp edge.

While making your own "Great Basin Rectilinear" petroglyph, note that while a casual scratch produces a visible mark, that easy mark also blows or wipes away just as easily, leaving only a faint permanent line. To make a more satisfactory line, it is necessary to bear down hard or to go over each line several times. It will next be noted that a repeated scratch makes a rather sloppy, fuzzy line and that curved lines require more care and effort than straight ones. You will also soon conclude that while such a medium may be a natural and almost inevitable first step in the creation of graphics, it is far from being ideal. The medium tends to encourage innovation.

Next try to make several incised petroglyphs, using each of the several techniques. Find a smooth, nicely varnished sandstone surface somewhere far from any real petroglyphs, then try making complete glyphs by hammerstone chipping, repeated abrasion, drilling, hammerstone-and-stone chisel, and maybe even using a chisel or drill made of antler or bone.

The first lesson learned will be that many ideal petroglyph sites do not have harder tool-rocks handy nearby. Petroglyph-making tools usually must be collected wherever they are available, given edges, then carried to where they are used. The next thing learned will be that while getting a first few dents or scratches through the thin desert varnish may be easy, making an entire glyph, with the lines as deep as with most prehistoric glyphs, is very hard, time-consuming, knuckle-busting work. Tests have shown that, depending on rock hardness, technique, skill and the craftsman's vigor, it takes from 25 to 100 dints or blows to make one inch of petroglyph line. This alone perhaps explains why little real interest was shown in the craft as a skill in itself, and why most glyphs are fairly small and poor in quality. Making glyphs was a chore, not a pleasure. Prehistoric glyphs show this, and yours will, too.

Other things will also be demonstrated by making a few glyphs. One is that rock hardness varies drastically, even in different places on the same rock surface, and that at its best, rock is a very obdurate graphic medium. Another is that care and experience must go into the selection and use of hammerstones and chisels, and that the hammer-chisel approach gives far better control and better results than the hammerstone alone. One researcher found that obsidian, a volcanic glass that is so hard that sharp chips of it can be used as scalpels in surgery, makes a very poor petroglyph chisel. It dulls too quickly.

Next, try making a few pictographs, preferably in a big alcove where the rock surface needs smoothing before painting. Next, find a natural mineral pigment and perhaps a colorful plant pigment, too, if you have the time for a lot of trial-and-error work. Then make a brush out of locally available materials.

Some immediate lessons learned will be that as with petroglyphs, everything needed is not available everywhere. Pictograph tools and materials must be gathered where they do occur, processed, then carried around. Pigments need to be ground. Only certain plant twigs make usable fiber brushes. And it is much handier to apply the paint with the fingers or by mouth-spray. It will also quickly be observed that pictographs are much easier to make than petroglyphs, so much easier that you may feel the urge to paint some really large and impressive figures, or even a whole panel. Doubtless a few prehistoric rock craftsmen noticed this, too, and responded to the urge by creating some really big figures, not because they were extraordinarily significant, but simply because it was fairly easy to do.

Once the experimental painting begins and the results are observed a few days later, it becomes obvious that some thought and experience must go into the compounding of pictograph paints. A few minerals will work very nicely with just water. Most, however, quickly flake or powder off of the work surface once dried unless some kind of binder is added or some other fluid medium is used. From such basic problems and attempts to solve them, the entire modern paint industry evolved.

The main lesson to be learned from attempting to actually create rock graphics first hand is that even with sophisticated modern understanding of the various elements of the process, the medium itself imposes severe limitations on what can be produced. Only a dedicated artist, with sophisticated graphic knowledge and plenty of time and energy available, could produce petroglyphic images significantly better than those produced by the Anasazis and Fremonts, using only naturally occurring materials. That such superior glyphs were not, in fact, produced leads to the inference that these prehistoric craftsmen did not possess the necessary combination of inspiration, time, knowledge and energy.

Another lesson that can be learned from personal efforts at producing rock art is that conventional scientific procedures can be applied to rock art research. It is possible to subject hypotheses to actual test in many cases, or at least to devise tests that will add inferential weight to an idea. There are, of course, limits to such extrapolations into the dim past from modern test data, but certainly at worst such extrapolations from solid, verifiable information are far more scientific than research based solely upon literature research. In sum, only field work of one sort or another can provide the new data needed if rock art problems are to be solved. Such field work will also serve to keep researchers in touch with the real world, to remind them that if answers are to be found to the puzzles of canyon country rock art, they will be found by hardheaded scientific research, not by armchair flights of fancy through esoteric realms far removed in time, space and concept from the primitive canyon country tribes of many centuries ago.

Salt Creek Canyon, Canyonlands National Park.

DATING

THE PROBLEM

The most vital element in rock art study is missing entirely, the ability to assign an absolute date to specific petroglyphs and pictographs with some fair degree of certainty. Standard archaeological dating techniques simply will not work with rock art.

Carbon 14 dating requires small but definite amounts of organic material, then measures the approximate length of time between the test and when the organic material died, whether plant or animal. Attempts have been made to C-14 date the traces of organic binders found in some pictograph paints, but the amounts of pigment available were too small to produce reliable test results. Even worse, gathering the sample damages or destroys the pictograph, something no researcher wants to do.

Ruins and other sites can be dated by dendrochronology, a very accurate method for fitting wood core drillings onto our calendar, but this works only with sizeable tree samples, such as the roof beams in dwellings. Obsidian hydration dating works only on obsidian. Dating by archaeomagnetism requires a fixed fire-hearth of baked clay, and other more experimental methods, such as fission track analysis and thermoluminescence, also have narrow applications, none of them suitable for rock art dating.

While these and other less direct methods have led to the fairly accurate dating of most prehistoric ruins and other artifacts, and hence to the cultures that created them, unless rock art can be just as accurately dated, there is no sure way to associate the rock art with its originating culture. A panel of spectacular pictographs found in the heart of Fremont country might have been made by Fremont craftsmen, or it might have been painted long before or long after the Fremonts occupied the region. Of course, even if the panel could be dated as contemporary with the Fremonts, that alone does not prove it was not done by the shaman of some intruding group of Plains Indians. Dating is only one aspect of the problem of associating rock art with its originating culture, yet a fairly reliable date could drastically narrow the field of possibilities in most cases.

Despite its vital importance to all serious rock art study, very little progress is currently being made toward devising accurate scientific methods for dating petroglyphs and pictographs, primarily because there is so little with which to work. Petroglyphs are nothing but grooves, lines, holes where rock is not. The only thing datable to test is the desert varnish that builds up in some glyphs, but this new varnish is in minute amounts at best, and its buildup rate is highly variable. There is nothing to pictographs except for their paint, which is theoretically testable, but again the amounts are minute and most potential age tests are destructive.

Thus, at present, a researcher can stand in front of a panel of petroglyphs or pictographs and not actually know, on the basis of unquestionable scientific evidence, how old that rock art is within a thousand years, let alone a couple of centuries. This baffling situation has led to the creation and use of several next-best methods for rock graphics dating, most of them based upon inference.

DATING BY INFERENCE

Dating prehistoric rock graphics by inference is largely a matter of assuming an association between the graphics and the nearest cultural remnants that are datable, although factors other than physical proximity are occasionally used.

Unfortunately, the validity of assumptions based upon proximity can vary drastically from one rock art panel to another and from one area to another. If an area has been used by only one prehistoric culture, it is fairly valid to assume, but still not certain, that most prehistoric rock art found there was created by that culture, provided it is possible to distinguish prehistoric from historic rock art that may be there, too. But in areas that were used by several cultures over the last two thousand years, dating rock art by assuming its association with nearby datable artifacts is highly questionable. In such areas, various "experts" differ wildly from each other as to the age of the rock art found there and its cultural affiliation, with no solid data supporting any of them.

There are other pitfalls to dating by association, even where the association may otherwise be fairly safe. For example, at one Anasazi site, Basketmaker III pot shards were found at a dwelling site five hundred years younger. In another case, a respected researcher surveyed a critical Anasazi occupation area, then dated its rock art by association with the nearest datable pottery fragments. Where sites had received multiple occupancy, he assumed that the majority users made most of the nearby rock art, a weak assumption at best. He then went on to perform a lengthy and detailed analysis based upon the inferred rock art datings, but deliberately left out of the analysis all rock art that was not near datable ceramic remnants. This major omission of data, of course, left his entire analysis in question. Since this rejection of data was arbitrary, and the researcher made no attempt to show that rock art diminished in importance if it was not near dwelling sites and pottery, his analysis was made without information that could have been critical. This same researcher then compounded his errors by using the results of his questionable analysis to extrapolate still further. Unfortunately, such ridiculous extrapolations are all too common within modern rock art literature, even that authored by otherwise sensible archaeologists.

To summarize, while prehistoric ceramics can be dated with considerable accuracy, dating rock art by association with ceramics is at best marginal as a scientific procedure. If this procedure is combined with other inferential techniques, then it can be useful in forming generalizations about the age of rock art within a region or area, but such generalizations should not be used as a basis for further conjecture. For example, several researchers have used inferential and relative age-dating methods to reach the general conclusion that the oldest rock art in the west is in the western Great Basin area. Some, however, go on to use that as a basis for proposing that the concept of rock art making spread outward from that area, ignoring highly probable alternate explanations, such as independent development at several times and places.

Attempts have also been made to date rock art by associating its apparent subject matter with similar subject matter shown on pottery designs. While some researchers have noted an evolution of design in pueblo culture pottery, from geometry to birds to animals to humans, no such steady progression of subject matter is apparent within the rock art of the same culture. Further, there is strong evidence that so long as rock art and its creation and use were ceremonial, rock art subjects were taboo to the women who designed and made pottery. If this concept is correct, a specific subject could only be used on pottery some time after it was no longer important in rock art, leaving a variable time mismatch that would preclude dating rock art by similar pottery subject matter.

Other attempts have been made to date rock art by cultural association with rock art crafting, technique, jewelry designs, sandal styles, architectural styles, migration patterns, lithic styles and by the simple expedient of sorting through prehistoric trash dumps. Surprisingly, this last approach has produced the best results at some locations. Cakes of paint pigments found in such dumps can associate the trash dump with nearby pictographs made with the same pigments, and trash midden layers can often be dated by any of several common methods, such as Carbon 14. The pictograph date would be almost certain if matching chemical analyses could then be made with the pigment lumps and the pictograph paint of the same color.

Another method commonly used to date rock art by inference is by its graphic "style." This approach is based upon the highly questionable assumption that within a particular time period, all of the rock art created by a distinct cultural group or subgroup will be uniform in graphic style. This assumption is discussed at length in the following chapter on style, but the concept of style and its application to rock art dating is so subjective, complicated and plagued by exceptions, contradictions and anomalies that its use is closer akin to magic than science. If the only clue to the age of a particular panel of rock art is its graphic style, then there is no scientific basis for estimating the age of that rock art.

Even so, established modern researchers commonly set about dating a particular "style" of rock art by nearby datable ruins, then blithely compound that error by transferring the date from the dated rock art style to other undatable sites near other rock art of similar style. This kind of fanciful "boot-strap" logic is not uncommon in rock art literature.

There is little doubt that within the broad sweep of time, rock art styles within Utah, the Great Basin and the general Four Corners region have changed. General patterns of change can be perceived, such as slowly increasing sophistication in site selection, subject matter, technique, design complexity, imagination, multiple-figure relationships, time and trouble spent, importance in use, proportions, multiple usages of sites and dimensionality. But each of these complex factors varied wildly in specific localities and with specific groups and individuals. The apparent general trend becomes so chaotic when viewed closely that it has no practical use in rock art dating beyond very limited inferential support of other dating methods.

One astute rock art researcher with a background in science summarized the matter of rock art dating by cultural association by saying, "There are absolutely no ways of tying a particular panel to a particular culture." It's as simple as that.

RELATIVE DATING

Although it is not at present possible to assign absolute dates to canyon country prehistoric rock art, in many cases it is possible to narrow the time span in which a particular site or figure might fall, to place limits on its age. There are many methods of such relative dating, many kinds of clues that can be helpful. Some tell that the rock art is older or younger than certain known points in time, or that one figure or panel is older or younger than another. Of course, such information may or may not be of any further use, depending on whether it can be integrated with other knowledge.

To give some examples of relative dating, if the graphics depict horses, guns, churches with crosses on them and caped humans wearing Sixteenth Century Spanish hats, then there is no doubt that the graphics postdate A.D. 1540, when these items were first introduced into the Southwest by Coronado's explorations. Cars, trucks, trains, airplanes and other modern machines date any rock art depicting them as fairly recent. Unfortunately, this kind of relative dating does not work in reverse. A lack of historic subject matter in rock art does not necessarily mean that it dates to prehistoric times.

Prehistoric "inventions" can also serve as rough time markers, although not as precisely as the prehistoric-historic interface. A certain special type of lithic point may not have appeared before a particular time, give or take a few centuries, so if that unique arrowhead or spearpoint design appears on a petroglyph panel, that panel is probably newer than the design's invention. The transition from atlatl to bow-and-arrow is another such time indicator when either is shown in rock art, although the use of these two weapons overlapped by hundreds of years, and the transition began at different times with different cultural groups. In some areas, the bow was used as early as A.D. 200. In others, the atlatl was still in use during early historic times. In the Four Corners region the atlatl-bow transition took place around A.D. 700, but still probably took at least a century. Thus, if a bow is depicted on a petroglyph panel, the glyph itself is probably newer than, say, A.D. 650. Adjacent glyphs that exhibit about the same amount of weathering and desert varnish buildup may be about the same age but with less certainty.

Petrolgyphs depicting bows and arrows, Behind the Rocks, Utah. Note that one bow hunter is disguised to resemble his quarry. A line from another bow apparently depicts the flight of an arrow.

The appearance of "shields" in some Utah rock art is used as a dating clue by some researchers, on the supposition that shields were introduced into the region by an outside culture around a certain time. While this inference may be true, many "shield" petroglyphs and pictographs could just as easily be something else, such as anthropomorphs with round, stylized bodies. Thus, dating rock art on the basis of "shield" subject matter can only be as accurate as the identity of the subject matter, which is often far from certain.

The appearance of macaws in Anasazi rock art leads to a fairly well established time limit. Other archaeological evidence indicates that these tropical birds were introduced to the pueblo cultures around A.D. 1100.

The Kokopelli figure also apparently migrated north from Mexico, with the oldest in this country dating around A.D. 700, although various authorities differ on this.

Rock art near ruins is difficult to relate to those who dwelt there, but now and then a petroglyph or pictograph is found that had been covered by a constructed wall, leading to a conclusion that the wall was younger. With pictographs and petroglyphs actually on constructed walls, the walls must be older, but only careful study could determine how much older.

The superimposition of one rock art figure over another can provide a clue as to the relative ages of the two figures, but can also be misleading and generally offers no indication as to the time gap between the two figures. If a pictograph is painted over a petroglyph, it may still appear that the picto is older than the petroglyph, because the paint may not have penetrated the glyph grooves or may long since have eroded out because of poor adhesion. This would make it look like the petroglyph had been cut through the pictograph and was hence younger, the opposite of the truth. The same problem occurs when newer petroglyphs are scratched over older chipped glyphs. The scratches do not enter the chipped lines, so they seem interrupted by the older glyph lines, leading to errors in relative dating. In other instances, a researcher may attach great significance to the fact that one pictograph figure overlies another, without even considering the possibility that they both might have been made within a few days, weeks or years of each other, and maybe even by the same craftsman. From all this, it can be concluded that the relative dating of rock art by superimposition should be done with caution, and that even at best the information gained may be of little value.

Typical superimposition of one petroglyph upon another. The desert varnish buildup in the bear image is lighter than that in the older images depicting a sheep hunt. Colorado River gorge, Utah.

Many kinds of geologic events can be dated with fair accuracy, but on a time scale that is generally ill-suited to the dating of human affairs. Geologists generally date events within thousands or millions of years, while archaeologists usually need dates within tens or hundreds of years. There are, however, several kinds of geologic events that can sometimes give relative dating clues useful in rock art study, and a few that can provide fairly accurate absolute dates, but it usually takes careful scientific detective work, plus a working knowledge of regional geology, to find such clues.

As noted in an earlier chapter, changed ground level below rock art is not a very useful clue to its age, but in some locations rock art has been discovered buried beneath alluvial fill that could be dated with some accuracy. Thus, the buried rock art had to be older than the catastrophic flooding that buried it. Glyphs buried by ash, cinders or lava from a datable volcanic event could be similarly dated. In one location, glyphs along the "shores" of a vast desert playa were dated as "before" and "after" a datable period of flooding, because some glyphs had mineral buildup within the glyph lines, while others did not. In some parts of the Western Hemisphere, such datable events as massive mudslides or landslides that engulf cultural artifacts have been used to date the artifacts, but such events as these are rare to nonexistent within the desert southwest. There, excessive rain, or rapid snow-melt, produces the catastrophic flooding noted above.

Attempts have been made to date petroglyphs that have lichens growing within the incised lines, but studies have shown that lichen growth rates are highly variable and hence not reliable indicators of age. Lichen growth rates vary, often drastically, with species, climate and the chemical composition of the rocks on which they are growing. In addition, there may have been a time gap of indeterminable length between when the glyph was cut and the lichen started growing into the cut, and within canyon country, the climate has changed considerably during the last thousand years. With all of these variables, it would take an intensive and time-consuming study of each site in order to derive a reliable petroglyph date from lichen growth rate.

Typical lichen growth in a petroglyph, Ninemile Canyon, Utah. Note the lack of lichens in the historic initials to the right.

One researcher has noted that Glen Canyon area petroglyphs roughly dated by other methods at less than 600 years old do not contain lichens. While this observation may have some use within the Glen Canyon area, it can only be as accurate as the other dating methods used, and cannot be applied to other areas.

Another approach to the relative dating of rock art is through careful examination of degrees of weathering, a factor that the famous European cave pictographs have escaped. But in canyon country, all rock art is exposed to one kind of weathering or another, no matter where it is located. Although an extensive natural cave system was recently discovered within one of southeastern Utah's several "salt valleys," such a cave is an exception within such geologic formations, and even so was largely vertical and hence not usable by prehistoric rock art craftsmen.

Thus, even the most sheltered pictographs within the Anasazi and Fremont territory that were placed in natural locations were exposed to wind erosion, and wherever wind can pick up sand or dust such erosion can be significant.

However, even though virtually all of the region's rock art is exposed to some form and degree of weathering, there are so many variables in this weathering that its usefulness in absolute dating is nil, and in relative dating very limited. Julian Steward summarized the matter very well in his 1936 report to the Smithsonian Institute:

"The degree to which petroglyphs have faded out through weathering has been examined with considerable care. This is one of the least reliable measures of age, for the mere appearance of antiquity is no proof whatever of great age. The writer has seen dates carved on rocks not over ten years ago which have weathered almost beyond recognition, whereas definitely pre-Columbian petroglyphs close by are still bright and fresh. The time required for weather to obliterate a petroglyph depends upon the kind of rock on which it is placed, the depth of the cut of the figures or the kind of pigment used, and the exposure to sun, rain and blown sand. Painted petroglyphs in caves of Europe have lasted nearly 25,000 years; in exposed places in America, some have practically disappeared within 50 years. Although degree of weathering may sometimes provide a clue as to age, it is never conclusive."

Other researchers have confirmed this. A very weathered and ancient-looking dated historic inscription on a relatively soft sandstone outcropping near Moab, Utah, was read as "1753" by local authorities, yet a later investigation proved the date to be "1953." Some obviously historic petroglyphs look as weathered as nearby prehistoric glyphs. Even so, within a single petroglyph panel, the weathering of the various glyphs may provide a clue as to their relative ages, that is, some are older than others, especially if that indication is reinforced by other evidence.

With pictographs, however, such relative dating is far less certain because paint composition is a major variable. A well compounded paint made with mineral pigments may still look fairly young after many centuries, while a paint that was made partly of vegetable pigments will look faded and very old in a much shorter length of time. A paint made without an adequate binder may not adhere well, and its flaking away may lend the appearance of great age.

Thus, weathering can give a clue to rock art age only if all the variables at each site are studied thoroughly, and even then the information gained may be of limited value and cannot be applied to rock art at other locations.

These same severe limitations also apply to dating a petroglyph by the amount of desert varnish built up within the incised areas since the glyph was made. Many researchers have discussed the problems inherent in this approach, and some have attempted to use renewed desert varnish as a clue to relative or absolute age of a glyph, but few have attempted to apply it scientifically.

As with other clues concerning the relative age of petroglyphs, varnish buildup has several variables that can drastically affect the actual growth of new desert varnish, and with this strange rock coating, none of the variables are well understood. The main factors that contribute to its growth — minerals, moisture, sunlight, air and time — are fairly well established, but how the process works is not. Without this knowledge, and how each factor affects the rate of buildup as it varies, varnish growth rate curves cannot be drawn, and it is simply not practical to gauge the age of a petroglyph by the amount of varnish renewal it exhibits. It can be generalized that if the varnish in a glyph is as dark as the surrounding undisturbed surface, then the glyph is pretty old, but on rocks of different composition and exposure, "pretty old" may vary as much as one thousand years on the calendar.

Desert varnish growth depends primarily upon the mineral content of the rock, and that can vary even within a small boulder. Either iron or manganese minerals must be present. Iron minerals make a brown-colored varnish, while manganese minerals make black varnish, which may have a metallic-blue or purple sheen if it is thick enough. Some varnishes contain both minerals, others only one.

85

Exposure of the mineralized rock surface to air and sunlight and the proper amount of moisture is necessary. A totally shaded surface will not build desert varnish. Too little moisture in the form of air humidity or precipitation will drastically slow or halt the process, while too much may actually reverse it. One researcher moved a heavily varnished rock from its desert location to one where heavy rainfall was normal. Within two years the varnish was gone. Another noted that varnish seemed to build up on rock only in regions where very hot summers were punctuated by occasional thundershowers. This is reasonable, because such showers would wet the rock but not for long enough to permit significant water erosion of existing varnish.

A change in climate, as the canyon country region has been experiencing over the last thousand years, will also affect the varnish buildup rate, and quite probably the rate will also vary with the rock's mineral concentration and the various iron and manganese mineral forms it may contain. Further, with some petroglyphs, water erosion can slow down or even prevent varnish buildup. The glyphs on one boulder exposed to mists from a river rapid were actually deepened. This would lead to the inference that the boulder was in some drier location when the glyphs were made, perhaps because the boulder was moved, or the river channel shifted. Glyphs have also been observed where historic or contemporary Indians had cut prehistoric petroglyphs deeper, thus removing any built-up varnish and making the glyphs look much younger than they actually were.

Typical refurbished petroglyph, with most of the original desert varnish removed from one figure. San Juan River gorge, Utah.

Typical "two-headed" animal petroglyph, Colorado River gorge, Utah. Note that the desert varnish in the righthand half of the figure is lighter and hence younger, perhaps by centuries.

In canyon country, it is not uncommon to see a petroglyph that has two distinct shades of varnish within the same figure. This can be used to infer that the original figure was altered, or something was added, at a later date. Many "two-headed" petroglyph animals were created by the later addition of a second head by a second craftsman, perhaps centuries later.

In spite of all the complications that arise in dating rock art by desert varnish renewal, and in spite of the lack of solid experimental evidence, archaeologists and others persist in making claims about this enigmatic process, and analyses based on these claims.

For example, one archaeologist states that in very arid areas, desert varnish takes from 1500 to 2000 years to form, and that in such areas petroglyphs that are as dark as the surrounding rock are 5000 to 7000 years old. Another researcher makes even wilder claims. He states, for example, that the color of desert varnish is a function of its depth, and that "purple-black" varnish is much older than "blue-black," this without any regard for how variations in chemical composition and rock and varnish surface conditions might affect color. The same archaeologist states that according to petroglyphs dated by nearby pottery, an association that is shaky at best, the darkest desert varnish takes about 1000 years to form.

In another strange case of petroglyph dating confusion, two "mastodon" petroglyphs in southeastern Utah, one near Moab and the other in Indian Creek Canyon, are thought by many researchers to be actual depictions of the elephant-like creature that once roamed this region. Paleontologists believe such "mastodons" (in this region, more likely they were one form of mammoth) went extinct at least 7,000 years ago, so it would be reasonable to assume that the varnish in a petroglyph this old would be just as dark as the surrounding varnish or very nearly so. Yet it is not, which leaves only one inference — the "mastodon" glyphs were done during late historic times by a craftsman who had either seen an elephant or a picture of one. In support of this idea, one writer noted that a "Don Castello's Circus and Menagerie" toured the Moab area in 1869. While the tour may have been made, it was not in 1869. Moab Valley was uninhabited at that time. A mistaken date, however, is not enough to dismiss the historic inference in general, or the circus tour in particular.

In sum, casual examination of the renewed varnish in a petroglyph is not enough to permit even a broad approximation of its age. One field observer reported seeing 400-year old Spanish petroglyphs with no trace whatever of new varnish within the glyphs. Within the Anasazi and Fremont cultural areas and periods, the extremes in elevation bring about wide variations in length of season, sunlight and moisture, while geologic differences result in wide variations in rock mineral content. These in turn, plus perhaps other factors not yet recognized, make desert varnish color a very unreliable indication of petroglyph age.

Tentative first steps have been taken toward a truly scientific testing of the desert varnish within petroglyph cuts, but much work remains to be done before the approach can become a useful field tool. Varnish was removed from within a glyph, then an attempt was made to age-date the material using a complex laboratory procedure called "neutron activation analysis." While this particular method may turn out to be impractical, it is nonetheless attacking the petroglyph dating problem by the only scientific approach possible — by an objective, repeatable test of the only thing datable a petroglyph offers — its renewed desert varnish.

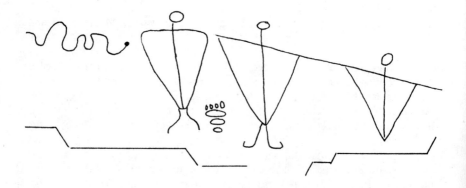

LIMITED SOLUTIONS

Other first steps are also being taken toward the scientific age-dating of pictographs. Unfortunately, so far all such experimental testing involves paint pigments removed from the pictographs, a practice that damages or destroys them for all other study except from photographic records. While the study of rock art photographs may be useful from the viewpoint of aesthetics and other esoteric aspects, direct examination of rock art and its setting is necessary for scientific study, because all the hard evidence other than graphic design and apparent subject matter must be obtained from the rock art itself in the field.

As noted earlier, attempts have been made to date the organic binders in pictograph paint fragments by the Carbon-14 method, but present techniques require more material than is normally available. There are several methods of detecting the minute traces of organic materials that may remain in pictograph paints, such as spectroscopic analysis, chromatography and electron microscopy, but detecting organic material does not automatically lead to age-dating it.

One researcher, however, discovered that a fairly common pictograph paint binder, egg albumin, decomposes at a rate that can be graphed, when tested using paper chromatography. The decomposition curve ended at about 1800 years, give or take 300 years, so the technique could not be applied to paints older than that. It was, however, successfully applied to the dating of a series of pictographs in Africa, but has apparently seen no use in dating canyon country sites. Further investigation of this technique could prove valuable to the serious study of canyon country rock art, even though relatively few pictographs in that region may be made using paints with albumin binders.

There is also an approach to rock art dating by inference that deserves further study, an approach that has largely been ignored by modern investigators. An understanding of the principles of how an isolated culture develops its knowledge of graphics concepts could become a tool that would at least be applicable on a general level to age-dating rock art.

This approach is based upon the testable assumption that within a primitive culture that is largely isolated from more advanced cultures — which certainly applies to the Anasazis and Fremonts — the development of graphic concepts will follow a predictable path. The path might be a matter of short periods of rapid change followed by long periods of little change, and would doubtless be complicated in many localities by cultural exchanges and overlaps, and by individuals who made short-term quantum leaps in imagination and understanding. But even with these complications, fairly clear, broad trends in cultural sophistication regarding graphic design could be established from the study of rock art, plus the graphics on basketry, pottery, clothing, kiva walls and elsewhere as these developed parallel to rock art.

Even within canyon country rock art alone, there are apparent phases in graphic design sophistication that could be used as a starting point for a more comprehensive study. These phases are:

PHASE 1:   Rock art designs involving straight and curved lines, dots, pits, grooves and miscellaneous simple geometric designs, limited to petroglyphs at first, then including pictographs. In this phase, the key design concept limitations would be: no idea of relating the rock art designs to things and events in the real world, no understanding whatever of third dimensionality, and a very limited understanding of how to depict areas.

PHASE 2:   Rock art designs that are representational as well as non-representational, including both petroglyphs and pictographs, with a gradual phasing in of the concept of depicting supernatural as well as natural subjects. This phase would still demonstrate no understanding of third dimensionality, would show only limited ability to relate multiple design subjects to each other on the same panel, and limited understanding of directionality.

PHASE 3:   Rock art designs developed as prehistoric kiva art by the Anasazis and perhaps other pueblo cultures farther south, but not by the Fremonts. This concept level would take two-dimensional graphic design and pictograph painting technique about as far as they could go within the scope of their inherent limitations, but would still not exhibit any basic understanding of third dimensionality in graphics.

PHASE 4:   Rock graphic designs and kiva art developed by the various Anasazi successor tribes and other historic tribes in the same region. This phase would be characterized by the gradual development of third dimensionality, probably stimulated if not initiated by repeated contacts with the graphics of European cultures and the more highly developed Indian cultures to the south in Mexico and Central America.

Within the four phases shown, the historic-prehistoric interface of A.D. 1540 would approximately coincide with the interface between Phases 3 and 4. A general time scale could also be applied to the other phase interfaces but only with the full understanding that such a scale could rarely be applied directly to the dating of specific rock art sites because of variations between cultural and subcultural groups and individuals within these groups. For example, the interface between Phases 1 and 2 might date around 2000 years ago, with the Phase 2 and 3 interface falling around A.D. 1200.

There are, of course, other ways in which the apparent levels of graphic concept sophistication could be formalized. For example, Phase 2 as shown could possibly be split into two phases with the first based upon representational natural subjects, the second based upon the appearance of representational supernatural subjects. And, theoretically, Phase 4 could be divided into several sub-phases, with each based upon some aspect of the developing understanding of graphic third dimensionality. It may, however, be impractical with the Anasazis to subdivide Phase 4, because of the complications introduced by the more sophisticated intruding cultures. The

Fremonts, of course, disappeared while still within Phase 2.

A noted art historian who has written extensively about rock art has noted that, "In the history of art there has been a noticeable tendency for forms to evolve from naturalistic through stylized, to abstract." This general trend would seem to be the opposite of the one just proposed, yet it must be understood that the suggested graphic development phases define pre-art stages, before these primitive cultures had started any significant use of graphics for aesthetic purposes. The chapter on interpretation explores further the concept of aesthetics and rock art.

It was noted in the earlier chapters on rock art locations and subject matter that most of the uncontestable factual information about canyon country rock art was its actual physical location and actual graphic design or image. Any additional hard data that may exist about a particular site can only be obtained from a detailed personal examination of that site and its rock art for some of the kinds of clues discussed in this chapter. At a few sites, there are enough such clues that, when considered together with other related solid information and inferences, fairly close estimates of age can be made. Few of these kinds of clues, however, are visible in photographs, no matter how carefully taken. This leads to the obvious conclusion that no serious researcher should even attempt to make any kind of rock art age determination from photographs alone, without first making a very careful study of the rock art itself, plus the immediate vicinity and general area. As noted earlier, rock art application techniques, apparent subject matter and graphic concept sophistication — the kinds of things that can be recorded by photography — can at best yield only general estimates of age, with numerous complications that can severely limit the reliability of such estimates.

Thus, the most vital need, the key, to scientific rock art study is still missing, with very little currently being done to fill this need. Yet without a reasonably reliable method of dating both petroglyphs and pictographs, other aspects of rock art study must continue to deal with little but inferences and assumptions, rather than solid, indisputable facts.

Colorado River gorge, Utah.

Horse Canyon, Canyonlands National Park.

92

STYLES

THE CONTROVERSY

It has truthfully been said that necessity is the mother of invention. Within the last two decades or so, frustration over the lack of hard data in the field of rock art research has mothered the concept of applying "style" and "style analysis" to the study of prehistoric rock art in the Southwest, or at least has adopted this concept from the supposedly related study of primitive art. Baffled archaeologists and amateur rock art enthusiasts, either unable or unwilling to perform the slow, painstaking field and laboratory research and analysis needed to obtain uncontestable scientific evidence, have conceived and developed a system for "studying" rock art from photographs and sketches, in a manner that requires little supplementary knowledge of archaeology in general, the culture that may have created the rock art in particular, or the many other scientific disciplines that can contribute to the study of prehistoric graphics.

During the last two decades, some who have taken this temptingly easy route to rock art study have carried it to ridiculous extremes, rarely pausing to view objectively the fanciful constructions they have built layer after layer upon patently false assumptions, unsupported inferences, and a complex nomenclature that has no relationship to the real prehistoric world.

Of course, not all serious rock art investigators subscribe to the assumptions and procedures of graphic style analysis as they are applied to the prehistoric rock graphics of Utah and the general Four Corners region. Opinions range across the spectrum from completely discounting style analysis as a useful tool, to blind faith so unquestioning that the procedures are used to the total exclusion of other valuable analytical approaches. This wide range of opinion among "experts" indicates, if nothing else, that the concept of style analysis is not Simon-pure or firmly established, and not without its faults in both concept and application.

Seasoned researchers who are well versed in scientific analytical techniques may make cautious and very limited use of rock art style analysis as a research tool, but they always bear in mind its inherent weaknesses and limitations. And they conscientiously avoid compounding those uncertainties by using style analysis inferences as a basis for additional extrapolations, conjectures and hypotheses that have no other support in fact.

Unfortunately, such scientifically conservative rock art researchers are in the minority. Most recent major published works on Southwestern rock art place heavy emphasis on style definitions and style analyses and are written in such scholarly language in a field so lacking in solid scientific investigations that they go virtually unchallenged by both amateur and professional rock art enthusiasts. In fact, since style systems are given such lovely, scientific-sounding names, and style analysis can generate such impressive-looking maps, charts and graphs, the amateur majority accepts the whole idea with enthusiasm, ready as always to believe without question anything that seems to offer a key to the lockbox of rock art "secrets."

Thus, at this stage, style analysis within the study of rock art could be characterized as "much ado about nothing." The amount of unassailable hard fact involved in the establishment of rock art styles and in making style analyses is virtually nil. Yet far-reaching conclusions are often derived, even though the assumptions are false, the data is almost all inferential and subjective, and the techniques used are anything but scientifically sound. Nonetheless, rock art style analysis is currently popular, and criticizing it is akin to throwing rocks at sacred cows — not conducive to making friends among true believers.

WHAT ARE STYLES?

What are rock art styles, who establishes them, and on what basis?

The concept of graphic "style" comes from the world of art, not the world of science. That alone should be enough to make it suspect in the minds of serious researchers. Art, by definition, is subjective and personal, while science strives to be objective and impersonal. Whether an idea born and nurtured in the world of art can survive the atmosphere of intellectual skepticism that is normal within the world of science remains to be seen.

As applied to rock art, "style" means some perceived difference between one rock graphic figure and another, between one panel and another, that can be used as a basis for sorting or grouping or categorizing a lot of other rock art. These categories, or "styles," are in turn used as a basis for further analysis which will, hopefully, reveal facts about the uses and meanings of the rock art and the cultures that produced it, facts that cannot be discovered by any other approach.

The first step in defining a rock art "style," that is, selecting a perceived difference that can be used to help sort other rock art, is an entirely subjective step, and the differences selected generally have nothing whatsoever to do with who created the rock art, what it really depicts, why it was made, what it means or how it was used. This basic element of subjectivity, divorced from the reality of the actual prehistoric world, has quite naturally led to a situation in which the number of rock art style systems roughly equals the number of investigators who take style analysis seriously. Although the leading proponents of style analysis have published copiously, and their several systems are encountered within virtually all recent rock art literature, other true believers seem unable to resist setting up their own new systems, or at least drastically modifying or augmenting someone else's.

Thus, at the present time, there are many rock art style systems, with little correlation between systems that represent different regions. They all have one thing in common, however. They all completely ignore the vital question — "Is there any demonstrable relationship between the style system and the cultures and individuals that created the rock art hundreds, perhaps thousands of years ago?"

What kinds of differences in rock graphics are used to establish "styles"? Since it need not relate to anything else, almost anything will do. In general, styles are established on differences in rock art apparent subject matter, location, application techniques and design elements, but within these categories still other variations have been used for defining styles.

For example, petroglyphs and pictographs are different "styles" of application, and style analysts attach great significance to the differences in the techniques, without any regard for the fact that in many instances the lack of suitable locations strongly biased technique selection, as did gross ignorance and the limited availability of paint raw materials in some areas. Three popular styles, "Great Basin Scratched Style," "Pit-and-Groove Style" and "Western Utah Painted Style," illustrate styles based largely upon technique. There are others.

Typical "Pit and Groove Style" petroglyphs, Green River gorge, Utah. Verne Huser photo.

Widely used styles that are based upon design elements are "Great Basin Rectilinear," "Great Basin Curvilinear" and "Great Basin Representational," meaning, respectively, that the graphics are made of straight lines or curved lines, or appear to represent an object in the real world. Other styles in this category may be based upon body shapes of anthropomorphs (e.g., round or trapezoidal or triangular or linear), their appendages (detailed, simplistic or lacking), their heads (round, square, triangular, linear, bucket-shaped or lacking), their accouterments, the presence or absence of animals on a panel, how realistically these may be depicted, the presence of negative handprints, the apparent age of the graphics, the presence of certain geometric shapes, and so on, ad nauseum.

The most widely used basis for a style is geographic location, although as discussed earlier, location is a very unreliable indicator of cultural origin. Dozens of rock art styles have been defined by the simple expedient of describing all the rock art in an area that seems to be similar in technique, subject matter and graphic design, then assigning a label to that complex of rock art. Sometimes the labels so assigned indicate cultural affiliation, even though that relationship has yet to be firmly demonstrated. Examples of styles based upon geography are "Tsegi Canyon Style," "Sevier Style," "San Rafael Style," "Classic Vernal Style," "Barrier Canyon Style," "San Juan Style" and "Glen Canyon Style." The latter is further divided on a chronological basis.

There are two major problems with establishing styles in this manner. One, most areas contain a lot of rock art that is at odds in one way or another with the major category being described. Two, rock art similar to the major category may also occur at other scattered locations, often far from the basic style area. Further, some geographic areas, such as the Maze area of Canyonlands National Park, may contain two or more distinct graphic styles of rock art. While most style analysts find it easy to ignore such exceptions to their rules, those exceptions tend to undercut the basic validity of the style concept, or at least indicate that the present use of style analysis is too simplistic to be scientifically meaningful.

It can be argued, of course, that describing and naming various distinct types of rock art provides convenient labels for verbal descriptions, and indeed, a considerable proportion of many rock art publications is devoted to such verbal descriptions. Most such verbalizing, however, has little real purpose that cannot be fulfilled far better by photographs and sketches. Although this kind of descriptive wheel-spinning is relatively harmless, the kinds of names often selected for rock art styles are not so harmless. Problems with semantics in rock art study were discussed in earlier chapters. Such problems also occur in the establishment and use of rock art style systems.

For example, a style title of "Great Basin Abstract" may have been intended only to describe the rock art from a modern-art viewpoint, that is, its meaning is as obscure as modern abstract art. But the inescapable implication is also there that the original rock art craftsman was deliberately and knowingly "abstracting" his subject matter, an idea that is ludicrous. While the originator of the style name may not be confused by this implied

Left, typical "Fremont Style" petroglyph, Fremont River gorge, Capitol Reef National Park. Right, typical "Classic Vernal Style" petroglyph, Dry Fork Canyon, Utah.

Left, typical "San Juan Style" petroglyphs, San Juan River gorge, Utah. Right, typical "Barrier Canyon Style" pictographs, Horseshoe Canyon (Barrier Creek), Maze district, Canyonlands National Park.

second meaning, others can be and are, once the term sees print. In this case, a more suitable term might have been 'Great Basin Crude" or "Great Basin Primitive." Either term would be more nearly correct and offer fewer unsupported inferences.

Other examples of style terms that contain questionable assumptions and inferences, or that create semantic confusion, are "Fremont Style," "Stillwater Faceted Style," "Desert Archaic Style," "Eastern Nevada Fremont Style," "Hohokam Style" and "Jornada Style." There are still others beyond the Anasazi and Fremont cultural regions.

Another major source of misleading semantics in rock art style naming is the implication that by naming a style, there is some kind of special significance to that style, something of importance to rock art study. All too many amateur enthusiasts, and no few professionals, fall prey to this implication, even though often the style definition is arbitrary and of itself meaningless. For example, no one has yet demonstrated that there is any special cultural significance to petroglyphs made only of straight lines, or curved lines, or that there is any reason whatever to differentiate between petroglyphs made of straight or curved lines. Yet, such style labels as "Great Basin Rectilinear" and "Great Basin Curvilinear" are widely used. As suggested in the chapter on rock art dating, there may be some general relationship between simple non-representational rock graphics and general cultural sophistication in graphics concepts, but it would be difficult to stretch the above style labels to fit that still unproven idea.

To understand how ludicrous some style definitions can be, imagine a tired Fremont hunter of some 1000 years ago who decides to call it a day and camp for the night by a seeping spring somewhere in what is now west-central Utah. His luck has been bad, so he decides to brace it up a bit with one of those magic figures he has seen others make. He picks up a sharp-edged piece of chert, then squats down and starts chipping away at a nearby sandstone cliff. He would like to make an image of the deer he is hunting, but his knowledge of graphics is not up to that. So he settles for chipping and scraping a few lines, hoping that by thinking about a deer at the same time he will invoke a bit of that badly needed supernatural help.

Now, if this ignorant native manages to make only straight lines, he is creating rock art in the "Great Basin Rectilinear Style," but if he manages to hack out a few curved lines, he is generating "Great Basin Curvilinear Style" graphics. Should a few of his lines happen by chance to intersect and make a geometric pattern for which some other culture halfway around the world has invented a label, he is making rock art in the "Great Basin Abstract Style." But, other than as illustrations of sheer chance and the degree of ignorance of this individual, what is the significance of these three distinctions?

While most other style labels are less obviously arbitrary and meaningless, the majority of them have little real reason for existing beyond a convenient way of saying "rock art that looks like this occurs in this area." The problems begin when researchers try to go beyond that simple descriptive use. Yet countless hours of study and discussion, and endless pages of print, have been devoted to looking for complex cultural meanings in rock art that probably originated in a manner as culturally meaningless as that just described.

There is another kind of rock art style analysis that has seen some use in recent years. In this approach, all the figures in one or more rock art panels are broken down into their geometric basics or "style elements." These are then counted, charted, listed, coded, named, shuffled and otherwise organized, then subjected to various statistical analysis exercises. While such analyses can look impressive on paper, and few people feel qualified to challenge them, style element analysis has absolutely no demonstrated relationship to the real prehistoric world in which rock art was created, and as a scientific tool it is roughly equivalent to such long used ethnic practices as reading animal entrails, tossing chicken bones or studying Tarot cards. That educated scientists should even consider applying statistical analysis of any sort to the study of prehistoric rock art is beyond understanding.

AN ASSUMPTION

What is the conceptual basis for rock art style analysis? Is that basis valid as applied? If not, is style analysis a total loss? The bottom line answers to these three questions are simple: style analysis is based upon an assumption transplanted from the study of primitive art; the assumption is not applicable to canyon country prehistoric rock art; and, style analysis could be a useful tool in rock art study, but not as currently applied by most researchers.

What is that basic assumption, and why is it not applicable to the Anasazis, Fremonts and their predecessors?

The present preoccupation with style analysis seems to be rooted in a 1953 paper on "style" authored by a Meyer Schapiro in "Anthropology Today," a publication of the University of Chicago Press. Most current authors who write about rock art styles quote that report almost reverently, then use the quotes uncritically as a basis for every kind of style analysis conceivable, without making any attempt to examine the validity and applicability of the assumption quoted.

In his report, Schapiro defined "style" in graphics as "the constant form — and sometimes the constant elements, qualities and expression — in the art of an individual or group." He then goes on to expand upon this concept by asserting, as paraphrased by one of his most outspoken proponents, that there is ample basis for "the assumption that every style is peculiar to a period of culture and that in a given culture or epoch of culture, there is only one style or at least a limited range of styles. Therefore, style can be used with confidence as an independent clue to the time and place of origin of a work of art. Thus its use as an archaeological tool is justified."

Since this assumption, however worded, is the basis for all current approaches to rock art style analysis, it would seem only logical to examine that assumption closely and in detail. While this volume is too limited in size for a thorough discussion of all questionable aspects of the assumption, several major weaknesses will be noted, any one of them enough to cast serious doubt upon the assumption's use in the study of Southwestern rock art.

First, as mentioned earlier and discussed at length in the next chapter, all evidence indicates that most if not all of the prehistoric "rock art" of Utah, the Great Basin and general Four Corners region is not actually art in the common sense of the word. The concept of "art" is inextricably linked with the intent of the person who creates it. While no one can know with certainty what was, or was not, in the minds of people dead for centuries (or even still living, for that matter), all secondary evidence points to non-aesthetic purposes and uses for this region's rock graphics.

Thus, while the quoted assumption may possibly be correct and useful when applied to actual primitive art, its applicability to graphics systems devised for other purposes is challengeable to say the least.

A second major weakness in the assumption is the assertion that within a culture or sub-group there are only one or a very few styles. This assertion, which is fundamental to the entire question, is erroneous in two ways — it is based upon a level of functional uniformity that simply did not exist in the Anasazis and Fremonts, and certainly not their Desert Archaic predecessors, and it omits all consideration of a very basic factor, human individuality.

One rock art stylist honestly notes that "stylistic uniformity results from a panregional information exchange network, and the degree of homogeneity in a region depends on the efficiency of the intergroup communications," yet style analysis proponents have failed to consider that throughout most of the Anasazi culture's history, all of the Fremont history and all the history of their predecessors, no "panregional information network" existed, and "intergroup communications" were virtually nil. Only toward the end of the Anasazi culture was there any significant communication network between some Anasazi sub-groups, and by then the use of rock art was dwindling rapidly, as was its cultural relevance.

One respected rock art researcher who has personally visited hundreds of Utah sites pointed out the lack of cultural uniformity in his region of study by saying that "there appears to be great variation in styles and motifs within a single culture," and that many style elements "may be found in panels assigned to any one of several cultures (with) little to distinguish among the techniques and styles of these common figures."

Cultural uniformity can and does exist, especially within some primitive cultures, and this uniformity can severely limit and control many facets of a culture, including its use of graphics. But such uniformity cannot extend beyond closely knit groups, because constant intercommunication is essential to the human instinct mechanism that seeks and enforces uniformity. In some parts of America, nomadic groups or clans of the same tribe had much better communications, and hence cultural uniformity, than did the various sub-groups and clans of the agrarian Anasazis and Fremonts. As noted earlier, the land itself served as a barrier to free travel and communications between settlements, and agriculture freed them from the need to migrate or even to travel beyond nearby hunting and foraging areas.

Language was another barrier between various canyon country sub-groups. Cultural uniformity is virtually impossible, and communications are difficult, without language uniformity, and it is well established that even within the Anasazi culture there were major language differences. Certain groups within the same "culture" could communicate only through translators, not because of minor dialect differences, but because their language bases were even different, as different as Farsi and Latin. This is known from the study of the languages of the several surviving remnants of the "Anasazi culture." And who knows how many languages did not survive the Anasazi cultural retreat? Who knows how many language bases and dialects there were within the "Fremont" culture, which was even more diverse and scattered through time and space, so scattered it is quite possible that some Fremont subcultural groups never even encountered each other.

Yet style analysis proponents assume cultural uniformity and significant uniformity in rock art styles within such scattered, isolated and linguistically different groups of prehistoric Indians, despite the fact that other cultural indicators, such as agriculture-forage ratios, architecture, tools, weapons, ceramics and clothing, show wide diversity, even within relatively small areas. There were, indeed, limitations imposed upon the creation of this region's prehistoric rock art, limitations that forced a certain uniformity, but these were the limitations of the medium itself, of the degree of graphic sophistication in general and of the region's geographic isolation, not of the cultures of the rock art craftsmen. These various natural restrictions were discussed in some detail in earlier chapters.

The second major factor that affects cultural uniformity — individualism — is almost completely neglected within modern rock art literature. Virtually everyone studying canyon country prehistoric rock art thinks of that "art" as an impersonal thing, the product of some ancient, enigmatic, faceless, monolithic, mysterious, cultural embodiment that functioned mindlessly on the basis of cultural limitations, cultural needs, cultural purposes and cultural skills. They fail to perceive that every scrap of rock art was made, not by such an amorphous, predictable cultural entity, but by an individual human being with all that this implies. They fail to understand and empathize with that individual human, what he was, how he lived and what his priorities were — and that aside from his cultural veneer, he was as human in every way as any modern American, and responded to the same basic human impulses and exhibited the same unpredictability in his behavior.

It was these impulses, and the absolutely assured variability among humans, that rock art style proponents overlook, that cut the ground out from under the assumption of cultural uniformity, and make a shambles out of virtually all style analyses based upon that assumption.

One astute researcher who did extensive field work on the rock art of western Colorado in 1922, but whose report to the Smithsonian Institute was lost until 1977, did at least recognize individuality as a factor. At the end of his report he concluded that "the occurrence of two or more peculiarly different general types (styles) of petroglyphs at one site may be due to individual peculiarity on the part of the workmanship of different artisans," but this recognition remains a rarity within rock art literature.

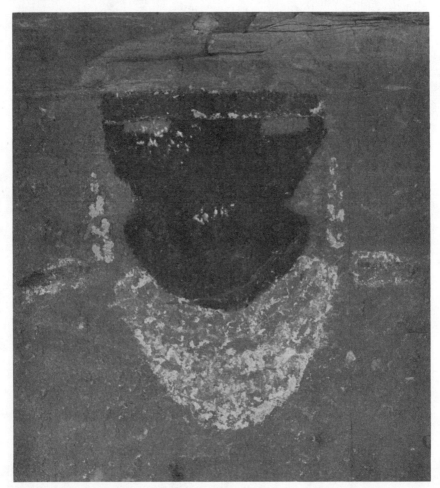

Horse Canyon, Canyonlands National Park.

INDIVIDUALITY

To date, no rock art scholar has seriously addressed the psychological and sociological impact of individuality on prehistoric rock art styles, subject matter, technique and other variables, yet individuality affects rock art study and style analysis in many ways, largely by throwing certain basic assumptions into question.

For example, quite a number of rock art subjects appear at widely scattered locations, without regard for the established style systems, subjects such as "Kokopelli" figures, "shields," crescents, "kachina" figures, "feathered serpents" and many others. Dedicated style analysts assume that such unique subjects were invented only in one place — usually in some other culture — and that the use of the subject spread by means of cultural infusion, migration and "colonization." A great deal of style analysis has been based upon this assumption of only one inventor for each graphic design, an assumption that rejects the concept of parallel but independent invention by two or more individuals, often widely separated in time and space.

Yet it is well known from the history of human creativity — whether in art, science or applied technology — that parallel and independent invention is common. To assume that this proven characteristic of humanity would not apply to the individuals who created prehistoric rock art is indefensible. Thus, style analyses based on the idea that a graphic figure was developed or invented only once, and that it then spread by cultural infusion, are highly questionable. While this doubtless did happen at times, it is equally certain that parallel and independent invention of graphic designs took place, and analyses in which this possibility is not considered are incomplete and their conclusions doubtful. With such complex rock art subjects as Kokopelli figures, multiple invention is less likely, but with simpler graphic designs, such as the "shields" and "sickle-shaped tools" found at widely scattered sites, single invention is far from certain.

Failure to consider the individuality factor also undercuts style analysis at its very roots, in the establishment of styles. Style systems are based on variations in technique, location, subject matter and design sophistication. But once the individuality factor is considered, it becomes readily apparent that such variations could as easily be based on differences between individuals as on differences between cultural groups. Many established rock art styles, which allegedly represent some cultural group not otherwise defined by archaeologists, could quite readily be nothing more than the work of one or a few dedicated craftsmen, or some inspired or inventive shaman and his disciples. Such a crew could hack out a lot of petroglyphs within a substantial piece of geography in a lifetime, even a short one. And with most rock art probably being created for religious, mystical, magic purposes, should such a possibility be ignored?

Another distinct possibility is ignored by style analysts. A single energetic rock art craftsman might produce a few figures or a panel on one boulder or stretch of cliff using one technique. He might then move a few feet, canyons or miles away for any one of a hundred mystical or whimsical reasons, and there, pulling a completely different technique out of his bag of shaman tricks, he might create another figure or panel. The second panel may have virtually nothing in common with the first, so to a stylist the two panels would be different "styles" and be assigned to two different cultures or the same culture but a different time, and these distinctions would be used as a basis for hypothesizing grandly about such serious cultural business as cultural trait infusions, game distribution, cultural sub-group areal limits, intercultural contacts, nomadic migration routes, regional climate changes, religious practices, and a host of other things that style analysts so blithely discuss. The clever and versatile old shaman who made both panels would probably be highly amused.

But the question remains — if two distinct "styles" of rock art appear on the same panel, could they not have been made by two craftsmen from the same local clan, perhaps a master and his apprentice, or by the same man on two different days? Could not different "styles" simply be the "signatures" of different contemporary craftsmen, rather than indicators of whole cultural variants?

Extrapolation into cultural matters solely from "evidence" derived from rock art style analysis is flagrantly unscientific, but it makes otherwise barren research papers look profound, and makes good reading in books published for popular sale. Even so, it ignores the laws of probability expressed by Ockham's Razor — that the simplest explanation for something has the best chance of being correct. If a distinct "style" of rock art is noticed, a scientist would first examine all likely explanations, then, lacking clues other than the special style, he would settle for the simplest explanation until more data could be found. In the case of many rock art styles, the simplest explanation is that the special style was the creation of one man plus, perhaps, a few copycats. The probability that the style represents a whole cultural sub-group or cultural intrusion would be low unless supported by some pretty impressive physical evidence.

Three examples within canyon country of generally adopted styles that could easily be nothing more than the work of one craftsman and a few apprentices or plagiarists are the Barrier Canyon Style, Cave Valley Style and Classic Vernal Style. There are many others throughout the Southwest.

It could reasonably be argued, on the side of style analysis and cultural uniformity and against the individuality factor, that prehistoric rock artists were not truly creative artists in that they did not produce art for art's sake, and that their graphic end product was less an end in itself than a means to an end, as with ceremonial use. This being quite likely, the argument goes, rock artists would not be the temperamental, creative individuals so typical of modern artists, but would be conservative, limited and bound by convention in their choices of technique, subject matter and graphic style.

While this may be true up to a point, humans are not rigidly bound in conformity by their instincts as are communal insects. Human individuals are and always have been rebellious, defiant, ornery, stubborn, creative, inventive, non-conformist, cantankerous, cranky, perverse, sneaky, hypocritical, innovative, bullheaded, curious and prone to be different for its own sake, in spite of all social pressures toward conformity. All of these very human characteristics can and do lead to wild and unpredictable variations in behavior — including the creation of rock art. Anyone who has failed to notice this variability has no business in any facet of anthropological study, including the study of rock art created by primitive cultures. It is thus a good bet that individuality played a large and continuous part in the variability of prehistoric rock art, perhaps a far greater part than any tendencies toward cultural uniformity. And it is a serious mistake and highly unscientific to indulge in rock art style analysis without giving careful consideration to that individuality.

THE BOTTOM LINE

In conclusion, the basic assumption upon which style analysis is based — cultural uniformity — is invalid as applied to the rock art of the Anasazis and Fremonts and their Desert Archaic predecessors. Conversely, it is just as invalid to assume that within this region all differences and similarities in rock art are due to individualism. There obviously is a general and unmistakable trend toward segmented uniformity in rock art technique, subject matter and graphic design, but in order to make analytical use of these general trends it is necessary to understand all of the factors that contribute toward them. Cultural conservatism and inertia is only one of these factors, and probably one of the least important. Another, of considerable importance, is individuality. The other three major factors are the constraints imposed by the medium itself, the general cultural level of graphic concept sophistication, and the geographic isolation in which these culture groups existed.

If appropriate weight is given to each of these five factors that affected the creation of distinct rock art "styles," then style analysis can be a valid, though highly limited, tool. Such a balanced approach has yet to be made, because in all too many cases it would lead to the conclusion that no meaningful style analysis was possible, something many baffled rock art enthusiasts would not like to admit. Yet those who do not give full consideration to all of the factors that contribute toward the establishment of apparent "styles" of rock art when they establish those styles, and who then use these styles for further analysis, are doing a severe disservice to the serious scientific study of prehistoric rock graphics, just as others who have reached extreme conclusions unsupported by hard fact have done.

Of course, some researchers who establish their own style systems do point out a few of the weaknesses of their systems, then go on to suggest how other researchers could create an improved system. Unfortunately, those "other" researchers who eventually attempt this Herculean task are few and far between, and the faulty style systems survive and thrive.

The most unfortunate aspect of such faulty style systems is that they are quite commonly used as a basis for making specific cultural extrapolations, conjectures and inferences. At its best, style analysis can be used to reach broad, general, non-specific, tentative conclusions. Scientists trained and experienced in scientific analytical methods generally recognize this, but enthusiastic amateurs usually do not. They make the mistake of assuming that tentatively established "styles" are significant cultural fact, that all analyses based on these styles are rational, and that the ideas produced by these analyses are true revelations, rather than the fanciful constructions they generally are.

As an example of how style analysis can bemuse even a respected scientist, the style system established by one during a salvage archaeology project led him to conclude that, because similar style elements were also found in other areas, "Anasazis colonization took place near Bishop, California, and, seemingly, southern Oregon," and that this "colonization" may have precipitated the southward migration of Athabascan nomadic tribes, a migration that later was to play a major part in the forced regression of the Anasazi culture.

While this interesting hypothesis may eventually prove to be true, basing it solely on the occurrence of a few rock art figures in California and Oregon that were similar to figures found in Glen Canyon is stretching a little hard data to the extreme. It is this kind of thinking that led humorist Mark Twain to observe:

"There is something fascinating about science; one gets such wholesale returns of conjecture out of such a trifling investment of fact."

Despite the fact that style analysis is a far more limited tool than commonly supposed, there are interesting and promising trends in rock art style that have not yet been explored. As noted briefly in the last chapter, distinct phases in graphic concept sophistication can be defined, in spite of complications caused by individuality.

A careful study of human visual perception, learning and conception processes, related to the development and use of graphics concepts in very primitive, isolated groups, could contribute toward the creation of graphic styles truly related to overall cultural development. Certainly, there would be considerable value to a style system based upon graphic concept transition points, quantum leaps in understanding, such as going from one-dimensional thinking (pits, grooves and assorted lines), to two-dimensional thinking (closed-area shapes of all kinds), to three-dimensional thinking (perspective, horizons, ground level, directionality, angled views of subject matter, hidden-overlapped parts, size proportions between related figures, complete realistic figures, gravity-balance, etc.), to four-dimensional thinking (duration — the depiction of the passage of time).

One respected art historian who has studied and written extensively about Western rock art has noted that "In the history of art there has been a noticeable tendency for forms to evolve from naturalistic, through stylized, to abstract." While this generalization is probably quite valid with respect to true art, the prehistoric rock graphics of the Four Corners states and the Great Basin are pre-art. They represent the very first dealings with graphics concepts that an isolated culture encounters. They are an evolutionary step prior to the use of graphics for art, for aesthetics, for decoration, for its own sake.

Thus, principles that apply to art as such do not apply to Southwestern prehistoric rock graphics. A whole new set of principles must be developed for this far more primitive stage of graphics understanding, before such fascinating remnants from the past can truly be understood.

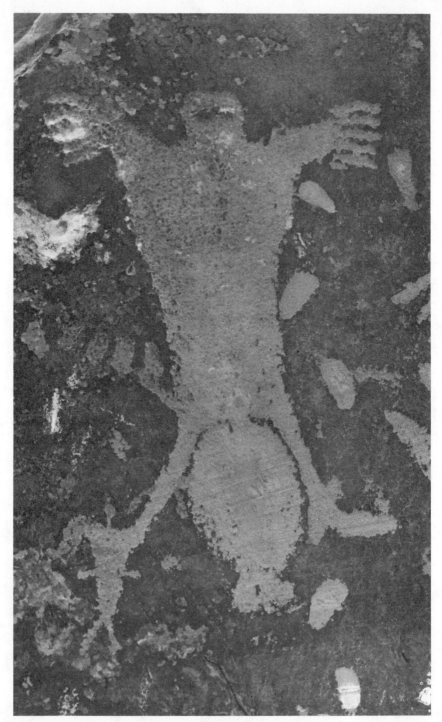

Cane Creek Canyon, Utah. A "birth certificate" petroglyph?

INTERPRETATION

QUESTIONS AND ANSWERS

When confronted with a display of prehistoric rock art, the first thing that a modern person wants to know is, "What does it mean?" The question is natural to anyone born and raised within a culture that is saturated with almost every conceivable kind of graphic display and use. The question is the same one most people ask when they see a piece of modern abstract art and for the same reason — our cultural background tells us graphics do have meanings and purposes.

Modern abstract art and prehistoric rock art are not exceptions to this, although their true meanings may be understandable only to the "artists," with the only possible meanings obvious to viewers being hints based upon the art's apparent subject matter. Such hints are far from reliable, whether derived from modern abstract art or prehistoric rock art.

Is it possible to interpret prehistoric rock art with any degree of assurance? Does it even have a cultural (as against individual) meaning that might possibly be interpreted? Can information of cultural significance be gained from the study of rock art that cannot be obtained any other way? Is the prehistoric rock art of Utah, the Great Basin and the general Four Corners region a crude "language," an early attempt at communications? These are the key questions that need to be answered if serious rock art study is to make significant progress, if this field of specialty is to gain the stature within anthropology-archaeology that its enthusiasts seek.

At present, there are almost as many sets of answers to these key questions as there are rock art researchers. In general, it could be said that Murphy's Law applies quite nicely to rock art meanings and uses — given millions of rock art images made by thousands of craftsmen over several thousand years, almost anything rock art COULD represent it DOES represent, with the most probable meanings and uses occurring many times and even the less likely appearing a few times. There are also, of course, quite a few very unlikely interpretations promoted by modern researchers who are more enthusiastic than knowledgeable. A few of these are discussed later in this chapter.

As noted in the earlier chapter on rock art literature, all too many archaeologists tend to avoid the serious study of prehistoric rock art because of the persistent cloud of nonsense that hangs over the subject, and of those who do enter the field, many seem to grow lax in their understanding and use of basic scientific disciplines and join the amateur enthusiasts in flights of unfounded fantasy, building layer after layer of shaky inferences upon the most minute traces of hard data. Yet often this is done with such seeming cleverness, depth of knowledge and command of archaeology's special language that others — even their fellow professionals — are bemused, overawed, that so much could be derived from so little. In simple fact, it can't.

This has created a situation in rock art literature that is reminiscent of the fable about the emperor who wore no clothes. It seems the emperor had been bamboozled by a nefarious tailor into thinking that his new uniform was ultra-fine, so fine that it might even be invisible to a few low-lifes. His Highness didn't dare admit that HE couldn't see it. And when he wore his invisible uniform in a parade, his loyal subjects were either so awe-inspired or brainwashed they didn't notice that the emperor was naked, or if they did, they dared not mention it.

Considerable modern rock art literature is equally "naked," in spite of having been written by awe-inspiring authors, and similarly, many rock art researchers are too bemused or brainwashed or polite to call attention to that nakedness. So the misconceptions published in polished archaeological prose persist, for lack of the modern equivalent of the guileless child in the fable who pointed, amazed, and said, "Look! The Emperor is wearing no clothes!"

While recently a few archaeologists, and quite a few others, have dared to walk where angels fear to tread in the matter of rock art interpretation, conservative scientists have had more realistic and pessimistic things to say about the subject.

Almost a century ago, Mallery put the matter of rock art interpretation into perspective by saying:

"But though (rock graphics) do not and probably never will disclose the kind of information hoped for by some enthusiasts, they surely are valuable as marking the steps in one period of human evolution and in presenting evidence of man's early practices. Also though the occurrences interesting to their authors and therefore recorded or indicated by them are not important as facts of history, they are proper subjects of examination, simply because in fact they were the chief objects of interest to their authors, and for that reason become of ethnologic import. It is not denied that some of the drawings on rocks were made without special purpose, for mere pastime, but they are of import even as mere graffiti. The character of the drawings and the mode of their execution tell something of their makers. If they do not tell who those authors were, they at least suggest what kind of people they were as regards art, customs, and sometimes religion. But there is a broader mode of estimating the quality of known pictographs. Musicians are eloquent in lauding of the great composers of songs without words. The ideography, which is the prominent feature of picture writing, displays both primordially and practically the higher and purer concept of thoughts without sound."

In his 1922 report on western Colorado petroglyphs, McKern expressed his honest bafflement about a particular petroglyph at Mesa Verde, a comment that could be applied equally to a great deal of rock art:

"It is hard to conceive of the producer expending his time and energy at such pains without the guidance of a definite idea and purpose. Such an idea is not, however, readily apparent to the

110

uninitiated eye. The drawing does not resemble a conventional-ized design. Its decorative value is indifferent. In such cases it seems safe to assume that the recording of some purposeful meaning must have motivated production."

He goes on to conclude, however, that:

". . . primitive art need not necessarily possess a meaning deeper than is superficially apparent, [and that while] . . . some (rock graphics) will readily fall into their proper places of classifica-tion, others will remain problematical of purpose with points of evidence indicating one or more possible uses. Where such points of evidence are nothing more than shreds of suspicion, it becomes unprofitable to lengthily debate purposes."

Boas, in his 1928 book on primitive art, pointed out a factor that confuses both style analysis and interpretation in the study of rock art:

"The essential conclusion drawn from our observations is that the same form may be given different meanings, that the form is constant, the interpretation variable, not only tribally but individually. It can be shown that this tendency is not by any means confined to art, but that it is present also in mythology and in ceremonialism, that in these also the outer form remains, while the accompanying interpretations are widely different."

If such variability in the meaning of graphic symbols exists within a single culture, as Boas contended, then it would be even greater in areas where the rock graphics are multi-cultural, as within the Anasazi and Fremont cultural territories.

In his 1936 Smithsonian report, Steward summed up his impatience with wild conjectures about rock art meaning by saying:

"Probably nothing in the entire field of archaeology has produced greater excesses of misinformation than the significance and authorship of petroglyphs. Unintelligible, mysterious and supposedly occult, they have stimulated a veritable orgy of mad speculation. Surely their primitive makers would have hesitated had they been able to foresee the furor their efforts were to cause."

Note that Steward called all rock art "petroglyphs." Turner, in his 1963 report on Glen Canyon petroglyphs, took an equally pessimistic view:

"Petroglyphs . . . can never be interpreted with the degree of insight that was in the mind of the creator. In other words, much of the importance and rich detail that were necessary to inspire the symbols on stone were lost when the artisan left the scene. They had significance only to him and his associates and now have become virtually mere curiosities, the total significance of which is lost or at best only guessed at. The thought which occurred when the design was executed is now impossible to recover."

Rock art researcher Meighan made a more optimistic, though still conservative summary of the interpretation problem in a 1978 report:

"The most we can hope for is a logical explanation of the (rock) art in terms of what is possible and probable for a given area and level of cultural complexity. And yet, while this approach is in part unsatisfying to all, and entirely unsatisfactory to some, what other path can be followed to go beyond mere description of rock art?"

There are, of course, still greater extremes of opinion about the question of the meanings and uses of Anasazi and Fremont rock graphics. These range all the way from "a bunch of prehistoric graffiti with no meaning at all except to the artist" to "a universal American Indian language of great complexity." As usual, the truth lies somewhere within the unexciting middle ground.

Is there any meaning to rock art, and is interpretation possible? "No," in the modern sense of its being a standardized form of intercommunication between humans who know the "language," but "yes," in the sense that most of it did have meaning to those who made it. As Turner pointed out, though each graphic no doubt meant something to its creator, the minute the craftsman walked away, the meaning was lost forever.

Can culturally meaningful information be derived from the study of Anasazi and Fremont rock art, information not obtainable by other means? Definitely yes. With careful scientific study, a great deal of information can be found in rock art that simply doesn't exist in other cultural remnants. For example, the development of graphic concept sophistication within a culture is very important, yet how could this be studied without a detailed examination of how it starts in many primitive, isolated cultures — with rock art? Rock art can also provide many clues and inferences useful in the study of such cultural facets as religious beliefs and practices (deities, ceremonies), agricultural development (continuing reliance on game and foraging), apparel (clothing, jewelry, sandal styles), weapons development and importance (atlatls versus bows), astronomical knowledge (star maps, solar calendars, celestial events), and many other things, some of them discussed in earlier chapters.

The value of prehistoric rock art as a unique key to cultural knowledge otherwise unobtainable is beyond question. The main problem is to get the right people working on the problem, and to maintain a healthy attitude of scientific skepticism about every hypothesis advanced, no matter who advances it. As Meigan pointed out, "What other path can be followed?"

MEANINGS AND USES

There is certainly no lack of ideas in modern rock art literature as to the possible uses and meanings of these prehistoric graphics. Few writers can resist the chance to conjecture about this basic puzzle, and their ideas range completely across the spectrum of sensibility.

There are many ways that the various possible meanings and uses of prehistoric rock art could be grouped or classified. Following is one of these. There is no particular significance to this grouping beyond the fact that it is a convenient system based upon conceptual classification of the suggested meanings or uses of rock graphics.

Ceremonial/Religious. This class includes all ceremonies based upon religious beliefs and practices, such as those related to planting and harvesting; male and female puberty; female fertility; the achievement of manhood; seasonal changes; propitiatory gestures; religious, allegorical or mythological tales; ritual coition with humans or animals; and images of gods, supernatural entities, Kachinas and shamans.

Anthropomorph, Ninemile Canyon, Utah. Human or supernatural entity?

Sympathetic Magic. This class could be included within the religious category, but in some primitive cultures is conceptually unique. Similarly, some of the uses listed under "religious" could instead be sympathetic magic in certain cultures. There is no way to determine whether sympathetic magic was distinct from religion in the Anasazi or Fremont cultures. Sympathetic magic graphics could include such applications as medical and healing practices, the manufacturing of hunting and fighting weapons, hunting and combat magic rites, and weather control ceremonies.

Communications. This would include such possible rock art uses and meanings as intergroup picture writing; terrain maps and indications of water sources, trails, etc.; teaching aids, especially for instructing shaman apprentices; and markings indicating clan boundaries, hunting and foraging areas and special campsites.

Social Events or Customs. These would include graphics apparently depicting war, combat or war trophies; friendship symbols; special events; special individuals; local customs; domesticated animals; special astronomical events; and game playing.

Individual Events or Customs. This class could include individual activities or customs such as rock art depicting a personal identity mark; apparent depictions of pregnancy and birth; symbols for virginity and other kinds of social status; "rock art" that is, instead, nothing but marks left from the sharpening of wood, bone or antler tools or weapon tips; apparent humor; mnemonic graphics (memory aids) such as counting; and meaningless doodling.

Aesthetics. This could, of course, be grouped with either the "individual" or "social" custom classes but is conceptually unique as to purpose. It would include rock art supposedly based upon creative, decorative and aesthetic impulses — art for its own sake, or at least as supplementary to some other primary purpose.

Acultural. This would include graphics supposedly placed on a panel by individuals from an intruding cultural group, or depictions of items definitely from some other culture.

It should be noted that none of the foregoing possible uses and meanings of the rock graphics created by the Anasazis, the Fremonts or their predecessors is certain. They are all just various possibilities suggested by serious researchers, with some of them having rather low probability of being true. Only further scientific investigation can establish the validity of the suggested meanings and uses.

It would be possible to write an entire book evaluating the various ideas that have been put forward about the meanings and uses of prehistoric Southwestern rock graphics, but discussion of a few is appropriate here. Some of the ideas that are fairly high or low on the probability scale are discussed under other headings later in this chapter.

HOW CAN WE KNOW?

Many factors complicate matters when it comes to outright resolution of questions about prehistoric rock art meanings and uses. Perhaps the greatest factor is the immense cultural gap — a veritable cultural Grand Canyon — that separates modern Americans from early Amerinds. Americans of the late Twentieth Century are the most sophisticated ever produced by the human race in such matters as graphics concepts, technology and understanding of the natural environment, while the Archaic and early Formative Anasazis and Fremonts were at the other end of the scale — with many thousands of years of painfully slow cultural development in between.

Because of this eons-wide cultural chasm, it is quite likely that not even the application of the best available scientific logic will produce reliable information about the actual meanings and uses of specific designs or panels of Southwestern prehistoric rock art. It is virtually impossible for a modern mind, scientifically trained or otherwise, to bridge the gap to a primitive mind of a thousand years ago or more. Even if we knew the precise state of knowledge and belief about the natural world then, and also knew all the details about that world, we still could not really understand how individuals and cultures perceived these realities, nor how they interpreted them by way of cultural and individual philosophies. We have trouble bridging this cultural-empathetic gap even between various modern nations and between members of the same family, so how could the immensely greater gap between modern and ancient Americans be spanned with any assurance?

Style analysis as a tool for doing this was discussed in the last chapter and found wanting. A few researchers with a mathematical bent have tried to apply the arcane methodology of statistical analysis to derive information from prehistoric rock art. This is roughly analogous to using a megabuck computer to search for meaningful patterns in a pile of chicken bones tossed by a witch doctor. It is possible to generalize from the act of tossing, but the bones contain no meaning to be found, and certainly cannot be used as a basis for constructing elaborate cultural hypotheses. A lot of prehistoric rock art could truthfully be characterized as the "chicken bones of cultures past."

It can safely be assumed that all of the rock art created during prehistoric times had some kind of meaning to its creators. This meaning ranged from aimless idle-time doodling to images fraught with import, depending on what the craftsman had in mind at the moment. But quite likely that meaning was not even apparent or clear to any others present when it was made, especially if they were ordinary clansmen sitting around watching a shaman in mystification, or in a stupor induced by some native hallucinogen. How, then, could a modern American expect to see the "true meaning" of such rock graphics millennia later, meaning that was quite possibly a "shaman's secret" even when created?

Nor, with some rock art, is it easy for a modern researcher to believe that the prehistoric craftsman had anything to say worth interpreting. It is quite common to find petroglyphs of deer, sheep and other large herbivores drawn with their hind leg "knees" bending forward, as with humans, rather than backward. It is difficult to assign much weight to anything a rock art craftsman might "mean" when he is so obviously naive about things common in his own daily life.

All efforts to interpret rock art meaning must, of course, be based upon what the graphics actually depict. An earlier chapter discussed how difficult this is to determine with any assurance. Is that "anthropomorph" a chief, shaman, Kachina, deity, spirit, venerated ancestor, hero or just an ordinary clansman who married the chief's homely daughter? If we know which, does that tell us why he was commemorated in stone? Or how the image was used and why? If it was, indeed, used at all.

Is that "shield figure" a warrior holding a war shield in valiant defense of his village, or a shaman holding a symbolic shield in a "peace" ceremony? Could the "shield" instead be a special kind of anthropomorph, maybe an obese chief or shaman, or some other being of special significance? Or did such round-bodied figures represent fat, well-fed people — a sort of clan "brag" about its prosperity? How can meaning or use be deduced if the actual subject matter is in question? Perhaps the last word on this was also one of the first. Mallery wrote in 1889 that "Perhaps the most important lesson learned . . . is that no attempt should be made at symbolic interpretation unless the symbolic nature of the particular characters . . . is known, or can be logically inferred from independent facts."

And when "experts" drastically disagree with each other on the "meaning" of the same rock art panel, who is correct? How expert are such experts? If one contends that the use of red in pictographs is related to blood, life, the body, renewal, birth and strong emotion, while another says that red was a predominant color in canyon country pictographs because red minerals were readily available and naturally durable, you have Ockham's Razor to help you decide between the two meanings. This principle of the simplest explanation having the highest probability of being correct could also help select between two proposed explanations for why most rock graphics of hands are pictographs, few are petroglyphs. If one expert contends that the hands must exhibit "earth colors" to be spiritually meaningful, while another says that hands are simply too detailed for easy petroglyph making, this simpler hypothesis is the best one, until additional solid data comes along.

How much credibility do various rock art "experts" really deserve when two of them interpret the same panel in two wildly different ways? If one sees the panel as a stylized graphic depiction of some complex religious allegory, while the other sees the graphic figures as universal Indian picture-writing symbols with entirely different meanings, which one, if either, is correct? At best, fifty percent of these experts are dead wrong, and quite possibly 100 percent. Throughout the history of science and technology, there are innumerable examples of "leading experts" with differing views contending publicly until one or the other retires in disgrace or disgust. History also reveals that the "winner" in such public disagreements does not always prove to be correct in the long run, even though his views may have

Salt Creek Canyon, Canyonlands National Park.

Uintah Basin, A. G. Pratt photos.

117

been widely accepted for decades by others in his field of study. The field of rock art research is proving to have more than its share of "experts" who cannot agree with each other, and so far there are no clear winners in the narrow specialty of rock art meanings and uses.

Another mistake commonly made in attempts to understand the meaning of rock art is to assume that the geographic setting when the rock art was made was the same as at present. That concentric-circle petroglyph on the canyon wall "must refer to the spring a few yards upcanyon." But did that spring even exist a thousand, two thousand years ago when the circles were incised? Was the land then so arid that a tiny spring was significant, yet still wet enough that the spring could exist? Or was the region's climate undergoing one of its periodic wetter cycles? Was it perhaps lushly wooded, with a perennial stream slowly carving this very canyon out of solid sandstone? Or could it have been even more arid, with no sign of a spring for centuries? If the spring was there then, as now, would a primitive, subsistence level clansman have been willing to share its life-giving waters with others by broadcasting its location? Unfortunately, many modern rock art interpretations are based upon just such uncertainties about the cultures, terrain, biospheres and climate of long ago.

Some researchers have attempted to determine prehistoric rock art meanings and uses by extrapolating back through time from the various graphics of historic American Indian cultures. While this approach may have some validity when the extrapolation is limited in time and scope, as between the early historic and late prehistoric periods of such surviving cultural remnants as the Hopis and Zuñis, its value rapidly diminishes with increased time and is virtually nil between cultural groups that have no direct lineage. While a certain amount of cultural continuity does exist between the several pueblo tribes of Arizona and New Mexico and their Anasazi predecessors, this continuity is now too tenuous for much practical use, and within Utah and the Great Basin region there are no known links between extant tribes and the prehistoric users of that immense region. In sum, there is no one left to ask about the meaning of the rock art there.

Again, Mallery pointed out two of the major weaknesses in this "ask an Indian" approach in his 1889 report:

"While the interpretation of petroglyphs by (local) Indians should be obtained if possible, it must be received with caution. They very seldom know by tradition the meaning of the older forms, and their inferences are often made from local and limited pictographic practices . . . An Indian, when in an amiable and communicative mood, (will) answer queries in a manner which he supposes will be satisfactory to his interviewer (and will) give any desired amount of information on any subject without the slightest restriction by the vulgar bounds of fact."

The questionable value of the "ask an Indian" approach is still further underscored by the fact that certain historic Indian tribes have strong taboos against going anywhere near prehistoric rock art. Doubtless, this cultural trait had its roots in prehistory and may then have been more the rule than an exception. Wherever it did exist, such an "avoidance custom" would have severely inhibited the transmission of rock art meaning information down through the centuries.

Extrapolating back through time, even where cultural continuity exists, and even using accurate and verifiable data, is therefore a very limited study technique at best. As noted earlier, symbol and design meanings change with time, and unless you subscribe to the unsupported assumption of cultural uniformity in rock art techniques, subject matter, meaning and use, other rock art craftsmen living in the same period of the prehistoric past or even in the same pueblo might not have known exactly what a particular rock graphic meant. How, then, could another Indian, a thousand or more years later in a culture severely diluted for more than four centuries, possess such knowledge?

One well known archaeologist solved the problem of rock art meaning quite handily, once and for all, by stating flatly that rock art "meaning" is the idea conveyed to the "interpreter" in response to his own established knowledge and background, "regardless of original intent" of the rock art craftsman. While this approach to "meaning" is very attractive in that it makes every interpretation correct by definition, and provides a meaning for every rock graphic, it furnishes no hints whatever of what the rock art meant to the originating individual and his culture, and is hence worthless as an analytical tool.

A more realistic archaeologist pointed out in 1936 that rock art researchers ". . . will never understand this phase of Indian life if we treat it as some unique product of the native mind that can be isolated from the culture of which it is a part." In spite of the obvious prerequisite of detailed knowledge about a culture before its rock art can be studied, attempts to investigate these challenging graphics as an isolated subject continue today. Even some rock art literature generated by professional archaeologists shows an amazing lack of understanding of the primitive cultures of those who created canyon country rock art, and the different and slowly changing environment in which they lived.

SOME GOOD POSSIBILITIES

Despite the problems inherent in determining the precise meaning and use of specific figures and panels of prehistoric rock art, it is still possible to assign general meanings to such graphics with fair assurance.

Such generalizing is based upon a lot of careful study of a lot of rock art, and considers factors such as apparent subject matter, design or subject matter repetition, its location and its relationship with other nearby rock graphics and other cultural artifacts. From the study of these kinds of factors, it is fairly certain that a lot of Anasazi and Fremont rock art was created for ceremonial purposes, whatever its figures depict. Other high probability meanings and uses are sympathetic magic (as depicted by innumerable hunting scenes), territorial claims (such as clan or dwelling area boundary markers), fertility symbols (coition, pregnancy and birth),

Apparent counting or record keeping, Black Dragon Canyon, Utah.

special individuals (highly decorated or unusual anthropomorphs), super-natural beings (definitely non-real figures, probably for ceremonial use), weather control (clouds, lightning, whirlwinds and rain), record keeping (counting marks), astronomical events (depictions of supernova and solar calendars), cultural intrusions (macaws), and a variety of other minor uses.

It should be noted, however, that while such a conservative approach can deal with what a specific rock graphic might represent and its probable general use or meaning, it makes no attempt to reach firm conclusions about exactly what it was or how it was actually used. If there are many figures in a region that show birds perched atop human heads, it is one thing to conclude that such odd juxtapositions probably have some symbolic meaning or ceremonial use. It is quite another to conclude that the birds were used in, say, harvest ceremonials, or with marriage rites, or that such men were shamans, with the head-perching birds representing the shaman's capacity for spiritual flight, unless other hard evidence lends weight to such detailed inferences. In another example, it is fairly safe to conclude that certain shallow, oval "petroglyphs" found on fairly level boulders beneath pictograph panels far from any habitation sites were probably used for grinding something used in ceremonials involving the pictographs. But conjectures about what products were ground, and for what kinds of ceremonies, are not warranted in the absence of further evidence.

Again, with the "Kokopelli" figures so common in Anasazi territory, it is feasible to reach the general conclusion that such figures had some kind of serious significance to those who made them, but there is far less certainty about conjectures that the concept migrated north from Mexico,

120

and that it symbolized a particular thing, such as fertility, weather control, a Kachina, interclan trading, a hunting magician, or a deforming disease. Various experts have suggested these and other possible "meanings" to the humpbacked flute player — who doesn't always have a hump, who may be walking, sitting or lying down, who may be playing or not playing his flute, who may or may not have a pet dog and who may or may not have a phallus shown, either tumescent or not.

The earliest proven Kokopelli in the U. S. — the name is Hopi and is spelled various ways — was found in Arizona on Hohokam pottery dated about A.D. 600, although certain Basketmaker rock art Kokopellis may be even older. As a historic Hopi Kachina, Kokopelli's "hump" is a bagful of babies and gifts used to seduce young maidens. The Zuñis see Kokopelli as a "rain priest," but the Hopis also use flutes in water ceremonies. Some researchers have contended that Kokopelli's hump is a sign of Pott's Disease, a form of tuberculosis that produces spinal deformity, but other rock art scholars with medical backgrounds have pretty thoroughly disproved that idea. They did not, however, entirely discount the chance that the hump might be from some other disease.

Arguments can also be made for and against each of the other proposed meanings and uses of the Kokopelli figure. For example, although many such rock art figures are shown with tumescent phalluses, this may not have had the obvious meaning of human coition and fertility. Some scholars have contended that when shown, human sex acts may sometimes signify an attempt to depict "original creation," a subject which seems to preoccupy all human cultures, primitive and modern. Further, did the Anasazis really have enough knowledge of human anatomy and the reproductive process to know about human sperm as "seed," or precisely how the fertilization process worked? Some of the "fertility" explanations presuppose a detailed understanding of human anatomy and function that came to our own culture only recently.

To summarize, the mystery of the canyon country rock art "Kokopelli" remains unresolved beyond the general conclusion that he meant something rather important to the Anasazis and other pueblo tribes, and that this meaning, or at least the use of the image, was slowly diffusing northward into Fremont territory.

In recent years, astronomers who have taken an interest in certain aspects of archaeology have established beyond reasonable doubt that prehistoric American Indians throughout the Western Hemisphere had and routinely used astronomical knowledge, in particular an understanding of the movement cycles of such major celestial objects as the sun, moon and Milky Way, plus a few major stars and planets. The Anasazis applied this knowledge in the construction of some of their more sophisticated pueblos and in a few petroglyphs. Various researchers have demonstrated that certain pueblo buildings at Chaco Canyon and Hovenweep National Monument, as well as at other locations, were built to mark summer and winter solstices and spring and autumn equinoxes, by means of shadow edges or narrow beams of sunlight through wall openings. At some locations, the buildings were constructed so that even the days between these seasonal indicators could be marked.

There are also petrolgyphs at Hovenweep, Chaco and other locations which serve as solar calendars. One type is located on a horizontal surface so that on the day of the solstice, if a person stands on the glyph at sunset on some, sunrise on others, the sun aligns exactly with some outstanding natural feature on the horizon, such as a rock spire or a notch in a cliff line. Another solar calendar at Chaco Canyon marks the four seasonal dates by daggers of light cast at high noon on a set of spiral petroglyphs in a shadowed alcove. The solar calendar petroglyphs at Chaco and Hovenweep appear to have been placed to take advantage of natural light-and-shadow effects, but the possibility that the massive rocks involved were adjusted for optimum effect cannot be excluded.

Although it cannot be inferred with certainty, it is highly probable that such architectural and petroglyphic solar calendars were used as planting and harvesting guides and for determining when to hold a variety of ceremonies. Ethnological studies and extrapolations into the past from surviving remnants of the pueblo culture all support this general inference. It is also quite probable that the petroglyph-in-natural-setting kind of solar calendar preceded those that were designed into pueblo dwelling and ceremonial structures, although it is possible that less durable pre-pueblo structures also contained solar calendar features but have not survived. On the basis of conceptual complexity, the solar-horizon calendar is the simplest of the three basic types and thus may have been the first devised. This type occurs many places in North America. Petroglyph calendars, like other Anasazi petroglyphs, may have become obsolete with the development of more sophisticated structural substitutes.

SUMMER SOLSTICE

Another highly probable but still controversial meaning of certain rock art figures found in canyon country and many other western locations is that such images depict the supernova of A.D. 1054. Accurate historical descriptions of this spectacular celestial event tell how it appeared in relation to our moon, which was in its last quarter at the time. Astronomical calculations indicate that the event could, indeed, have been witnessed by western prehistoric Indians. R. A. Williamson, an astronomer who has a special interest in archaeoastronomy, described the event and its probable depiction in prehistoric rock art this way:

". . . on the morning of 5 July 1054 a star of spectacular brightness appeared within 3 degrees of the waning crescent Moon in western North America. The nearness of this event to the time of the summer solstice and the great brightness of the star leads us to suspect that it was noted and recorded in one of the few permanent media available to the Indians of North America. We recognize that our hypothesis cannot be proven, but the circumstantial evidence for this point of view is growing."

That was 1979. The evidence is virtually overwhelming now. For readers who wish to know more about prehistoric astronomy in America, the Ballena Press book, *Archaeoastronomy in the Americas,* edited by Williamson, is highly recommended. The book's extensive bibliography can lead to still further information.

SOME LOW PROBABILITIES

Literature, recent and past, abounds with speculation about the meanings and uses of prehistoric American Indian rock art. Most of those proposed and promoted are arrant nonsense, but they persist because, while unsupported by hard fact, they are difficult to disprove, and a few are so ridiculous that serious scientists prefer to ignore them entirely. However, some of the worst ideas are so appealing to the uneducated public that serious rock art researchers simply cannot ignore them.

Some of these curious low-probability ideas are fairly simple and narrow in scope, while others have broad significance. As an example of a limited idea, many petroglyph figures appear to resemble terrain maps and are accepted as such by many rock art enthusiasts. Yet upon careful study, such "maps" do not seem to correspond in any significant way to nearby geographic features. There are also other major arguments against the "map" interpretation. If a modern American, highly sophisticated in graphics concepts and the use of maps cannot "read" such a map, how could a primitive Indian, unfamiliar not only with mapping techniques but with the very basics of graphics, make use of the map? Further, map-making requires an understanding of third-dimensionality that prehistoric Indians notably lacked. And even assuming he could, would an Anasazi or Fremont clansman want to share his hard earned knowledge of the land with just any stranger that came along? In most primitive societies, information vital to survival is carefully guarded, not advertised.

In sum, all three aspects of map-making — motivation, execution and use — seem to be very weak in the "map" interpretation of the masses of squiggly lines that appear on many petroglyph panels. But either way, the "map" idea is not earth-shaking in importance.

On the other hand, the idea that most if not all rock art — prehistoric and historic — comprises a form of "universal Indian language" or "picture writing" would have immense significance if it could be supported by fact. The principal advocate of this proposal bases his concept on extrapolations and inferences from historic Indian graphics. As noted earlier, such inferences can be made within narrow time limits and where cultural continuity exists, but beyond these limits and without cultural continuity such conjecturing enters the realm of very low probability.

Many rock art researchers have felt constrained to comment about the "language" concept:

Siegrist said, in his 1972 report, ". . . there is no shred of firm evidence that North American rock art is any form of writing or abstract communicative system. . ."

In McKern's 1922 study he noted that "The tendency to treat all primitive picturing as attempted chronicles or graphic symbols . . . has done much to discredit the scientific worth of pictograph study and has tended toward discouraging serious research . . ."

Nordenskiold discussed the rock art-language possibility at length in his 1893 report, and while conceding that further studies might bring new data to light, he expressed his skepticism by saying that ". . . it is scarcely probable that any interpretation of them will be discovered."

The Shutlers agreed with this in their 1962 survey of southern Great Basin rock art sites by concluding that "Their lack of pattern makes it positive, however, that they do not represent a written language."

Steward in his 1936 report also discussed the language possibility at length, even referring back to Mallery, another cool head in rock art research, and concluded about prehistoric rock graphics that "When, therefore, anyone not excepting Indians, pretends to interpret these, unless he has the direct testimony of the original artist, one may be assured that it is merely his own entirely unfounded guess."

As with so many aspects of American rock art, Mallery's 1889 report still remains a solid and quotable authority. In his chapter of general conclusions Mallery wrote:

"Interest has been felt in petroglyphs, because it has been supposed that if interpreted they would furnish records of vanished peoples or races, and connected with that supposition was one naturally affiliated that the old rock sculptures were made by peoples so far advanced in culture as to use alphabets or at least syllabaries. . ."

He also pointed out that ". . . even in limited areas of North America, diverse significance is attached to the same figure, and differing figures are made to express the same concept," thus attacking the very roots of the "universal language" idea. If the meanings of symbols changed from place to place, time to time and tribe to tribe, how would meaningful communications be possible?

Dozens of other rock art researchers could be quoted on this matter, with virtually all of them extremely skeptical about the language-communications hypothesis. This writer is no exception.

Another low-probability interpretation or meaning to rock art is "humor." Very few images that could be remotely considered humorous have been found, although doubtless a modern humorist could, if pressed, find a great deal of amusement in some of the crudely wrought figures with their disproportionate bodies in ridiculous postures apparently doing silly things. However, the question is — was humor intended by the rock graphic craftsman? That prehistoric Indians had senses of humor is beyond dispute, although what they found funny probably differed wildly from modern Indians, as it does even among modern Americans. But is that petroglyph of two Kokopellis, each blowing on opposite ends of the same flute, intended to be humorous? Or was it depicting a special flute actually designed for two players, to be used in very sacred and solemn ceremonies? It is too early to write off the concept of humor in rock art, but so far the evidence is extremely thin. The same can be said for aesthetics, which is discussed further in the next section of this chapter.

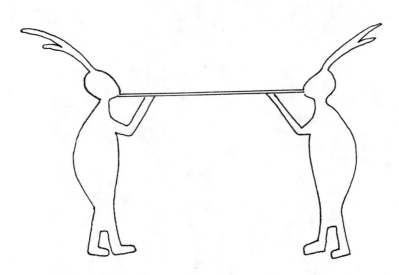

Another possible interpretation of certain rock art images is that they depict combat or war. Again, the probability of this is low but not zero. While violent cultural contacts did occur late in the Anasazi development, for most of their Formative history their nearest neighbors were also peaceful puebloans, and war was apparently not a part of their culture as it was with contemporary nomadic tribes in other parts of North America. Anasazi weapons were quite crude by comparison with similar weapons used by nomadic tribes. Apparently the Anasazis had "beaten their swords into plowshares" quite early in the development of the bow, after finding that agriculture provided a better living in the rugged land they occupied, and that they didn't need to pursue hunting weapons development. They evidently were under no cultural pressure to develop defensive weapons.

The Fremonts seemed also to be relatively peaceful, although they may have had more contact with nomadic tribes in surrounding areas, and may have done more hunting because of a smaller agricultural base. The question remains, however, whether the occasional prehistoric "combat" scenes depict actual combat, or merely ceremonial combat dances or even ritualized religious allegories involving spiritual combat. All of these possibilities occur within primitive cultures. Thus, so far, the preponderance of circumstantial evidence points to stylized rather than actual combat for most such rock graphics.

At the lowest end of the probability scale there are endless fantastic ideas about rock art meaning, including "maps to buried treasure," "writings by or about extraterrestrial beings," "extinct animals," and countless fanciful constructions based upon one religion or another. They all have two things in common — none have even the slightest basis in fact, and none find the slightest support within the scientific community.

Petroglyph figures in "combat"? Behind the Rocks, Utah.

One of two "mastodon" petroglyphs, Colorado River gorge, Utah. The second is in Indian Creek Canyon, Utah.

AESTHETICS?

As noted several times earlier, the use of the word "art" in connection with the prehistoric rock graphics of Utah, the Great Basin, and the general Four Corners region is common, but semantically confusing and based upon an assumption that neither has been nor can be proven.

Most writers of rock graphics literature use the term "art," but few attempt to analyze the question of whether this region's prehistoric petroglyphs and pictographs are in fact true art. Presumably most trained archaeologists do not feel qualified to address a subject as slippery and subjective as art, especially since our own modern culture, highly sophisticated in graphics, has yet to settle on a single, uncontested definition of the term.

This reluctance to take positions on matters outside of their own field has not, however, inhibited artists and art historians who have become interested in prehistoric graphics, most of whom firmly proclaim that such graphics are, indeed, art in every sense. One such art-oriented researcher put it this way:

"There are many examples of rock art, such as those featuring crude stick figures or curvilinear meanders, that no one would classify as art; but the moment an aboriginal craftsman bothered to pick out a particularly smooth and colorful piece of rock on which to peck a carefully conceived and decorative figure, you are dealing with an artist. True, he may have been a tribal shaman whose main concern was to put down a visualization of a certain supernatural being for ceremonial use, but if he was concerned in the least with composition, design or craftsmanship, his work has to be considered art."

This statement, while well thought out from the viewpoint of a historian accustomed to dealing with primitive art from cultures elsewhere in North America and the world, demonstrates the highly subjective aspects of art study and indicates that artists are no better qualified than archaeologists are to make sweeping conclusions about this region's rock art-aesthetic questions. As pointed out in earlier chapters, the terms "carefully conceived," "decorative," and "composition, design or craftsmanship" can rarely be applied to the rock graphics of the Anasazis, Fremonts and their Archaic stage predecessors. The terms may perhaps be fairly applied to some late prehistoric Anasazi kiva art, but most if not all Anasazi and Fremont rock graphics appear to be entirely devoid of the qualifying characteristics of intent noted in the quote, as are all still older rock images.

The art historian's position is also weak from another viewpoint. He contends that graphics are "art" if the craftsman cares in any way about the quality of the final image. While this definition is popular with some artists these days, it is nonetheless debatable. Another definition of art holds that technique does not, of itself, make art — that the artist's intent is the critical factor, that the end product must have been produced for aesthetic purposes, must be art for art's sake. There is little doubt that art-for-art's sake develops from decorative graphics for other purposes. Anasazi kiva art was developing in that direction, and the art of the several Central American cultures was well along the way.

Even in modern America, decorative graphics are in common use for many other purposes than aesthetics, such as for architecture, religious and political propaganda, nostalgia, product design, advertising and promotion, the translation of instrument data into something that human senses can perceive, graphical representations of abstract mathematical and physical concepts, and countless other uses. Of course, a few individuals do claim that such graphics for non-aesthetic purposes are also "art," but this position is at best rather contrived, strained and highly subjective. Is a graphic "art" if even one person sees some aesthetic value to it, regardless of its creator's intent? Taken to its logical extreme, this concept would make art out of everything, and artists out of every living thing, including plants.

Basing the definition of "art" on creator intent would, therefore, seem to be a more objective, rational and limiting approach. Art historians object to this by pointing out that the complex art in many cathedrals primarily has a religious intent but is still undeniably art. This argument overlooks the fact that if the artisan has the capability, a graphic may have two intents — one religious, one aesthetic.

But the rock graphics craftsmen of the prehistoric West did not have this capability. They lacked both graphic concept understanding and technique, and their rock medium tended to inhibit artistic innovation. The poor results produced would soon discourage any budding artisan who was concerned over the quality of the end product. The Anasazis apparently gave up serious rock graphics as soon as they developed a better medium — smooth, plastered kiva walls.

There is little doubt, of course, that artistic concepts were developing within the region's prehistoric cultures, primarily in such utilitarian items as basketry, apparel and pottery. As long as the making of such items was strictly the province of women, they were free to be decorative, with purely aesthetic intent. Later, men got into the act and transplanted their very serious world views into such decorative art, so the intent became dual, as with cathedral art.

It might also be argued that prehistoric rock graphics cannot be judged non-artistic just because they are crude in design and execution. The point has some appeal, since most rock art is no cruder in apparent design and execution than a lot of the art that graces our modern galleries and museums. But again the creator's intent comes into play. Such modern art is "crude" by intent, and if examined carefully reveals immense sophistication in design. Prehistoric rock craftsmen had no such sophistication. They lacked the intent and ability to exercise close control over the end results, and those results were crude because the medium permitted little else. Again, intent is the factor that brings order out of confusion.

A strong argument against any intent to make rock art solely for aesthetic purposes is that its subject matter was so limited. Why would a prehistoric canyon country artist interested in aesthetic beauty completely neglect the wide range of natural beauty that surrounded him on all sides? Why are there no spectacular rock art sunsets, or soaring cliffs, or awesome gorges, or painted deserts, or breathtaking panoramas, or gnarled juniper trees, or snowcapped mountain peaks, or the myriad other forms of beauty that abound in the land of the Anasazis and Fremonts? It doesn't take a modern education to perceive natural beauty.

Another aspect of the "art" controvery that has been touched upon in earlier chapters is "abstract art." The word "abstract" is widely used in rock art literature and has even been built into certain rock art style definitions. Even so, the term is unwarranted. It implies that the craftsman had an understanding of the principles of abstracting or simplifying to the bare essentials, that he had the knowledge and mental ability to actually perform this abstraction process with real-world three-dimensional objects, to reduce them to their two-dimensional components in a form suitable for the crude painting or rock-pecking techniques he had available, and that he then had the skill to faithfully produce this abstract design true to his abstract concept.

To attribute all this knowledge and ability to a primitive, Stone Age native pounding a rock or smearing some minerals on a cliff face would seem to be stretching the laws of probability to the extreme.

From the viewpoint of modern researchers who are highly sophisticated in graphics concepts, much non-representational prehistoric rock art is, indeed, "abstract" in that it is not a living, breathing, realistic depiction of something in the physical world, but that concept is strictly a subjective interpretation that has nothing whatever to do with the intent or

Horseshoe Canyon, Canyonlands National Park. For aesthetic purposes?

ability of the person who made the graphics. It is virtually certain that when a prehistoric rock art craftsman produced a set of figures, those figures closely represented the craftsman's state of understanding of graphics concepts and the technique used, and that the crafting process was not preceded by any deliberate cerebration process designed to reduce conceptual complexity to a design suitable for the simple medium being used. In sum, what he made was quite likely the best he could conceive and execute.

Of course, in discussions about prehistoric humans, "primitive" refers to cultural differences and their relative lack of knowledge, not their lack of intelligence. It is quite likely that such primitive cultures had the same proportionate distribution of intelligence as we have in modern society, so that even then exceptional curiosity and creativity were factors with a certain percentage of individuals. Thus, in a very few cases, where this exceptional creativity and the opportunity coincided, there might have been a few early glimmers of dual-purpose intent — religious purpose but with a little caring about the aesthetic qualities of the end result — but with this culturally premature creative impulse largely stifled by the severe limitations of the rock art medium. It can safely be assumed that this did happen a few times — Murphy's Law — and that this facet of individuality was responsible for the production of the few rock art displays that seem inspired beyond the general cultural level of the prehistoric inhabitants of the Anasazi and Fremont territories. Historic rock art, of course, and even late prehistoric graphics in kivas and on ceramics, baskets and other items, exhibited decorative-aesthetic characteristics to a much higher degree, and with some, much earlier.

In conclusion, to modern eyes, a lot of prehistoric rock art may have artistic merit, aesthetic qualities, but that is a subjective judgment that has nothing to do with the intent of its creator. Any aesthetic value in such rock art is serendipitous, an aspect of individuality and thus culturally meaningless.

While viewer interpretation may be one valid measure of aesthetic merit, when it comes to the study of prehistoric graphics the best measure of cultural significance is creator intent. Within such graphics in Utah, the Great Basin and the general Four Corners region, the selection of locations, subject matter and techniques, apparent meanings and uses, the common factor of superimpositions, and the universal crudity of results, all point to intents other than aesthetic, with little if any secondary concern over aesthetics.

It is thus safe to conclude that within this vast region of the American Southwest, rock art for aesthetic, decorative purposes — art for art's sake — did not develop on a cultural basis, although a few scattered individuals may have made temporary strides toward dual purpose rock art in advance of the general cultural pace. These few exceptions that seem to show some aesthetic intent — such as some of the "Classic Vernal Style" petroglyph figures and some of the "Barrier Canyon Style" pictographs in Horseshoe Canyon — tend to underscore the main conclusion. The Anasazi and Fremont cultures simply did not progress in graphics sophistication to the stage where their rock art could have a dual purpose, that is, aesthetic in addition to its primary purpose.

It is quite possible that the first cultural efforts toward dual purpose graphics expression were made by the women of these tribes, who decorated the baskets, pots and other utilitarian items they made. Then, apparently, in late prehistoric times, the male rock graphics craftsman "discovered" new media — primarily plastered kiva walls — and abandoned the meaningful creation of rock graphics. This cultural sequence of development is, of course, hypothetical, but does fit a lot of existing data.

Only continuing objective scientific research can provide valid answers to questions about the development of graphics concepts within the primitive cultures of canyon country.

SUMMARY

It is possible, by combining extensive rock art study with detailed knowledge of the cultures that created the graphics, to reach general conclusions about their meaning and use, even though specific figures cannot with certainty be identified as to subject, meaning and use. Such general conclusions can reveal or at least suggest cultural information not otherwise accessible, which makes the serious scientific study of prehistoric rock graphics worthwhile, despite the fog of fantasy and pseudo-scientific nonsense that continues to obscure and complicate such study. It is encouraging to note that a growing number of competent scientists are reaching the same conclusion.

It is not feasible to apply valid generalizations about rock art meanings and uses to the detailed analysis of specific images or panels. Such generalizations are reached by way of a great many inferences that support each other, with relatively few apparently contradictory inferences, but this logical process is essentially one-way. The general conclusion that much rock art was related to religious ceremonial activity cannot be used to conclude that a set of graphics that appear to be ceremonial actually are. It can be said that the panel might be ceremonial, but only additional hard data could strengthen that inference.

Some of the cultural generalities that can be drawn about the meanings and uses of the rock graphics of the Anasazis, Fremonts and their Archaic predecessors are:

1. The development and use of rock graphics seems to have been following a natural evolutionary trend from no graphics at all, to crude no-meaning petroglyphs, to meaningful petroglyphs and pictographs, to moderately sophisticated pictographs and the first hints of the relief-style of rock carving that Central American cultures had already developed to a high degree.

2. Much of the rock art had ceremonial/religious meanings and uses, but not all. Other uses were for territorial marking, record keeping, sympathetic magic, depicting special persons and events, solar calendars and, beyond doubt, some doodling that had no meaning at all.

3. Much of the earlier Archaic stage rock graphics, and most of the late Anasazi petroglyphs, may have had meaning only to their individual creators, with little or no cultural significance other than the reasons for the lack of meaning. Possible explanations for this probable lack of cultural purpose were discussed in earlier chapters.

4. Rock art was not a form of communication; not used for aesthetic purposes; not a secret code to anything whatever; not by or about extraterrestrial visitors; not any kind of divine manifestation by ancient or modern deities; not a guide to water, game or good forage; and not subject to detailed, specific interpretation of any sort. Only the rock art creators could have done that.

The general conceptual approach to rock art meanings and uses is supported by the respected California researcher C. W. Meighan, who noted in a 1978 study that:

"If we can accept the notion that there are broadly shared and basic belief systems . . . then we can analyze those belief systems to give us some clue of the meaning the rock art may have had for the people who made it. With all its limitations, such an approach represents an attempt to find the cultural meaning of rock art, and it appears a more fruitful approach than discussion of aesthetics, or still worse, merely interpreting what we see in terms of our own cultural beliefs."

Meighan was discussing the hunter-gatherer cultures of Baja California, but the same concept is true of other primitive cultures, whether Archaic or early Formative, as with the Anasazis and Fremonts. His comment about subjective interpretation was also highly cogent. Basing an interpretation upon just what can be seen by looking at a rock art panel or, worse, just its photograph, is simply not rational or scientific. Various observers might see a particular mass of squiggly lines as a map, a fishing throw-net, a supernatural spirit, a clan symbol, a hunting-magic talisman, a maze-game or — perish the thought — as simply a meaningless squiggle of lines made by an aspiring or apprentice shaman practicing his technique, or some prehistoric idler killing time.

With such ambiguous rock graphics — which are all too common — many researchers select meaning on a subjective basis, but an honest scholar will consider all possible meanings in his analysis and maintain a healthy skepticism about all of them until more unchallengeable data can be acquired. A researcher who considers only one of several equally probable meanings is simply not being scientific, and where that single possible meaning is used to build an elaborate hypothetical superstructure, the researcher is leaving the world of science for the realm of faith and fantasy. In the esoteric study of rock art meaning, it is well to bear in mind that things are rarely what they seem to be.

In sum, when it comes to the interpretation of individual rock graphics and panels, a quote attributed to Thomas Jefferson is quite appropriate:

"Ignorance is preferable to error, and he is less remote from the truth who believes nothing, than he who believes what is wrong."

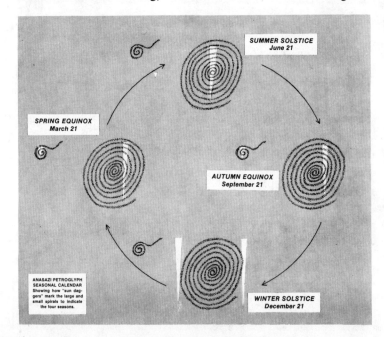

Recently completed research has shown that this Chaco Canyon petroglyph was also used to mark a nineteen year lunar cycle, making it the only presently known prehistoric calendar in the world that indicates both solar and lunar cycles.

133

Spanish Valley, Utah.

DESTRUCTION AND PROTECTION

THE BIG PICTURE

Prehistoric rock art, like everything else humans create, is ephemeral — here today, gone tomorrow. For some human constructs those tomorrows come later than with others, but they always come. In time, a span of time quite short when compared to the measured pace of such natural events on this planet as geology and the continuing development of life, no trace of mankind's works will remain on Earth. Somewhere in the future, some say the not too distant future, our species will have finished demonstrating its lack of fitness for long-range survival on spaceship Earth. Then, within a few tens of thousands of years — a mere instant in the life of a planet — even man's most enduring and defacing artifacts, his massive concrete dams, will have disappeared, perhaps eroded back into their component particles, perhaps buried deeply within the wounded Earth by catastrophic natural events.

Rock graphics, while far from being the least enduring of human artifacts, began their slide toward oblivion the moment they were made, and in some cases the seeds of their destruction were planted by the rock art craftsman by his choice of location, or by the quality of his craftsmanship or materials. Petroglyphs made on boulders too near a stream or river risked premature damage from water erosion or flash-flooding. Those built on cliff faces susceptible to fracturing or collapse risked early total destruction, first from falling, then from the accelerated decomposition of sandstone lying against moist ground.

Petroglyphs made too shallow, or pictographs made from inferior paint or on scaling surfaces, faced early deterioration from wind erosion or the kind of surface exfoliation that moist sandstone exhibits. Pictographs in caves or alcoves formed by seeping moisture, or by regular or intermittent flowing water, were in immediate jeopardy, because these natural forces continued, even though their rates varied as a region's climate varied.

Well made rock graphics placed in locations less exposed to the natural elements had longer life expectancies. In general, much of Anasazi and Fremont territory is rocky and relatively arid. Plentiful exposed rock of moderate hardness encouraged the development of rock graphics in the region's human cultures, and its general aridity helped preserve these fascinating but enigmatic cultural remnants. Although at best all rock art is ephemeral, some of it could last for still more thousands of years if all it had to endure was the elements.

Still, it is highly probable that quite a bit of prehistoric canyon country rock art did not survive into historic times. Most of such losses would have been pictographs, but some petroglyphs were also lost to such catastrophic

Typical pictographs damaged by rock exfoliation, Temple Wash, Utah.

Typical petroglyphs damaged by natural rock exfoliation, Spanish Valley, Utah.

natural forces as flash-flooding and rock falls. Numerous split petroglyphs testify to this. Both kinds of rock graphics have also shown signs of accelerating deterioration within recent times. Researchers have compared current photographs with older photographs of the same rock art panels and found appalling deterioration, even within a few decades. The reasons for this accelerating deterioration are not natural.

NATURAL LOSSES

Rock graphics are exposed to the same natural forces that turn buried rock strata into soaring cliffs, these cliffs into giant boulders, the boulders into smaller rocks, the rocks into sand and silt, and then carry these sediments out to sea. The general term for this is "erosion," and the major elements of this process are wind and water, although occasionally other natural forces such as volcanoes, faulting and earthquakes may contribute.

Water from rain, snow, ice, fog or mists, and even from high humidity, can cause damage to rock art, especially pictographs. Water can also damage rock art by causing exfoliation as it seeps out of rock, or by causing massive collapse from rapid runoff and flash-flooding. Water can weaken the chemical bonds that hold sandstone together, causing it to disintegrate. In some coastal locations tides, and waves with entrained beach sand, wear away at hard granites and igneous rocks, and the deeply cut petroglyphs some have on them. Water also weakens slopes, causing landslides that can bury rock art along a river or stream, perhaps permanently. Water freezing in the tiniest cracks can fracture rock and cause fragmentation or collapse. An exceptionally violent storm can carry windblown rainwater directly into a shallow cave, to erode pictographs normally well sheltered. Water can also cover rock art with mineral deposits, thus either hiding it or destroying it by chemical action or the promotion of plant growth.

Wind can also be destructive without water, by carrying sand and grit and thus becoming an enormous sandblasting machine. Pictograph paints are highly susceptible to such airborne abrasives, which can reach into all but the deepest caves. Some large canyon country caves have been virtually filled by windblown sand, burying the eroded remnants of cave-wall petroglyphs and indicating a change of climate since they were made. In general, the closer rock art is to the ground, the more wind abrasion it will get, but desert winds are often so powerful that dust and sand are carried hundreds of feet into the air, so virtually all canyon country rock art is exposed to some wind erosion. Great Basin rock graphics are even more exposed to wind abrasion.

Even graphics in locations seemingly protected from the prevailing winds can be fiercely abraded by the kinds of random gusts and whirlwinds that cliffs and canyons generate. A few oddly shaped canyons, and high cliffs that are positioned just right, can even act as venturis, accelerating moderate winds to sandblasting speeds. This wind-tunnel effect has doubtless hastened rock art erosion in some locations.

The sun has little erosional effect on petroglyphs, and may even strengthen them where desert varnish is added with the sun's help, but direct sunlight can quickly destroy any organic components in pictograph paint and can accelerate erosion on moist surfaces of caves and alcoves by creating wet/dry cycles which cause surface flaking. Microscopic surface plants also contribute to this process. When pictographs were located in places sheltered from the summer sun but exposed to the lower winter sun, a situation fairly common in canyon country, solar aging and fading takes place. Although some pigments made only with chemically simple mineral components are unaffected by sunlight, more complex minerals will change composition and color when exposed to moisture and direct sunlight. It is thus fairly certain that many surviving pictographs are not now their original color, either from organic deterioration or from chemical changes induced by moisture and sunlight.

Another natural force that attacks rock art is vegetation. The attack may be either mechanical or chemical. Roots penetrate even the slightest cracks in rock, forcing them open and causing further cracking and even rockfalls. The rootlets of the many kinds of mosses and other tiny plants that grow on the moist walls of caves and alcoves contribute toward the surface scaling that damages pictographs.

The juices and saps of some living plants can chemically attack rock surfaces and thus erode petroglyphs, and rotting dead vegetation releases organic acids that can do this, too. The microscopic plants that thrive on the moist surfaces of caves also attack those surfaces chemically, and when dried by direct sunlight or seasonal changes, cause surface flaking. Windblown tree limbs and stiff plant stems can also cause mechanical damage to rock art by abrasion. Many panels are obscured, and thus endangered, by seasonal growth and by trees that have grown since the rock art was created.

Although in time all rock art would be destroyed by natural elements, the process would still be relatively slow for well-crafted graphics placed at locations protected from the worst natural hazards, were it not for another major destructive factor — modern man.

HUMAN DESTRUCTION

Nature destroys rock art very slowly but surely. Modern man is destroying rock art just as surely but at a pace that makes natural deterioration seem insignificant.

Deliberate damage or destruction to canyon country prehistoric rock art comes from two sources — individual vandalism and economic vandalism. Within these general categories, the destruction takes various forms.

Individuals may damage or destroy rock art during scientific research (either deliberately or carelessly), during attempts to copy or collect it (again carelessly or deliberately), by adding graphics to a panel deliberately, or by deliberate destructive vandalism.

Scientists, careless of any purpose or use but their own, have added permanent marks to many rock art figures and panels, usually as an aid to easy measurement or the cataloging of figures, and have abraded petroglyphs by chalking them. Some individuals, whose interests were more aesthetic than scientific, have copied petroglyphs using techniques that damaged the glyphs, or that left defacing materials behind.

Typical permanent defacing marks left by scientists (P34A), Dry Fork Canyon, Utah.

Collecting canyon country rock art is notoriously difficult because most of it is on cliff faces or boulders too large to move. Even so, graphics on smaller rocks have disappeared into private collections, their scientific value to mankind lost forever. In some parts of the West, where petroglyphs on smaller boulders are common, these are being illegally collected from both public and private land at an appalling rate, or destroyed in the attempt.

The commonest type of individual vandalism is the addition of dates, names and other graffiti to rock art panels, using either metal tools, paint or other marking materials. As an example of this, the first road into Utah's Nine Mile Canyon can be dated (1880) by the names and dates added to its numerous petroglyph panels. Some of those names now have historic value, if that is any compensation. Still other individual vandals deal solely with the senseless destruction of rock graphics. Bullets are commonly used to deface rock art too high above the ground for direct access, and spray paint is a favorite where access is easy. Even researchers in the early 1900s reported bullet holes in rock art panels.

Another strange kind of individual vandalism probably began in prehistoric times and has continued into the present. Some researchers have called this "ritual obliteration," and have suggested that in primitive cultures such destruction has religious meaning, or a purpose based in superstition. Thus, an Indian who believes that certain rock graphics are causing him spiritual or physical harm may ceremonially negate that power using a method acceptable to his beliefs, such as superimposing another supposedly benign figure, or completely obliterating the "hex" figure. A well known pictograph panel in Arches National Park that was destroyed in 1980 may have been the victim of a ritual obliteration. Certainly, whoever committed the crime must have had some extraordinary motive because he put far more time and effort into it than common vandals normally devote to their mindless craft.

Typical defacement of petroglyphs by an early name and date, Ninemile Canyon, Utah.

Typical petroglyph defaced by the material used to copy a figure, Colorado River gorge, Utah.

140

Even though some individual vandals, such as scientists who place permanent marks on rock art panels, certainly know the cultural value of the graphics they are defacing, it is often claimed that most individual vandalism is done by people who simply "don't understand" the real value of what they are damaging or destroying. While this may be true of the few ignorant people who just can't resist adding their names to a panel, it is highly doubtful if the kind of warped mind that wantonly destroys rock art with paint or bullets would be deterred by knowing its value.

Nor would those who are responsible for the other major destructive force, economic vandalism. Economic vandalism is performed by people who are quite capable of understanding the scientific and aesthetic value of prehistoric rock graphics, yet who value economic gain still more. Such people place economic gain far above such esoteric values as knowledge and aesthetic beauty, and they are quite willing to sacrifice rock art and other scientific values without a second thought. If forced to by law, they will make a halfhearted attempt at "salvage archaeology," but grudgingly, minimally, and with good public relations as their primary goal.

There are all kinds of economic vandalism. Most of them are presently running rampant in Utah, the Great Basin and the general Four Corners region because of the preponderance of public land there. Almost any kind of development or use of land that contains archaeological remains jeopardizes those remains. Anything portable is "collected." Commercial collectors steal whatever private collectors can't manage, sometimes using bulldozers and power drills to collect rock art panels. Anything not portable, such as much canyon country rock art, is soon damaged beyond any possible scientific study or aesthetic use.

Some economic projects are double threats to rock art previously protected by isolation — they do damage during the construction phase, and they provide easy access from then on to other kinds of vandals. Road building, mineral search and development, livestock grazing and other such activities are examples of double jeopardy threats, as is reservoir building.

Other economic threats to rock art are posed by the construction of industrial parks, strip mines, residential subdivisions, power plants, ore refineries, mining camps, tailings piles and ponds, ore collection depots, radioactive waste dumps, powerline and pipeline corridors, railroad lines and other such developments in areas that contain rock graphics.

Even stock grazing on public land jeopardizes the rock art there, because stockmen commonly use caves and alcoves for storing feed or sheltering their animals, and they promote water development projects and such massively destructive practices as "vegetation manipulation." This means the removal of all trees and large shrubs from large areas of land using giant bulldozers, then planting grasses that domestic animals will eat. Such practices destroy thousands of archaeological sites a year on both public and private land in the Four Corners states.

In almost every case of economic development within an archaeologically sensitive area, the first damage is done by the construction crews, either as a part of the construction or in the form of off-hours vandalism. The destruction continues, then, as the new development provides access to other vandals. This process started early in canyon country and continues at a mad pace today. As an example, the vandalism to the famous rock art panels in Thompson Canyon, Utah, began when the coal mine opened there around 1930. In this case, most of the rock art is still there, although terribly damaged. Rock art in the way of more recent industrial projects is gone entirely.

Even transient uses of public land can jeopardize rock art. Seismographic blasts can topple boulders or crumble cliffs, movie crews on location have been known to deface prehistoric graphics, and off-road vehicle event participants sometimes collect or damage rock art in remote locations.

One type of economic vandalism that is causing growing damage to rock art is air pollution and the resulting acid rain. On certain kinds of rock, such as limestone or marble, acid rain can cause devastating damage. On the granites, igneous rocks and sandstones that dominate canyon country, the effect is less but not zero. Sandstones, most of which are chemically bonded with little or no metamorphosis (bonding created by prolonged heat and pressure) are fairly susceptible to acid rain. With air pollution from southern California and Nevada already reaching canyon country, and with a dozen or more immense coal-burning power plants already operating within or planned for the region, it will soon be drowned in an aerial sea of acidic pollution, and acid fallout will pose a rapidly growing threat to all rock art on surfaces exposed to rainfall or runoff. Pictographs will, of course, be more susceptible to air pollution and acid precipitation than petroglyphs.

As serious as this threat may be, it is minor when compared to the destruction already done by the worst economic vandalism of all — dams and reservoirs. Prehistoric Indians had a natural affinity for flowing water in the arid to semi-arid lower terrain in the southwest, in particular in the canyon country of the general Four Corners region. Thus, reservoirs built in this region inevitably inundate an appallingly high percentage of the region's most meaningful archaeological sites, including rock art. There, virtually every major reservoir represents an enormous loss of antiquities, all too often including much of the area's most significant rock art.

Such huge reservoirs as Glen Canyon, Flaming Gorge and Hoover Dam brought equally huge losses of irreplaceable archaeological treasures. The Glen Canyon dam was by far the worst because it drowned out almost 200 miles of main canyon to depths of more than 400 feet, plus many hundreds of miles of tributary canyons to lesser depths, all in the heartland of the Anasazi culture. Many of these canyons were heavily used by the Anasazis because they contained the perennial water sources vital to their agrarian lifestyle.

Other reservoirs that have brought the permanent loss of antiquities, or soon will, are Cochiti, Navajo, Elephant Butte and others in New Mexico; Blue Mesa, Morrow Point and McPhee in Colorado; White River, Strawberry and many smaller ones in Utah; virtually all of the reservoirs in central Arizona; plus a host of others under construction, in the planning stages or proposed by agencies of the Four Corners states and the federal

government. Some of the reservoirs have even backed water into supposedly protected National Park areas, inundating large quantities of unique rock art in at least one national monument.

The worst part about rock art losses to reservoirs is that the loss is virtually total. As noted in earlier discussions, the kinds of information about rock graphics that can be preserved by photography are quite limited and of minimal usefulness to meaningful scientific research. The really useful clues remain behind at the site. They cannot be captured by photography and are subsequently inundated and destroyed, lost forever to science.

LEGAL PROTECTION

Prior to the Twentieth Century, the United States had no laws protecting its antiquities, whether paleontological, paleobotanical, archaeological or historical. By the turn of the century, however, the magnificent Anasazi pueblo ruins in the Four Corners area were being stripped so blatantly by private and commercial collectors that public indignation forced Congress to pass a law protecting all antiquities on federal land. Few states followed this example until very recently, thus leaving the antiquities on thousands of square miles of state land open to exploitation for more than half a century after the need for protection became obvious.

The federal government has recently enacted still other laws aimed at inventorying, protecting and studying the antiquities on public land under the jurisdiction of such federal land administration agencies as the U. S. Forest Service, National Park Service, Bureau of Land Management,

Department of Defense and others. Some western states now have adequate laws and regulations governing antiquities on state-owned lands, but to date there are no laws protecting antiquities on the private land which dominates most states of the nation, and even some states west of the Rockies. On private land, the owner is free to destroy, sell, commercialize or otherwise exploit antiquities that should be preserved and studied for the benefit of the entire nation.

In most European nations, such as England and France, all antiquities are highly valued and the central governments assume the responsibility for their protection, wherever they may be. Even on private land, such prehistoric treasures as ruins and rock art are physically protected from both trespassing vandals and the landowner's activities. It is unfortunate, indeed, that the citizens and government of the United States are not equally concerned with providing legal and other protection for this nation's invaluable and irreplaceable antiquities.

DO THE LAWS WORK?

Are existing federal and state antiquities laws adequate as written, and are they working to protect the antiquities on public land? For the most part, the laws as written are suitable, although in many instances the implementing regulations are far from adequate. But the laws are not providing effective protection for this nation's rapidly dwindling treasury of prehistoric and historic remnants. This failure is due to the democratic nature of our government and as such, reflects the actual sentiments of the majority of this nation's citizens concerning the relative importance of antiquities.

The problem parallels the truism that you can lead a horse to water, but you can't make him drink. Minority citizen groups can get legislatures to enact laws, but they can't force the implementation of those laws in the face of massive passive resistance. Relatively small groups of dedicated, far-seeing citizens have got state and federal legislatures to pass fairly good laws, but have failed in the long run to get these laws enforced on the practical level.

Even a good law can only be as effective as subsequent legislatures and administrations want it to be. If a legislature does not fund enforcement, or even if it does but the administration is philosophically opposed to the intent of the law, that law is simply not enforced, or the barest of lip service is paid to enforcement, and the default is concealed by cynical public relations programs. Only long, expensive lawsuits that are pursued to the U. S. Supreme Court level have any chance of overcoming such "benign neglect," and generally by that time the damage is done, and the victory — even if won — is Pyrrhic.

A legislature, state or federal, may enact an antiquities protection law in response to pressures, but then usually shows its true sentiments by providing little or no funding for enforcement. Administrations change. Some value such things as antiquities and do their best within the funding limitations imposed by their legislatures. Others are more in thrall to economic interest and may not only fail to provide the funded level of antiquities protection, but may actively seek the destructive development of public lands under their administration.

Such political realities have to date held the enforcement of antiquities laws to a bare minimum. As the result of a series of precedent-setting lawsuits, the federal government has been forced by the courts to pay some minimal attention to the several federal antiquities laws, but such limited efforts tend only to further underscore the abysmal neglect that is the general rule. Most states still do not implement their antiquities laws much beyond the public relations level, that is, plenty of publicity but little real action, and especially none that would get in the way of economic developments.

Of course, with none of the present antiquities laws applicable to private land, Murphy's Law comes into play — anything that could happen does. Ranchers dynamite boulders with prehistoric rock art in order to rid themselves of annoying trespassers who want to see the ancient graphics. Entrepreneurs develop archaeological sites into tourist traps, or sell off anything that is portable. A few, of course, try to provide reasonable protection for the antiquities on their lands, but eventually fail or grow tired of the thankless effort.

But at best, the protection offered by a conscientious private citizen can only last a generation or two. Then, land ownerships change, and new owners have their own development plans, priorities and personal philosophies — which may not include a burning interest in preserving a bunch of faded old "Indian signs." Thus, in the long run, antiquities on both private and public land can only be protected by good public laws that are consistently and rigorously enforced. This nation has still not enacted comprehensive public antiquities protection laws, and has barely started enforcement of the limited laws already on the books.

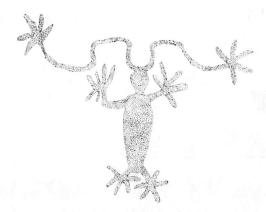

OTHER PROTECTION

Efforts have been made to protect rock art by methods other than ineffectual antiquities laws. Unfortunately, most of these methods apply only to rock art in or near well developed areas of public land, such as parks and recreation areas. For the vast majority of rock art on public land, its isolation is its only protection. When that goes, in one manner or another, the protection goes and the destruction begins.

Where some reasonable measure of control over a rock art site is practical, protection measures can take three forms — physical protection (fences, ranger patrols, reduced vehicular access, on-site interpreters, or perhaps a permit system for access); education (public relations, educational literature, signs and, again, on-site interpreters); and diversion (providing a harmless outlet for those who simply must leave their own marks). As an example of diversion, visitors to El Morro National Monument are invited to give vent to their rock graphic urges on a big boulder in front of the visitor center, rather than among the historic and prehistoric rock graphics on El Morro itself. The museum boulder gets plenty of use, and El Morro suffers very little vandalism in spite of heavy visitation.

This rock at the El Morro National Monument visitor center gives "creative" visitors an outlet and thus helps protect the monument's prehistoric and historic rock graphics.

Unfortunately, simply being within an established state or federal park is not much protection for rock art. It is axiomatic that to create a park or other special area around a rock art site, without also providing other forms of protection, is little more than an invitation to vandalism. This is underscored by the fact that few panels of rock art in western park areas are free of such damage unless they are also protected by sheer isolation. At Arches National Park, the destroyed pictograph panel was in a conspicuous place, within plain sight of a heavily traveled highway, yet it was completely obliterated, and the vandals were never caught.

Some rock art scholars advocate that in the long run the only way to protect rock art is to inventory it thoroughly, then document it completely. In one sense they are correct. But, as discussed earlier, photography alone documents only a small and relatively limited part of the total potential knowledge at a rock art site. Only a very meticulous, skilled, detailed and time-consuming scientific study of each site and its surroundings can extract and document the less obvious hard data. Unfortunately, neither the personnel, skills, funds or time necessary for such a monumental task are available now, or likely to be in the future.

This leads to the conclusion that "salvage archaeology," whether done in a leisurely manner in advance of natural deterioration and individual vandalism, or in panic programs just ahead of an onslaught of economic vandalism, is not going to go very far toward saving this nation's prehistoric heritage of rock graphics.

SALVAGE ARCHAEOLOGY

Salvage archaeology, in the usual sense, is an attempt to salvage or save archaeological values in an area ahead of some planned and scheduled industrial project that will destroy such values. If federal or state lands, funds or permits are involved, the regulations that implement antiquities laws permit and require that salvage attempts be made. Generally, little thought is given to the thoroughness or success of the attempt, which tends to imply that the whole process may be more of a gesture than an attempt at complete salvage.

What is salvage archaeology, then? It is different things to different people.

To development interests it is a pacifying gesture toward the citadels of science, an altruistic offer to pay the bills while academe labors to save all that is archaeologically valuable in an area that is about to be destroyed by a vital scorched-earth project like a dam, highway, power plant, utility corridor, strip mine, industrial park, retirement subdivision, dump for chemicals or radioactives, or a state-sized missile base.

To the government agencies that control the lands or funds, or who must issue permits for such projects, salvage archaeology is a reasonable and prudent effort to comply with existing antiquities laws and regulations, to mollify outraged environmentalists, to buy the silence of academe, yet still dance to the sub rosa tunes played by the industrialists who are so generous at election campaign time.

To many archaeologists, salvage archaeology is a valiant effort on the part of academe to fight on the frontiers of science, to save what can be saved in the face of the advancing industrial juggernaut. To a few more realistic archaeologists, it is a take-it-or-leave-it last chance to salvage at least a little something from destruction, with industry's legally mandated money for such salvage being far better than the pitiful funding they would otherwise receive for field work.

To environmentalists, salvage archaeology is a clever and cynical political ploy designed to buy the silence of academe while paying bare lip service to antiquities laws which flatly forbid the destruction of "objects of antiquity" on public lands, without regard for economic rationalizations or weasel-worded regulations.

Which of these viewpoints is the truth? An objective observer, aware of what actually happens with salvage archaeology operations, would see elements of truth and elements of self-serving hypocricy in each position.

What actually happens is this:

A project is planned by an industry or government agency, with the cooperation of other industries and government agencies, especially those who will be providing land, funds or permits. Once the planning is well underway, with little standing in the way but a handful of incensed environmental activists, funds are allocated and a contract let to do the salvage archaeology. The contract is usually granted to universities of the state or states in which the project will be constructed. This is primarily for political purposes, but also because basic antiquities laws limit serious (destructive) study of antiquities to such academically accredited institutions.

The contract is then fulfilled by qualified archaeologists either associated with or hired by the university, who then write a lengthy and detailed report. This report becomes a part of the project's basic environmental documentation and the project rolls on.

But an objective observer will note that while salvage archaeology on very small projects may be fairly effective, on big projects the end results are usually far from satisfactory.

On projects that involve a lot of land, such as reservoirs or major utility corridors, there are early signs that the environmentalists had some valid points. In such cases, no intent is demonstrated on the part of industry, government or academe to make even a thorough archaeological survey, let alone an attempt at comprehensive salvage of all antiquities, not even the most obvious. In no case are the funds and time allocated for the salvage work enough to do more than a small fraction of the entire job.

In compensation to the concerned public, and as a public relations gesture of benefit to all project participants, a part of the salvage funds may be allocated to the construction of a public display of some sort. While such displays may be educational in themselves, and certainly better than nothing, they are very poor compensation for the immense amount of archaeological data that is totally destroyed by the projects, for the unmeasurable and

148

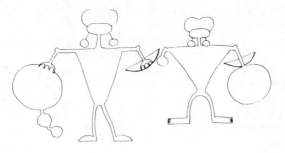

unique aesthetic values in such antiquities as rock art and pueblo ruins, values that are lost entirely and forever.

That objective observer of the salvage archaeology scene may also be bemused by the strange behavior of the academics who are involved in salvage archaeology. Some rarely venture into the backcountry of a region rich in archaeological treasures unless paid to do so out of public or industrial funds provided for salvage. Few if any express any concern over the enormous losses of antiquities to major industrial projects, nor do they make any efforts to combat the highly questionable porkbarrel projects so popular with legislatures and certain government agencies. They bring no lawsuits demanding the enforcement of existing antiquities laws, nor do they lobby for improved laws and regulations and better funding for enforcement. Rather, they remain silent in their ivory towers of objectivity, while thousands of unique and irreplaceable archaeological sites are drowned by reservoirs or bulldozed to rubble in remote places out of sight and mind, unknown to the public — but not unknown to academe.

Archaeologists just quietly take the funds allocated for salvage and, making no protest about what will not be salvaged, go quietly about saving what they can within the time available. It has been said by some that such archaeologists are in conflict of interest, that their salvage contracts buy their silence and that of their universities. While this may be an oversimplification, the argument has merit, because regardless of the diverse purposes of individual archaeologists, a lack of effective public hue and cry is the effect desired by project planners, and that effect is obtained by funding limited archaeological salvage.

In defense of the strange silence of academe it could be argued that they understand the futility of combating the development juggernaut and so choose to simply take what they can get, whatever that may be, without jeopardizing that by agitating for more or by protesting the losses. Perhaps this is a distasteful truth in the hard, cruel world of politics, but it leaves an objective observer with the impression that academe agrees with the principle that economic values should always take precedence over historic, scientific and aesthetic values, over knowledge of any sort. And this academic position is not preventing enormous and continuing losses of antiquities. Other sectors of American society fight for antiquities they think worth saving, such as historic structures, but too few people know about the prehistoric treasures being lost daily in the lands of the ancient Anasazis and Fremonts to be effective, and those who do know — a handful of archaeologists — stand silent, watching this American heritage fall to roaring bulldozers, or sink beneath dark waters.

Despite salvage archaeology, which has photographed a few hundred rock art panels, thousands of prehistoric rock graphics have already been totally lost to development projects, most of them not even photographed, and none of them studied in the manner necessary for the extraction of all the knowledge available. If salvage archaeology is cavalier with other prehistoric sites, it is downright disdainful of rock art sites, as tens of thousands of inundated carved and painted images can attest from the black depths of Lake Powell, Lake Mead and others on the Colorado River; Flaming Gorge Reservoir on the Green River; Navajo Reservoir on the San Juan River; Cochiti, Elephant Butte and others on the Rio Grande; Morrow Point and Blue Mesa on the Gunnison; Roosevelt, Apache and others on the Salt River and its tributaries; plus countless other artificial bodies of water in the lands of the Fremonts, Anasazis and other pueblo cultures farther south in Arizona and New Mexico.

Such losses were final and almost total, because the percentage of available scientific knowledge saved by salvage archaeology was exceedingly small. Even less aesthetic value was saved. Can the colorful splendor of a thousand year old pictograph panel on a soaring sandstone wall be captured on a 35mm slide? Can the mystery and three-dimensional beauty of ancient petroglyphs cut into an age-blackened boulder beside a rushing canyon stream, survive being reduced to a grainy, blurred monochrome photograph?

At least one attempt has been made to preserve a magnificent petroglyph panel that was to be intermittently drowned, then exposed, in a reservoir. It was carefully and heavily coated with penetrating, water-resistant plastics prior to the first immersion, then observed again after the next seasonal water level drop. While this research might yield some information useful in other applications, it could not possibly save petroglyphs subjected to periodic inundation. Eventually, the standing water would cause the massive collapse of the wall, or the lack of transpiration through the plastic coating during drying cycles would cause its selective separation from the sandstone.

It is thus easy to conclude that from the viewpoint of rock art study for science or aesthetics, salvage archaeology is a farce and a crime, both literally and figuratively. It does not provide the protection mandated by law for all antiquities.

Colorado River gorge, Utah. Thousands of prehistoric Anasazi and Fremont petroglyphs and pictographs have already been drowned beneath reservoir waters. Few were even recorded properly first, let alone studied scientifically.

151

RESTORATION

Efforts by various governmental agencies and individuals to restore damaged rock art to some semblance of its original appearance have been more successful, although often frustrated by lack of incentive, funds and proven technology. Rock and desert varnish are difficult to repair, and it is far easier to duplicate the paints used by classical painters than those compounded by primitives out of available organic and mineral materials, especially when the organic components have long since decomposed.

In the case of the pictograph panel at Arches National Park, the figures were scrubbed, using some kind of cleaning abrasive. The restoration efforts consisted largely of removing the white cleanser left on the rock. This revealed several interesting and previously unknown facts about the panel. For example, the dark red pigment used was quite tough and resistant to the scrubbing. There were indications that several cultures had contributed to the panel over a long period of time, possibly up into late historic times. Some of the additions may have been "ritual obliterations." No attempt was made to restore the panel to its original appearance.

In support of petroglyph restoration, the Bureau of Land Management, U. S. Department of the Interior, has issued a "technical note" discussing the various aspects of petroglyph restoration and providing a bibliography of related literature. The technical problem of restoring damaged desert varnish, or of creating it on simulated petroglyph displays, has been solved by Australian government agencies that have been active in the restoration of prehistoric glyphs there.

As with the damaged pictographs at Arches National Park, much of the restoration of petroglyphs consists of the removal of the materials added by vandals, such as spray paint, without damaging the underlying desert varnish and rock. The filling of bullet pocks is not difficult, but color-matching the surrounding desert varnish is tricky.

The complete restoration of pictographs is possible if good color photographs are available of the graphics before they were damaged, and if authenticity of pigment is not required. While this may restore the aesthetic and educational value of a pictograph, it does not restore lost scientific data. To date, most such restorations have been done by individuals skilled at reconstructing damaged historic art, but in time there may be specialists in rock graphics repair.

In practice, each damaged pictograph presents a unique problem in restoration, with many technical and philosophical factors involved. Standard policies for the resolution of such problems, and standard restoration techniques, should be formulated by governmental agencies that administer public land that has rock art as a known resource.

The Courthouse Wash pictograph panel in Arches National Park before it was vandalized. The white outlining around the figures was probably chalk added by some photographer years ago.

The vandalized Courthouse Wash panel after the defacing material had been cleaned off. Note that some figures previously hidden are now revealed, and that the outlining chalk is gone.

PROGNOSIS

The prognosis for the protection of prehistoric rock art is dismal. Despite the earnest efforts of a few professional archaeologists, academic institutions and public organizations, real no-nonsense scientific study of most rock art has barely started and is sporadic at best. Although the trend toward serious study is slowly growing, human destruction of rock art is growing explosively.

Other factors also affect the maddeningly slow rate of scientific rock art study. One is the term "rock art" itself, which implies that rock graphics are a form of art. To all too many scientists, this implication alone is enough to deny rock graphics any chance of serious consideration. "Art" doesn't have scientific value, and scientists simply don't mess with art — just as few artists hold science in great esteem. Some states and universities even place rock art affairs under their arts and humanities departments, rather than scientific. Thus, semantics again serves to confuse and inhibit rock graphics research.

Another factor is massive academic and public ignorance about rock art in general, and the prehistoric rock art of the Four Corners states and Nevada in particular. This vast, arid region was the last to be thoroughly explored in the contiguous United States, and its varied resources are still largely known only to those who would exploit them for economic gain. A recent federal law required that all federal land be thoroughly inventoried for all resources, specifically including all antiquities, but this has yet to be done, funding continues to be minimal, and destruction has accelerated.

The economic vandalism that is the source of this destruction, and the general lack of opposition to it, are indicators of our modern culture's general level of intellectual/scientific/aesthetic attainment. Collectively, as a nation, we have yet to mature to the point where we can decide that some things are more valuable than economic gain, then forego that gain in order to retain what we value more highly. Although many of us have reached this point as individuals, we are nonetheless a tiny minority. The majority are still governed by their relentless survival instincts for more and more security, which in our culture takes the form of money, things, progress, continual expansion and the immediate development of every natural resource on the planet — or its destruction if it gets in the way of development.

Thus, the prognosis is that the cultural clash between modern America and prehistoric American remnants will continue virtually unabated, and at an accelerating rate, until little is left of aboriginal America to study, until all rock art is destroyed, or damaged beyond any civilized use, this long before it would have been obliterated by natural forces.

The best that can be expected is that those who care about rock art — for whatever reason — will be able to fight an effective delaying action. But economic vandalism will ultimately prevail. A century from now, virtually the only remaining trace of rock art that had endured the natural elements for hundreds, even thousands of years, will exist only as dusty files of photographs and scientific reports. The individuals who created the graphics will have vanished without trace into antiquity, and the Americans of that future time will be poorer for our present lack of collective foresight.

Behind the Rocks, Utah. Note the crude modern attempt to make a desert sheep petroglyph.

Colorado River gorge, Utah. Note defacement by materials used in copying several petroglyph figures.

Colorado River gorge, Utah. Telephoto picture of petroglyphs high above the present ground level.

RECORDING TECHNIQUES

TYPES OF TECHNIQUES

There are a number of techniques for recording rock graphics. These vary widely in accuracy and usefulness. Some do not require touching the graphics in any way and hence do not damage or endanger them. Others require some gentle contact and hence involve some small possibility of damage and the chance that foreign materials could be left on the graphics. A few methods require excessive contact and the use of potentially damaging materials. Such methods are not advocated for general use and will not be discussed in detail in this book.

In general, photography and sketching are the principal no-contact recording techniques. Rubbings and tracings involve minimal contact. Various molding techniques can be used to duplicate petroglyphs in negative form, then these molds used to cast positives, but some molding techniques and materials can affect the rock graphics and should hence be used only under the direction of an experienced archaeologist who has a permit for the operation from the appropriate land administration agency or property owner.

Accuracy and usefulness can vary with recording techniques. Some methods are not accurate enough for scientific record-keeping or study, but may be satisfactory, or even preferred, for aesthetic purposes.

The most accurate method for recording both petroglyphs and pictographs is stereo color photography, provided this is done skillfully and with attention to detail. Each photograph must contain an indication of scale, be sharply focused and properly exposed for accurate color reproduction. Other problems and variables in photography are discussed later in this chapter.

Since stereo color transparencies have more limited usefulness than ordinary color negatives or positives from which printing is possible, this second approach is more commonly used but still requires care and skill if it is to record accurately everything that photography can capture. Black and white photography can be as thorough at this as color photography with petroglyphs, but fails to capture pictograph colors. Black and white negatives and prints, however, generally produce more detailed pictures in printed publications, although special, more expensive measures can be taken to produce detailed monochrome prints from high quality, large format color transparencies. Black and white photography has another advantage in that common darkroom techniques can be used to improve the visibility of a faint rock graphic image, either for publication or study purposes. With color negatives, special darkroom techniques can be used to enhance contrast, but few photographers possess such skills and the process is not available from most commercial film processors.

While sketching rock art is at best less accurate than photography, and is inherently incapable of accurately recording such characteristics as color, erosion, lichens and desert varnish or its lack, if done properly sketching can have some usefulness to science. For such usefulness, the sketching must be complete and done to accurate scale, which means that the artist must be highly skilled and conscientious. Sketching rock art freehand can produce results useful for aesthetic and display purposes, but is too inaccurate for scientific documentation.

Rubbing and tracing techniques also fall into this category — not accurate enough for science, but highly satisfactory for display, educational and artistic applications. Molding cannot be used with pictographs, but if skillfully done can produce highly detailed three-dimensional copies of petroglyphs that are scientifically useful and aesthetically pleasing, especially if efforts are made to accurately color-tone the surface of the positive cast. Such accurate casts can be especially educational in museum displays, where they tend to divert casual attention from fragile original rock art while still serving educational purposes.

At best, however, no recording technique, however accurate, can capture more than a small percentage of the total relevant scientific data at or near a rock art site. Only meticulous, knowledgeable study of the original graphics, the immediate area and general vicinity — in coordination with other cultural studies of the area and region — can obtain a high percentage of the potential data. And even then, research techniques and knowledge developed later may lead to still more data from rock art sites — if they have survived the bulldozers, dam builders and other vandals.

SAMPLE METHODS

There are any number of methods for recording rock art within the general approaches noted, but a few samples will be described here.

For accurate sketching, it is necessary to superimpose a grid of squares over the figures or panel to be sketched. For large areas, this can be done by placing a string grid against the panel. If the area being copied is only a few feet in either dimension, a wood-frame grid, with the string wound around tacks in the frame at two, three or four inch intervals, is satisfactory. Smaller frames with one-inch string grids can be useful with one or a few graphic images. The smaller grid will permit greater accuracy.

For irregular rock surfaces, string grids on frames are not practical but can still be made by carefully attaching the strings directly to the rock surface at intervals with tape, making the grid squares as accurate as practical. Techniques for free-hand sketching for aesthetic purposes can be found in many art books. With sketching of any type, it is wise to also photograph the graphics being sketched. Photographs can be useful during subsequent sketch detail work away from the field site.

Two tracing techniques are often used. With one, a textured paper of appropriate strength, such as rice paper, is taped over a petroglyph to be copied. A marking substance, such as a common wax crayon, is then

Note: This figure
should be 2X larger

This scale drawing of a large pictograph panel in the San Rafael Swell in central Utah
was made by the following steps:
1. A 4-mil sheet of clear vinyl plastic was taped over the panel. Other sheet
    plastics, such as mylar or acetate, are also suitable.
2. The pictographs were traced, using a felt-tipped marking pen. Marking pressure
    was kept to a minimum to avoid any damage to the pictographs. Different
    colored pens may be used to indicate various pictograph colors. Bright reflec-
    tions on the plastic surface can be reduced by shading the immediate work area
    and by wearing polarizing sunglasses.
3. The completed tracing was removed from the panel and checked for accuracy
    and completeness. It was then placed flat on a suitable work surface and an
    accurately dimensioned square grid of lines added. The size of the squares
    will depend upon the overall size of the panel and the amount of detail it
    contains. This particular panel was 5 feet by 2½ feet, except for the larger
    figure, so two-inch grid squares were adequate.
4. To make the smaller drawing which is reproduced above and on the cover of
    this book, a sheet of drawing paper was marked with the same number of grid
    squares that the full-scale tracing had, using a soft pencil. The squares were
    ½ centimeter on a side.
5. The pictographs were then carefully drawn onto the paper, using the two sets
    of grid lines as a guide. The figures were then inked to represent the original
    pictographs. After the ink was thoroughly dry, the penciled grid lines were
    erased.
This procedure, if carefully followed, will produce an accurate full-scale positive
transparency and an accurate reduced-scale opaque drawing. Both can be used for a
variety of scientific, educational and aesthetic purposes. As alternates to the grid
system, if a pantograph of adequate size is available, it can be used to make an
accurate reduced-scale drawing from the full-scale tracing without the use of grid
lines, or the tracing can be photographed and the negative used to make prints of any
scale desired.

Steven J. Manning

rubbed across the paper until the petroglyph image becomes apparent. Skilled use of the marker can accent the glyph image so that it is distinct from the background color of the rubbing. Other rubbing methods and materials are used, but great care must be exercised in making rubbings or the glyphs can be damaged.

A less hazardous approach is to tape a sheet of transparent plastic over a petroglyph, then trace the glyph with a soft-tipped marker pen. Transparent tracings of this type can later be photographed against textured rock or copied by other methods for artistic applications. In effect, an ink tracing on clear plastic is a full-scale positive film of the rock art that can be stored easily and used in many ways.

As noted earlier, molding techniques can be hazardous to rock art and should be employed only by skilled specialists who have the appropriate permits for the activity. Molding can be done using paper mache, clay, latex or certain plastics, but often involves potentially damaging parting agents and hence should not be attempted by amateur rock art enthusiasts except under professional direction and supervision.

There are countless techniques for recording rock art for aesthetic purposes. Most of them are adaptations of standard skills that can be learned from art books and classes. Techniques that might jeopardize the rock art being copied should not be used.

In the long run, photography is the most accurate and practical method for recording rock art, whether petroglyphs or pictographs or a combination, and the resulting photographs can then be used for both scientific and aesthetic purposes, conveniently and without hazard to the original rock graphics.

PHOTOGRAPHY

There are many variables in recording rock art photographically. Some are inherent in the rock art itself and must be overcome by photographic skills, ingenuity and physical agility. Others have to do with the photographic equipment and the photographer, and can be overcome by knowledge, experience and the right equipment.

Rock art may be in brilliantly lit or deeply shaded locations, making it difficult to capture balanced color. Even worse, an area to be photographed may be partly sunny, partly shaded, making exposure control difficult, especially with automatic-type cameras. On some rock art, contrast is low. Pictograph paint may be faded or eroded. Petroglyphs may be too shallow to exhibit shadowing, or may be so old their desert varnish matches that on the surrounding rock.

Rock art in caves can be too dimly lit for normal photography, and heavily overcast days can reduce lighting and unbalance color rendition of pictographs and desert varnish. Rock reflectivity on bright days can cause definition and contrast problems, especially with heavy desert varnish.

Access to the rock art can be a real problem, too, because for accurate, undistorted photography, the camera must be held at 90 degrees to the rock surface and the proper distance away. With rock art above narrow ledges, in confined places or high above the ground, correct camera alignment can become very difficult or impractical.

Another hazard to photography, of course, is the graffiti so common on rock art panels. Other recording methods can ignore such unsightly and obscuring acultural blemishes, but photography cannot. The fact that such graffiti are simply objective evidence of cross-cultural impact is hardly compensation for ruination of this sort. While we may learn from such vandalism that a "Jim Blackmun" viewed this panel in 1972 and felt impelled to bid for posterity by cutting his name and the date across a pictograph painted fifteen centuries ago by a prehistoric shaman of a relatively unknown culture, somehow the 1972 event does not seem to have any great historical significance. Mr. Blackmun would have done more for history had he fallen down a nearby cliff before he found the pictograph panel.

The major variables within photography itself that can affect the accurate depiction of rock art are the film used, the accessories available, the camera's versatility and the photographer's skill. Even after the pictures are taken, faulty film handling and processing can defeat everything else. Such things as letting film get hot before or after exposure can ruin it, as can poor quality processing and physical handling of developed film.

The basics of good photography can be acquired by reading, formal training and experience, but it is appropriate to discuss here some of the solutions to problems specifically related to rock art photography.

Extremely brilliant lighting can be brought under control with photographic filters. Yellow filters are suitable for black and white film, while any of several chromatically neutral "sky" or "haze" filters can reduce glare for color film. A polarizing filter is even better, giving control by degrees, and can be used with most standard films without causing chromatic imbalance.

Rock art in full shade that is well lit by reflected light from the sky, ground or a nearby canyon wall can be photographed by available light. If not enough reflected light falls on the panel, it can be augmented with an aluminum foil reflector or daylight flash. If a flash is used for photographing petroglyphs, holding the flash several feet to one side will prevent the flash from filling the glyph grooves and thus reducing contrast. Angled lighting will actually increase glyph shading and hence contrast and visibility.

There is no perfect answer to a shadow crossing a rock art panel. Close framing can avoid the contrasty lighting, but where it cannot be avoided only half-measures can be taken. Using a low-contrast film is one. Lighting the shaded part with a reflector or flash will help but not very much unless the supplementary light can be kept from the sunlit side of the panel. With black and white film, proper exposure and clever darkroom work can produce a fairly balanced print, but with color negative film the color balance will be affected. A camera with automatic exposure control will not

Cane Creek Canyon, Utah.

produce a suitable picture with either kind of film. The meter will average the light, then over-expose one part and underexpose the other. In any case, unless time is a critical factor, the best approach is to take the picture later, when the panel is all sunlit or all shaded.

With low-contrast pictographs, only special films and light sources can improve the situation, a combination usually found only in scientific laboratories. Petroglyphs that are shallow, or whose desert varnish matches the surrounding rock, can have their low contrast enhanced by any of several methods. Extreme sidelighting, either from the sun or an artificial source, can increase shading and contrast. With most petroglyphs cut into desert varnish, a polarizing filter will increase contrast in direct sunlight, but will not help in the shade or with artificial lighting.

Traditionally, photographers have chalked-in petroglyphs to enhance their contrast, but this practice is now known to damage the glyphs and is no longer used by responsible photographers. A substitute for the chalk is sometimes used if other techniques for improving contrast are not practical. Finely powdered aluminum is stirred into water, then carefully painted into the glyph grooves with a soft brush. This is a time-consuming operation but provides excellent contrast. Once dry, the aluminum powder can easily be brushed away with a big paint brush or flushed away with water, with no damage to the petroglyph. This technique does, however, obscure relative patination and weathering within the glyph lines and is thus not entirely

162

suitable for scientific recording.

Positioning the camera the desired distance from rock art to be photographed, and at a right angle, can also at times be impractical. A high, narrow ledge may be the only access to a panel of rock art, or it may be in a narrow cave or between two close boulders. Since carrying big ladders around, building scaffolding up a cliff or blasting open a narrow enclosure are seldom solutions to be considered, photographing such rock art at an angle less than 90 degrees may be the only practical answer. For pictures taken at less than 90 degrees, the use of a slower shutter speed and smaller lens opening will usually provide enough depth of focus to keep the entire picture area sharp, provided the angle is not too acute (less than about 45 degrees) or the distance too short (under about 8 feet). Note that these figures will vary, depending on the camera's focal length. The depth of focus table that comes with every good camera should be used as a guide. Medium and large format cameras with tilting backs can compensate for angular distortion and focus with this mechanism. As a further complication, if the shutter speed required to get suitable depth of focus is slower than about one-fiftieth of a second, or if a wind is blowing or the photographer's footing is unsteady, the picture will still be blurred unless the camera is placed on a tripod and a cable-release or built-in shutter-delay mechanism is used.

In some cases, an angle closer to correct can be obtained by photographing from a greater distance, using a telephoto lens and fairly fast shutter speed. In cramped locations, a wide angle lens is useful but will produce some image distortion. Many kinds of exotic special gear could be devised for solving the common problem of proper angle and distance for the best photography, but few such ingenious solutions can be adapted to the realities of canyon country terrain.

The only practical way to keep graffiti out of a photograph is to avoid pointing the camera at it. With many close-up photographs, it is fairly easy to leave out unwanted images, but with larger areas or full panels, the signs-of-our-times must simply be accepted. In a few cases, it may be possible to touch out unwanted graphics from negatives or prints, but this requires special skills not commonly available.

The photographic variables — film, camera, accessories, photographer and processor — can be controlled or standardized many ways, with each experienced photographer having his or her own working system. Still, when it comes to photographing rock art in primitive areas, the conditions encountered tend to establish certain practical limits if good results are desired. Optimum scientific photography will, of course, be more demanding than photography for aesthetic or educational purposes.

If color accuracy is important, then selection of film and its processor is critical. Some films do not give good color balance under the light conditions often encountered in canyon country, nor do all films respond to filters in the same way. Each photographer will need to find by trial and error which film is suitable for his or her purpose, then find a processor who produces consistently good results with that film.

Many cameras are suitable for general photography, but good rock art photography imposes a few non-negotiable requirements. The camera must have adjustable focus, user control over aperture and shutter speed, a sharp and moderately fast lens, and be able to accept a tripod, filters, a sun shade and auxiliary lenses. Desirable features found only in larger format cameras are a tilt back, a selection of accurate slow shutter speeds and very small lens apertures.

While the many kinds of point-and-click cameras that take standard or self-developing film may be fine for photographing rock art for aesthetic purposes, they are not suitable for scientific or educational applications.

Accessories can also vary to tastes, but serious rock art photography requires a sturdy tripod, at least a polarizing filter, a sun shade, wide angle and telephoto lenses, a padded, pack-type camera case, a ruler to show scale, a cable release, a detachable flash and a lens brush. One good variable focal length lens can cut the total number of lenses carried to two, but to date no single variable focal length lens can cover the entire range that may be needed.

The photographer variable can only be optimized by suitable training and experience. No matter how good the equipment, if the photographer is not skilled, the results will not be consistently good. With many modern "fool-proof" cameras, almost anyone can get some pictures to "turn out," but if extraordinary effort is to be spent getting to remote rock art sites to record them photographically, then it is only sensible to invest similarly in good equipment and skills. Canyon country conditions often defeat even good photographers who are unfamiliar with the region's unusual conditions, so rock art photographers should be prepared to make the special effort necessary to accommodate to those conditions.

The optimum camera for photographing rock art will vary, depending upon purpose. For limited visual use, a stereoscopic camera with color film

A 4×5 camera is about the largest practical for field use in the canyon country hinterlands. Photographer Tom Till shown in action at a remote site in Arches National Park.

will give the best results. For non-stereo color or monochrome photography for accurate scientific purposes, a large format camera with tilt back and high quality lens is best, with the 4x5 inch format being about the biggest that is practical to carry into the field. The smallest size suitable for this purpose would be the 2¼x2¼ inch format, preferably with a tilting back to compensate for camera angles less than 90 degrees to the subject.

For non-scientific display, educational and aesthetic purposes, a good single-lens reflex 35 mm camera is suitable, provided its focus, aperture and shutter speed can be controlled manually, it has the required accessories and it is skillfully used. For such less demanding uses, color balance and quality are not as important, making film and processor selection less critical.

SUPPLEMENTARY DATA

If the rock art being recorded is to have any scientific use at all, supplementary information about the site must be documented in addition to the photographs or scale sketches. Such documentation may include many things, depending upon the specific intended scientific purpose, but should at least cover the following:

1. Exact location on 1:62,500 scale (1 mile equals about 1 inch) U. S. Geological Survey topographical map.
2. Location on the same map of other archaeological sites within a few miles of the rock art site.
3. If the rock art is not on a cliff face shown on the topo map, indicate what direction it faces.
4. Supplementary photographs of the rock art setting, taken from various distances and angles.

The systematic survey and documentation of rock art sites should be done under the direction of professional archaeologists in coordination with the appropriate land administration agencies or owners. Such surveys generally use standard forms listing the supplementary information desired. Public organizations and universities involved in such projects are generally willing to issue such forms to serious amateur rock art enthusiasts, but amateurs will serve the cause of rock art study and preservation better if they join and work directly with such public organizations or university scientists.

In the long run, while willing and capable amateur rock art enthusiasts can do much to support professional research and arouse public attention to the need for better protective laws and enforcement, only competent, highly trained scientists have the capabilities needed for the serious scientific investigation of rock art. Only they have any chance of deriving hard facts from our rapidly dwindling heritage of prehistoric graphics, of sorting fact from fancy in the masses of literature already generated on the subject. Serious amateurs can help, but scientists must solve the problems — if they can be solved at all before the rock art is gone forever.

Salt Creek Canyon, Canyonlands National Park.

PROTECTED ROCK ART SITES

ARIZONA
COLORADO
NEVADA
NEW MEXICO
UTAH

Detail of Thirteen Faces pictograph site, Horse Canyon, Canyonlands National Park.

PROTECTED ROCK ART SITES

STATE	SITE NAME	ROCK ART LOCATIONS AND ACCESS	COMMENTS
ARIZONA	Canyon de Chelly National Monument	See monument literature for locations accessible only by off-road vehicle or guided tour.	Authorized tour guides must accompany private vehicles into Canyon de Chelly.
	Navajo National Monument	See monument literature for locations accessible only by ranger-guided hiking tours.	At times, some sites within the monument may be closed to the public.
	Petrified Forest National Park	See park literature for locations accessible by easy walking.	Some rock art is also on display at the south entrance museum.
COLORADO	Mesa Verde National Park	See park literature for locations accessible by ranger-guided easy walking.	Park also has backcountry sites accessible only by hiking. Contact park rangers for details.
	Colorado National Monument	See monument literature for location in No Thoroughfare Canyon accessible by hiking.	Monument also has other rock art in backcountry sites accessible only by hiking. Contact monument rangers for details.
NEVADA	Lehman Caves National Monument	See monument literature for locations accessible by easy walking or hiking.	For backcountry sites accessible only by hiking off of established trails in monument and vicinity, contact monument rangers.

Red Rock Canyon	Numerous locations within the canyon and vicinity are accessible by easy walking or hiking.	Side road to Red Rock Canyon is about 17 miles west of Las Vegas on Nevada 159.
Valley of Fire State Park	Locations at Atlatl Rock, Petroglyph Canyon and other sites accessible by easy walking.	Park also has many sites in the backcountry accessible only by hiking. Contact park rangers for details.
NEW MEXICO — Bandelier National Monument	See monument literature for locations accessible by easy walking or hiking.	Monument also has backcountry sites accessible only by hiking off of established trails. Contact monument rangers for details.
Chaco Canyon National Monument	See monument literature for locations accessible by hiking.	Monument also has backcountry sites accessible only by hiking off of established trails. Contact monument rangers for details.
El Morro National Monument	See monument literature for locations accessible by easy walking.	Monument also has backcountry sites accessible only by hiking off of established trails. Contact monument rangers for details.
Gila Cliff Dwellings National Monument	See monument literature for locations accessible by hiking.	There are other rock art sites within the surrounding wilderness primitive areas that are accessible only by hiking and backpacking. Contact forest rangers for further information.

Site	Access	Location
Indian Petroglyphs State Park	Easy walking trail to petroglyph panels.	Park is in West Mesa area of Albuquerque.
Three Rivers Petroglyph Site (BLM)	Numerous sites along a ridge-top trail are accessible by easy walking.	The site is 5 miles east of the town Three Rivers, which is about 30 miles north of Alamogordo on U. S. 54.
UTAH		
Arches National Park	See park literature for locations accessible by easy walking.	One location is near the trail to Delicate Arch. Another is above U.S. 163 just north of the Colorado River bridge.
Canyonlands National Park	See park literature for locations accessible by hiking or off-road vehicle. See river guide books for locations accessible only by boat.	Principal locations accessible by hiking or off-road vehicle are Salt Creek, Horse, Davis, Lavender and Horseshoe canyons and The Maze. There are numerous other backcountry sites accessible only by backpacking or boating.
Glen Canyon National Recreation Area	See recreation area literature and commercial guide books and maps for locations accessible by boat and hiking.	Much of this region's rock art is now beneath the reservoir waters, but many sites still remain. Some can be reached by boat and hiking, some only by off-road vehicle or backpacking. Backcountry locations are found only in archaeological reports.

Capitol Reef National Park	See park literature for locations accessible by easy walking or hiking.	Principal locations accessible by walking are beside Utah 24. There are numerous other back-country sites accessible by hiking or off-road vehicle. Contact park rangers for details.
Zion National Park	See park literature for locations accessible by easy walking or hiking.	Principal locations accessible by walking are within the main canyon. There are many other sites accessible by hiking or off-road vehicle. Contact park rangers for details.
Dinosaur National Monument (located in Utah and Colorado)	See monument literature for locations accessible by walking or hiking. See river guide books for locations accessible only by boat.	Monument has numerous locations in the backcountry accessible only by hiking, boating or off-road vehicle. Contact monument rangers for details.
Hovenweep National Monument	See monument literature for locations accessible by walking or hiking.	Monument also has many back-country locations accessible only by hiking off of established trails. See monument rangers for details.
Natural Bridges National Monument	See monument literature for locations accessible by hiking.	Monument also has many back-country locations accessible only by hiking off of established trails. See monument rangers for details.

Newspaper Rock State Historical Monument	Roadside display beside Utah 211, the paved road between U.S. 191 (formerly U.S. 163) and the Needles district of Canyonlands National Park.	An outstanding display of easily accessible prehistoric and historic rock art. There are other smaller panels within the same stretch of Indian Creek Canyon.
Grand Gulch Primitive Area (Bureau of Land Management)	See primitive area literature for locations accessible by back-packing or guided tour by horseback.	The Grand Gulch canyon system is accessible from three points: Utah 261; Utah 263 and the Collins Spring road; and the San Juan River. Prior registration with BLM rangers is required.
San Rafael Swell (BLM)	Rock art panels at Temple Mountain Wash and Buckhorn Wash are beside paved or dirt roads accessible to highway vehicles.	The Swell also has many back-country locations accessible only by hiking or off-road vehicle. See Utah Multipurpose Map #2 for road information and locations of Buckhorn and Temple Mountain panels. Backcountry locations are found only in archaeological reports.
Utah 279 (adjacent land is under BLM administration)	Roadside displays beside this paved highway, down the Colorado River gorge, beginning about 4½ miles from U.S. 191 (formerly U.S. 163).	Rock art panels beside Cane Creek Road, on the opposite side of the river, are on private land. Some panels along U279 are above the road level, because talus was removed during road construction.

SPECIAL
ROCK ART AREAS

Cub Creek, Dinosaur National Monument. Verne Huser photo.

Albuquerque and Santa Fe Area

The desert lands along the Rio Grande from south of Albuquerque to north of Santa Fe are rich in prehistoric native petroglyphs and pictographs. The dark basalt or lighter sandstone outcroppings that are a frequent occurrence in the area make superior surfaces for pecked, scratched, or abraded petroglyphs; the occasional overhang or sheltered sandstone faces that are also common in the region serve as excellent "canvas" for the few painted designs that can be found.

The style of the glyphs is distinctive and is characterized by highly decorative, stylized designs. Though they display clearly defined connections with the rock art of other regions, particularly southern New Mexico and western Texas, their special characteristics set them apart from the rest of New Mexican art. Masks, shields, and shield bearers are common designs. Birds, hands, serpents, and lizards are often found, sometimes in pairs or in mirror images. Among the most typical geometrical designs are stars, equi-armed crosses, circles, and spirals. The glyphs most commonly appear on the south, east and west sides of boulders, usually near habited areas, but also along game trails. Designs are most often found grouped together in panels with little or no obvious relationship to one another.

Until recently, the sites have been well preserved, but encroaching civilization has caused many sites to be destroyed (for roads, rights of way, etc.) or to be threatened by nearby development. Some glyphs have been used for target practice, others have received modern additions or have simply been defaced.

In recent years, in addition to being appreciated for their artistic value, the glyphs of the Rio Grande have also been studied for what they can tell us of prehistoric ritual behavior and migration patterns of the prehistoric Pueblo peoples. The masks of the region are particularly noteworthy. They demonstrate that a katchina cult similar to that of the Western Pueblos of Hopi and Zuñi existed in the Rio Grande area in the late Fifteenth Century, although it had all but disappeared by the turn of this century, when anthropologists began studying the Tiwa, Tewa, and Keres Pueblos of the area. The glyphs themselves can be dated very roughly by their proximity to datable dwellings. This, together with comparisons of the styles and content of the rock art is evidence that the Pueblo ancestors of the historic groups were influenced strongly by their neighbors to the south, even into Mexico.

Dr. Ray A. Williamson
Center for Archaeoastronomy
University of Maryland

All photographs in this section are
by R. A. Williamson.

Galisteo area.

San Cristóbal area.

Galisteo area.

Española area.

Galisteo area.

San Cristóbal area.

La Cieneguilla area.

Galisteo area.

177

Galisteo area.

Española area.

San Cristóbal area.

La Cieneguilla area.

Galisteo area.

Española area.

Galisteo area.

Galisteo area.

San Cristóbal area.

Galisteo area. For more photographs of rock art in this region, refer to "Rock Art of New Mexico," by Polly Schaafsma.

Arches National Park

Arches National Park in prehistoric times served as a gathering and hunting area for peoples passing through the area or, later, the Pueblo Indians living in the Moab Valley. Consequently there are rock art examples scattered throughout the park, mostly associated with good rock-shelter camping sites or near convenient trail routes.

At the mouth of Courthouse Wash is a famous panel of pictographs with several large Barrier Canyon type figures; a few shields added to some of them may represent latter Ute or Fremont use. Also included are a few pecked horned figures of either Mesa Verde Anasazi or Fremont style. The panel has been placed on the National Register of Historic Places because of its significance. Unfortunately it was recently vandalized by someone, and at some expense, the National Park Service has partially restored it.

Near Wolfe Cabin are a series of petroglyphs along Salt Wash that depict horseback riders hunting or herding some variety of sheep, possibly mountain sheep. Undoubtedly these are late Ute glyphs as they did not have horses prior to about 1700 A.D.

Near the Dark Angel there are panels of petroglyphs pecked into the heavy desert varnish on sandstone cliff faces. These mostly represent Mesa Verde and some Fremont style glyphs with many anthropomorphs, deer and mountain sheep. Near the park visitor center there are several isolated rocks and cliff faces with petroglyphs on them. Most of the glyphs are mountain sheep. Similar small panels of glyphs with some Kokopelli figures are scattered along the lower canyon of Courthouse Wash and its side canyons.

Lloyd Pierson, Curator
Moab Museum

Courthouse Wash, panel detail, before vandalized.

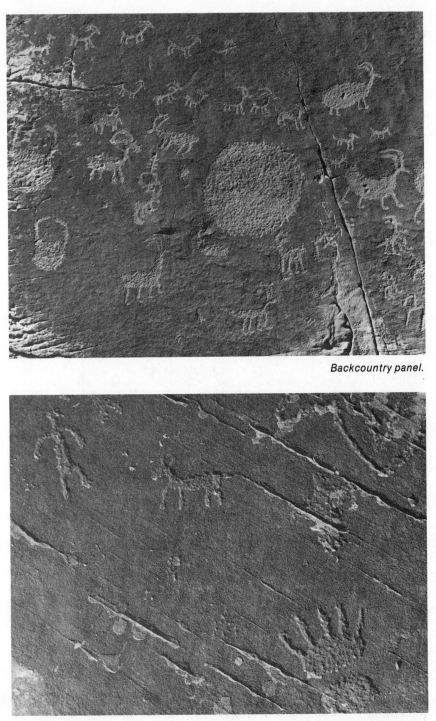

Backcountry panel.

Backcountry isolated boulder.

183

Salt Wash, historic petroglyph panel.

Dark Angel area.

Courthouse Wash, petroglyphs of sandal prints.

184

Courthouse Wash, panel detail, before vandalized.

Bandelier National Monument Area

The Pajarito Plateau, in northcentral New Mexico near Santa Fe, is rich in evidence of prehistoric Pueblo people. Scattered over the plateau are thousands of ruins. Some are large villages containing hundreds of rooms, but most are small structures of only a room or two. Archaeology shows that, although people have lived in the area for at least 3000 years, the time of heaviest population began in the Twelfth and Thirteenth Centuries and drew to a close about the middle of the Sixteenth Century. This time period follows that in which the great Anasazi centers of the Four Corners area (Mesa Verde, Chaco, Aztec, etc.) were abandoned. By the time that Spanish explorers entered northern New Mexico in the mid-1500s, the Pajarito Plateau was nearly abandoned. Present-day pueblos along the Rio Grande, including Santa Clara, San Ildefonso, and Cochiti have traditions that their ancestors moved to these villages from the plateau.

Bandelier National Monument, administered by the National Park Service, and Puye Cliffs, administered by Santa Clara Pueblo, offer good examples of ruins from the late prehistoric period. Both contain large excavated pueblo ruins, reconstructed talus houses, cave rooms, and plentiful petroglyphs. Bandelier also has a visitor center, museum, introductory slide show, and self-guiding booklets to the ruins trail. Interpretive programs are given during summer months. The visitor center is open year-round, and rangers there can provide directions to sites that are open to the public.

The Anasazi of the Pajarito Plateau followed the familiar agricultural way of life, growing corn, beans, squash, and perhaps cotton, keeping domestic turkeys and dogs, and utilizing wild plants and game. They had no metal except for an occasional copper bell, apparently traded from Mexico. Their environment was much like that of most southwesterners: pinyon-juniper forest, with Ponderosa pine, firs, and spruces at higher elevations; little rainfall, but summer storms that made agriculture possible. The elevation of the plateau, 6,000-8,000 feet, made for cold, snowy winters and cool summer nights.

The plateau itself, on the flanks of a gigantic volcano, is composed of compacted volcanic ash or tuff. This tuff is usually tan, brown, or pinkish in color, with an appearance similar to much of the sandstone found in the southwest, but it is much softer and lacks the layering characteristic of sandstone. Tuff boulders were cut into rough bricks for housebuilding. On sunny south-facing canyon walls and mesa sides, cavities in the tuff were enlarged and used as dwellings, often with a masonry structure, or talus house, added on the front. Obsidian, basalt, and rounded river stones were available nearby for use as tools.

Rock art is abundant throughout the plateau. Petroglyphs are found on boulders, canyon walls, cliff sides, and inside of caves used as dwellings. The soft tuff was easy to peck or scrape to make petroglyphs. But, because it is easily eroded and has little patina, nowadays many drawings are difficult to see. Rubbings or latex molds should not be made because they can cause severe damage to the images. Along the Rio Grande and in some side canyons the underlying layer of basalt is exposed. The people also drew on this harder, darker rock, and these images are usually clearer, but they are also less abundant and accessible.

Many of the pictures appear quite crude and rough. People and animals are often represented as simple outlines, with little attempt at realism. Many are isolated figures, although there are some large panels. Some still show evidence of having been painted. Among the most common figures are birds, animals, people (often with one or both hands raised), masks, spirals, concentric circles, and steps. Humpback flute players and serpents (both horned and plumed) appear in many forms. Some figures appear to have been made in historic times, as they include horses, churches, and other items introduced by Europeans.

Cave rooms often functioned as kivas. In some of these cave kivas, petroglyphs were carved through the soot on the ceiling, exposing the white stone beneath. The resulting design stood out sharply even in the gloomy room. At least two of these decorated kivas contain designs that appear to show influence from Mexico, including spotted animals that some say may be jaguars.

There is evidence that pictographs, mostly painted on the plaster of room walls, may have been common. Unfortunately, since the villages were in the open, few walls have survived. Some cave rooms show multiple layers of plaster, but even the caves are so shallow that little has survived. In Frijoles Canyon in Bandelier, one cave has dim figures of a plumed serpent and a person's head, painted on different layers of plaster. Another has a series of triangles around the inner surface of the cave. One section of wall plaster that remains from a house built against the cliff shows red and buff stepped shapes. South of the plateau at the ruin of Kuaua, now part of Coronado State Monument near Bernalillo, sections of kiva wall murals are on exhibit in the museum. The kiva from which they came has been reconstructed and repainted with many of the original designs and is open to visitors.

The rock art of the Pajarito Plateau has special significance due to the link it provides between the early Anasazi and the present-day Pueblo people. Figures seen carved into cliff walls are seen now on dance costumes and pottery. The people and their art and traditions are still very much alive.

L. Christine Judson
Park Technician
Bandelier National Monument

Left, Ancho Canyon, petroglyph scratched in cave-ceiling soot. Right, Tsankawi Ruin.

Tsankawi Ruin.

Long House Ruin.

188

Tsankawi Ruin. Fran Penner photo.

Tsirege Ruin, near White Rock.

189

Long House Ruin.

Tsankawi Ruin. Tracey Morse photo.

Tsankawi Ruin.

Tsankawi Ruin.

191

Canyon de Chelly National Monument

There was a great rock art tradition in Canyon de Chelly as evidenced by close to two hundred known sites. Some locations consist of only a few figures while one area, called Newspaper Rock, is over twenty-five meters wide. Art abounds in work areas and around dwellings as well as at other widely scattered sites — sites of possible religious or political significance.

Anasazi inhabitation of Canyon de Chelly spanned more than a thousand years. The entire cultural calendar from the Basketmaker era through the period of Cultural Decline is represented in rock art and the remains of their material culture. Although the most visible remnants of the Anasazi culture are the dwellings built during the Great Pueblo period, these sites yield little elaborate rock art. Art of this period was carelessly produced, highly abstract, and in the case of pictographs, almost entirely monochromatic. It appears that with the increasing specialization in pottery and kiva art, the discipline associated with rock paintings and carvings was removed.

Pictographs account for three-fourths of the rock art in the canyon. The people of the Basketmaker and Early Pueblo periods produced the majority of this work. Drawn primarily in white, red and yellow, the mineral-based paints have survived, while seemingly half-drawn turkeys and human figures attest to the instability of vegetable paints.

Early Anasazi rock art is the finest. The designs are limited, and the sites are few, but much time was devoted to each art production. Basketmaker people produced large, intricate human figures and decorated them with designs in a variety of colors.

The frequency of animal figures, including turkeys, ducks, and mountain sheep, reveals their importance in the Anasazi lifeway. Throughout the cultural calendar, however, human figures remain the most common motif. In healing rituals, hunting scenes, or isolated studies, these subjects, along with the handprint signature of the "Ancient Ones," are found in all sections of the canyon.

The rock art here is remarkably free of vandalism. Safeguarded in the past by its obscure location, the sites now lie within the protective custody of the National Park Service. To protect the Anasazi sites, as well as the privacy of the Navajo people who live there today, access into the canyon is limited. Participation in an organized tour, with a National Park Service ranger, or with a permit and an authorized Navajo guide, are the only ways to visit the major sites.

David P. Fletcher
Canyon de Chelly National Monument

All pictures in this section are National Park Service photos by David P. Fletcher.

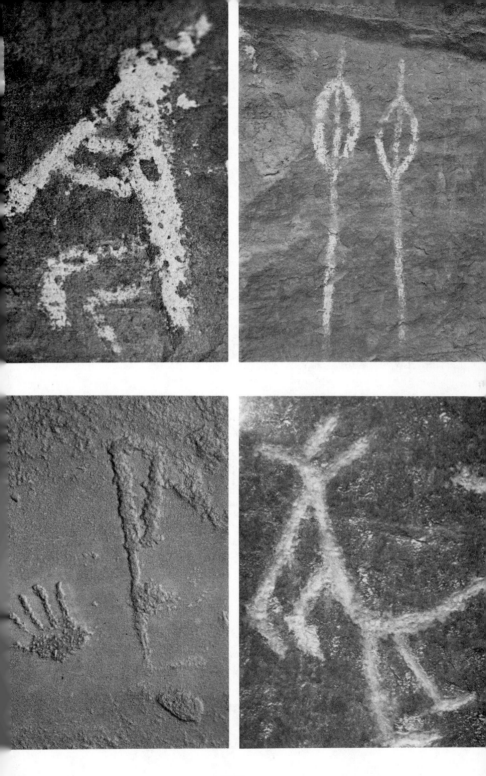

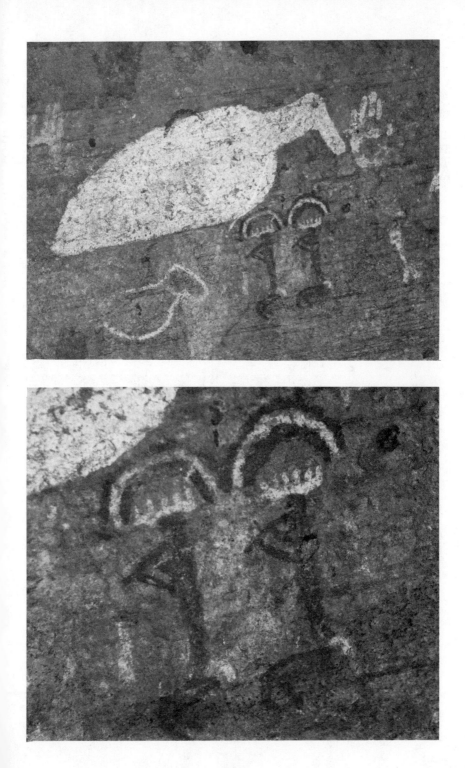

For more photographs of rock art within this national monument refer to "Canyon de Chelly, Its People and Rock Art" by Campbell Grant.

Canyonlands National Park
THE MAZE AREA

The Maze area in Canyonlands National Park contains some of the most visually outstanding prehistoric rock art in Utah. The "Great Gallery" in Horseshoe Canyon and the "Harvest Scene" in The Maze are large panels of pictographs depicting human-like and animal-like figures, some larger than life-sized.

Although the area is basically Fremont territory, it is within a cultural overlap zone and fairly near mountainous regions to the east that were used by prehistoric nomadic tribes. Thus, the cultural origin of the area's rock art is uncertain and probably mixed, as it is throughout the Anasazi-Fremont overlap zone. While the large panels of pictographs in the area illustrate a somewhat different graphic style, most other rock art there is more typical of Anasazi and Fremont craftsmanship.

Because of the unique style of the main panels in the Maze area, a few researchers have assumed they were made by an intruding culture. This and their sheer size and aesthetic appeal has led some researchers to assume that the "style" has extraordinary significance, even though no one has yet established any relationship between image size and cultural significance. The unique graphic style could easily be nothing more than an expression of the individuality of one prehistoric shaman plus, perhaps, a few dedicated followers. There is no hard evidence dating these controversial "Barrier Canyon Style" pictographs, but their graphic sophistication would seem to preclude any pre-Fremont Archaic origin, and no evidence has been found to support the "intruding culture" hypothesis. Thus, while the puzzle of the cultural origin of this graphic style has not been resolved, there is nothing to indicate that the solution to this somewhat academic problem would have any special significance.

The "Harvest Scene" and "Great Gallery" and other rock graphics near these outstanding panels are within Canyonlands National Park and can be reached by hiking established park trails. Other rock art in the area is in remote locations that can only be reached by hiking into primitive and very rugged backcountry.

Horseshoe Canyon.

Horseshoe Canyon.

201

Horseshoe Canyon.

Horseshoe Canyon.

202

Horseshoe Canyon.

The "Harvest Scene," The Maze.   Steven J. Manning photo.

Canyonlands National Park
THE NEEDLES AREA

The Needles area of Canyonlands National Park is within the Anasazi cultural region, but its rock art shows Fremont influence. Such mixing of graphic styles is to be expected within overlapping cultural zones.

Most of the area's rock art is found in the canyons that drain northward from the Abajo Mountains, then westward into the Colorado River gorge. The picturesque labyrinths of Salt, Horse, Lavender and Davis canyons and their numerous tributaries contain many but widely scattered petroglyph and pictograph images, as do a few of the "grabens" farther west. Many of the pictographs display graphic styles reminiscent of Fremont design, but other cultural remnants are clearly Anasazi.

Perhaps the most visually fascinating pictograph panels in the area are the "Five Faces" of Davis Canyon, the "Thirteen Faces" of Horse Canyon, and the "Four Faces" and "All American Man" of Salt Creek Canyon. The Salt Creek figures are associated with dwelling ruins, but the others are not.

Even though most of the area's rock art is in remote locations within the national park and in relatively unspoiled condition, there have been a few instances of vandalism. Most sites can be reached only by four wheel drive trails or by hiking into primitive and rugged backcountry, and many of the sites are difficult to locate.

"Five Faces," Davis Canyon.

Salt Creek Canyon.

Salt Creek Canyon.

Horse Canyon.

Salt Creek Canyon.

Nine of "Thirteen Faces," Horse Canyon.

Salt Creek Canyon.

Salt Creek Canyon.

Capitol Reef National Park

Capitol Reef National Park is renowned for its extensive, outstanding prehistoric rock art sites generally attributed to the Fremont culture. Over 90 simple to elaborate rock art sites have been identified within the 240,000 acre parkland area. Continued studies are revealing additional data that suggest the presence of more varied cultural activity than was previously suspected. In addition to the rock art attributed to the Fremont culture are depictions representative of possible Archaic Barrier Canyon, Anasazi, Paiute and/or Ute styles.

The majority of the rock art sites located along the Fremont River are characterized by large, front-facing anthropomorphic figures shown pecked with elaborate facial and body decorations. Smaller anthropomorphs and stylized desert bighorn sheep often accompany the major figures, with many of the sheep illustrated in active, side-view positions. The large anthropomorphs are mostly illustrated in shallow-to-deeply incised format, with some depictions being both pecked and rubbed. These figures usually wear masks shown with slit or dot eyes and horn or feather headdresses; chest decorations consisting of necklaces with arrangements of dots, circles, and parallel lines; and kilt-like torso coverage. Stick-like arm and leg appendages appear in various lengths, with the hands generally shown with splayed fingers.

In other areas of the park, large Fremont-style anthropomorphs appear as a combination of petroglyphs and pictographs. Many of the reddish-brown and white painted features have eroded away, leaving abbreviated renditions of the figures. These "pictoglyph" anthropomorphs are often accompanied by a wide variety of pecked desert bighorn sheep and various abstract figures. Generally, the large Fremont-style anthropomorphic depictions are situated near permanent water sources where agricultural activities may have been conducted.

Elsewhere in the park where hunting and gathering activities were principally conducted are petroglyph panels that vary significantly from the large Fremont-style anthropomorph panels. At such sites the rock art consists of anthropomorphs and zoomorphs that are often associated with abstract or geometric designs. Some panels at these locations may contain only a few elements, but many consist of numerous figures that approach or exceed the density of element illustrations associated with the large Fremont-style anthropomorph panels. Anthropomorphs and zoomorphs at the hunting/gathering sites are generally shown in active, side-view positions, and often there is superimposition of newer petroglyphs over older depictions suggesting long-term use of these locations.

Many of the rock art sites at Capitol Reef National Park remain relatively unknown and contain little vandalism due to their location in sparsely visited areas of the park.

John S. Noxon & Deborah A. Marcus
American Indian Rock Writing
Research
Monticello, Utah

Fremont River gorge.

Fremont River gorge.

Left, Capitol Gorge. Right, Fremont River gorge. Noxon and Marcus photos.

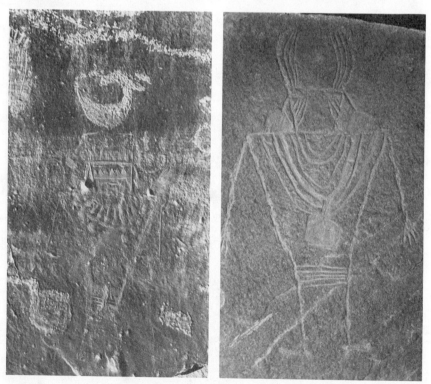

Fremont River gorge. Noxon and Marcus photos.

Pleasant Creek. The crescent and concentric circles on the right are believed to depict the AD 1054 supernova.

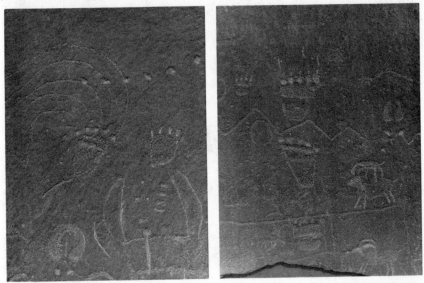

Pleasant Creek.

Pleasant Creek.

211

Noxon and Marcus photo.

Noxon and Marcus photo.

Noxon and Marcus photo.

Capitol Gorge. Noxon and Marcus photo.

Central Utah Area

The rock art of central Utah is dominated by the finely executed work of the prehistoric Fremont Indians, with a few panels of beautiful "Barrier Canyon" style pictographs. Also located in the area are a few inscribed names old enough to be considered historic, dating back to the early 1800s in the instance of the famous Roubidoux inscription.

Central Utah is dominated geographically by the San Rafael Swell, a large kidney-shaped "bubble" or anticline, which contains many canyons with dark cliffs which made excellent places for the prehistoric inhabitants of the area to use in making their rock art.

Foremost in the execution of rock art is the Fremont culture, which inhabited Utah from 400 A.D. to about 1300 A.D. but dominated central Utah from 950 A.D. to about 1250 A.D. Fremont rock art is characterized by large anthropomorphs, many of them decorated with earbobs, necklaces, kilts and other regalia, and often depicted holding shields, bows and arrows, and other items. The fancy attire pictured in the petroglyphs probably represents ceremonial garb, because it is highly doubtful that they wore such apparel on an everyday basis.

Not all Fremont rock art is characterized by large anthropomorphs, however. That located in Nine Mile Canyon and the San Rafael Swell area is characterized by small, simple anthropomorphs, animals, geometric designs and other nondescript elements.

Adding a welcome flair to the rock art of central Utah are the little understood "Barrier Canyon" style rock art panels. Named for the beautiful pictographs beside Barrier Creek in the Horseshoe Canyon annex of Canyonlands National Park, this style of rock art is instantly recognizable wherever it is found. The well executed panels are characterized by bug-eyed anthropomorphs with long, tapering bodies, often heroic in size (up to 14 feet tall), that are embellished with ornate clothing or body decorations. These panels are often located in deep canyons or alcoves or hidden away in remote places. Some Barrier Canyon style panels are in large amphitheaters that could have been the settings for ceremonies that were later depicted on the cliffs.

We do not know much about the culture that made the Barrier Canyon style rock art, but some evidence shows that it may predate the Fremonts and may have been made by a hunting and gathering culture. This is inferred from the presence of wild grasses and seed-beater implements in some of the panels. Although the originating culture is unknown, the figures exhibit sophisticated graphic knowledge.

Many panels of rock art have been found in Central Utah, and many more undoubtedly remain to be found. Because of its deep canyons and hidden crevices, many areas are yet to be thoroughly explored. A few of these will surely yield other panels for the appreciation and bemusement of modern man.

Layne Miller, Committee Chairman
College of Eastern Utah
Prehistoric Museum

Sheep Canyon. Layne Miller photo.

Bullard Cove.

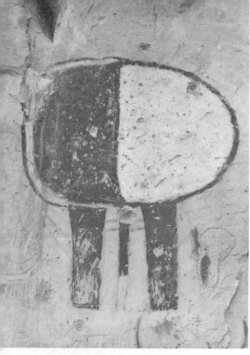

Bullard Cove.

Black Dragon Canyon.

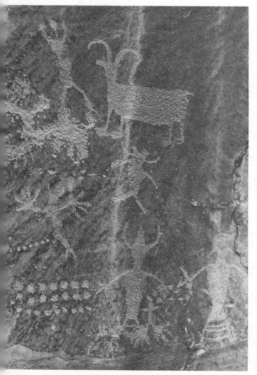

Ninemile Canyon.

Hog Springs. Layne Miller photo.

216

Price River gorge. Layne Miller photo.

Price River gorge. Layne Miller photo.

San Rafael Swell. Layne Miller photo.

217

Buckhorn Wash. Layne Miller photo.

Buckhorn Wash. Layne Miller photo.

Cottonwood Canyon. Layne Miller photo.

218

Ninemile Canyon.

Ninemile Canyon. Layne Miller photo.

Ninemile Canyon.

Buckhorn Wash.

Buckhorn Wash.

Rochester Creek. Layne Miller photo.

Ninemile Canyon. A. G. Pratt photo. For more photographs of rock art in this region and throughout Utah refer to "Petroglyphs and Pictographs of Utah" by K. B. Castleton (two volumes) and "The Rock Art of Utah" by Polly Schaafsma.

Chaco Canyon Area

Chaco Culture National Historical Park, formerly Chaco Canyon National Monument, contains remains of Anasazi and Navajo occupation. The park was created to preserve the spectacular ruins of the Chaco culture, a development of the Anasazi people which reached a high level of complexity about AD 900 to 1300. Heavily influenced by trade connections with the more sophisticated cultures of northern Mexico, the Chaco people developed their basic Basketmaker culture traditions into a regional network of towns and villages, with Chaco Canyon at their center. Within the park, more than 2300 archaeological sites are recorded, many of them huge greathouses with hundreds of rooms such as the famous Pueblo Bonito. With its estimated 600 to 800 rooms, Pueblo Bonito remained the largest apartment house in North America until the last half of the 19th Century. The abandonment of all the Chaco sites in the region started by about AD 1200, and by AD 1300 the area was deserted until the arrival of the Navajo about 200 years later.

The sandstone cliffs within the park abound with petrographic art, including Anasazi, Navajo and Euro-American. There have been several attempts to study the many figures over the years, but only recently has an inventory been completed. The results of the inventory are overwhelming in the diversity of figures, but to date no scientific study has been made of these figures. There are no petroglyphic panels specifically integrated into the park's interpretive program, although some panels are visible from the self-guided tour trails. The fragile nature of the environment prohibits visitors from leaving the trails, but petroglyphs are observable from the trails at Chetro Ketl, Pueblo Bonito and Penasco Blanco.

As nearly as can be determined, the earliest petroglyphic figures in the park date from the Basketmaker period, AD 400 to 750, and the latest, alas, are graffiti by recent visitors. In between, the characteristic pecked Anasazi figures are dominant. Later, Apachean, or Navajo, figures were incised, like Euro-American graffiti, with sharp metal objects. The Navajo figures rank second to the Anasazi figures in frequency. Most of the Euro-American graffiti were made by Hispanic sheepherders passing through the area during the last quarter of the 19th Century and the first quarter of the 20th.

While many of the Anasazi panels apparently represent intelligible activities, e.g., hunting, the majority are enigmatic as to both subject and intent, and many seem to be no more than symbolic cyphers whose meanings disappeared with the last Chacoan. Navajo panels are more representative of their subjects. Horses, dances, trucks and names are common, although some Navajo figures have only idiosyncratic meaning. The Euro-American graffiti are mainly names and dates, with occasional home towns or simply initials.

C. Randall Morrison
Chaco Culture National
Historical Park

Chaco Culture National Historical Park, near campgrounds.

Una Vida ruins.

Una Vida ruins.

Desolation-Gray Canyon
of the Green River

The Desolation-Gray canyon system of the Green River begins a few miles downstream of the town of Ouray, Utah, and ends where the river emerges from the Book Cliffs a few miles upstream of the town of Green River, Utah. Major John Wesley Powell, the first explorer to chart this stretch of the Green, called the upper part "Desolation Canyon" because of its extremely wild and rugged nature. He named the lower few miles "Gray Canyon" because of the grayish colored mineral deposits that dominated the gorge there.

The Fremonts, their Archaic predecessors, and possibly a number of wandering nomadic groups from the north or east, all left rock graphics in the canyon and its major tributaries. With this mixed usage, it is not possible to assign a cultural origin to specific rock art with certainty, although most of it is probably Fremont.

Three of the Green's tributaries in this stretch — Nine Mile Canyon, Range Creek Canyon and Price River Canyon — contain great quantities of rock art, while many others have lesser amounts. Most of the rock art in the Desolation-Gray Canyon system can be reached only by rubber raft and hiking. Part of upper Nine Mile Canyon is traveled by a public dirt road, but much of Nine Mile, Range Creek and Price Canyons are privately owned and off-limits to the public except by special permission. Beginning not far below the Nine Mile confluence and downriver to about four miles below Range Creek, the east bank of the Green and all of its eastern tributaries are within the Uintah and Ouray Indian Reservation. A tribal permit is required for exploring.

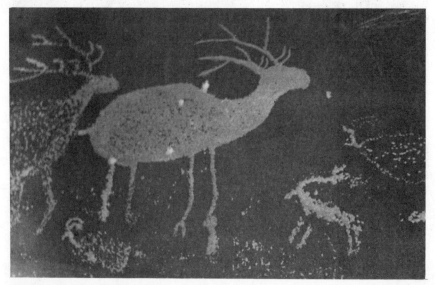

At Nefertiti. Verne Huser photo.

Rock Creek Canyon.

Flat Canyon. Verne Huser photo.

227

Maverick Canyon. Verne Huser photo.

Flat Canyon. Verne Huser photo.

228

At Nefertiti. Verne Huser photo.

At Nefertiti. Verne Huser photo.

Grand Canyon National Park

During the past three or four thousand years, Grand Canyon has been occupied by several groups of Native Americans. The earliest of these, makers of split twig figurines of animals, left no other artistic record.

After A.D. 500, the depths and rims of the Canyon were inhabited by Anasazi of the Kayenta and Virgin traditions and by the somewhat enigmatic Cohonina people. Virgin Anasazi Indians occupied the northwestern reaches of the Canyon while the Kayenta utilized both north and south rims as well as the inner portions of the gorge. The Cohonina were mainly restricted to the South Rim and to Havasu Canyon.

Anasazi petroglyphs and pictographs in Grand Canyon are similar to those in the Kayenta heartland. Painted depictions of bighorn sheep and human hands are common, although human representations such as the humpbacked flute player are rare. Petroglyphs of spirals, concentric circles, and other geometric forms are frequently found.

The Cohonina, who lived as friendly neighbors of the Anasazi, developed their rock art, especially pictographs painted on protected surfaces of the canyon walls, in a more complex manner. The artists usually used red and white pigments and painted many geometric design motifs. Frequently one sees a number of more complex and esoteric combinations of forms.

Following the abandonment of Grand Canyon about A.D. 1150 by the Cohonina and Anasazi, no human groups inhabited its vastness for some 150 years. Then, shortly after A.D. 1300, the ancestors of the Southern Paiute settled the North Rim, and the precursors of the Walapai and Havasupai moved along the South Rim. Rock art of the Paiute has not been recognized in Grand Canyon, but that of the Havasupai has been found in rock shelters in their territory. This consists mostly of pictographs, usually in red, sometimes white, of deer and other animals. At some sites, large circles with quadrilateral designs were painted on the cliff walls.

Fortunately, most of Grand Canyon's native rock art has remained free of vandalism. It is only those examples near well-used hiking trails that have had recent names, dates, and other graffiti added.

Dr. Robert C. Euler
Research Anthropologist
Grand Canyon National Park

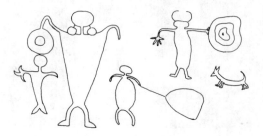

Attributed to the Cohonina culture.

All pictures in this section are National Park Service photos by Robert C. Euler.

Attributed to the Havasupai culture.

Attributed to the Virgin Anasazi culture.

Attributed to the Cohonina culture.

Attributed to the Virgin Anasazi culture.

233

Attributed to the Kayenta Anasazi culture.

Attributed to the Kayenta Anasazi culture.

Attributed to the Kayenta Anasazi culture.

Grand Gulch Primitive Area

Grand Gulch and its tributaries is a network of canyons and washes that rank as some of the roughest yet most beautiful in the Southwest. The main canyon, from Kane Springs to the Collins Spring tributary, is about 35 miles long and contains some of the most unusual as well as some of the grandest rock art in canyon country.

Grand Gulch became famous in the 1800s when Richard Wetherill noticed a non-pottery culture buried beneath the Anasazi culture that he was excavating. His comment about the "basketmakers" stuck and is the name we now use to refer to an ancient people who created exquisite baskets but who had not yet invented ceramics. Very little was ever said about the rock art in the papers that Richard Wetherill wrote, but as a trip down the canyon testifies, it is very abundant and quite different.

Some figures appear in Grand Gulch that do not appear anywhere else. Some of these are a two-headed man, a green mask, and mountain lion tracks. Many of the figures were done during the Basketmaker period. Some figures most likely executed during Basketmaker times are large anthropomorphs, atlatls, and yucca plants complete with blossoms.

Grand Gulch has been inhabited from Basketmaker times through the late Pueblo periods, consequently the rock art is representational of all these periods so it is a fine area for the serious student of rock art to study styles and representational elements and superimposition. It is very possible that a thorough study of the rock art in the canyon could clear up some of the questions now facing the rock art student about the similarities in style between Basketmaker, Fremont and Anasazi rock art.

Layne Miller
Committee Chairman
College of Eastern Utah
Prehistoric Museum

Bullet Canyon.   All photographs in this section are by Layne Miller.

236

Bullet Canyon.

Bullet Canyon.

Bullet Canyon.

Bullet Canyon.

Main canyon.

Main canyon.

239

Hovenweep National Monument

Hovenweep National Monument is best known for its square, round, and D-shaped towers built by Anasazi Indians 750 years ago. The area also contains small, well preserved rock art sites. It is extremely difficult to know what the designs and pictures mean at these sites. They range from geometric shapes of squares and lines with right angle turns, to spirals and circles, pictures of animals and their footprints and men wearing headdresses. Geometric designs appear everywhere, while spirals are usually found near features used to store or channel water. Pictures of animals, and their hoof or paw prints usually occur near storage rooms. The pictures of people, most of them wearing headdresses, are located near small isolated camping and living sites that may have been used for ceremonies.

Most of the rock art probably dates from the Anasazi era. For the Hovenweep area this means between A.D. 1000 and A.D. 1300. The pictures of the broad shouldered people wearing headdresses may be earlier, either Basketmaker or Fremont people. If this is true, then the men who wore these headdresses performed their ceremonies between one and two thousand years ago.

The Four Corners area has a well deserved reputation for its rich archaeological resources, but few people are aware of the rock art in the Hovenweep area. The National Park Service protects and interprets some of this prehistoric art at Hovenweep National Monument.

Roger L. Trick
Area Manager
Hovenweep National Monument

Little Ruin Canyon. Note the three faint "bird" figures across the center of the photo.

All pictures in this section are National Park Service photos by R. L. Trick.

Near Hovenweep, N. M.

Near Hovenweep, N. M.

Near Hovenweep, N. M.

Near Hovenweep, N. M.

Near Ismay Trading Post.

Near Hovenweep, N. M.

Indian Creek Canyon

Indian Creek descends the north slopes of the Abajo Mountains of southeastern Utah, then heads west down a spectacular canyon for many miles. It then crosses open country for a few miles before cutting deeply into red sandstone formations, then plunging into the deep Colorado River gorge within Canyonlands National Park.

Utah 211 travels the length of the upper canyon, which has many rock art sites. The best known of these, Newspaper Rock State Historical Monument, is within sight of the highway and is a mixture of prehistoric and historic petroglyphs. Other sites are more difficult to find and reach.

There are no major dwelling sites in upper Indian Creek Canyon, but the lower canyon saw considerable occupation and use by the Anasazis. Numerous ruins were reported by the 1859 Macomb expedition. The expedition's chronicler named the canyon "Labyrinth," but the name did not stick. Lower Indian Creek Canyon is accessible only by hiking. It has many rock art sites.

Upper Indian Creek Canyon contains one of the controversial "mastodon" petroglyphs, but the glyph seems to be no older than other nearby historic glyphs, and its graphic style seems far too sophisticated to have been contemporary with these extinct, elephant-like creatures.

Shay Canyon.

244

Shay Canyon "mastodon."

Shay Canyon.

Shay Canyon.

Newspaper Rock State Historical Monument.

Shay Canyon.

247

Shay Canyon panel.

Shay Canyon.

248

Newspaper Rock detail.

Moab Area

All of the various periods of prehistoric culture except the Paleo-Indian stage (5500-9500 B.C.) are represented in the rock art of the Moab area. Archaic culture (450 A.D. - 6000 B.C.) rock art is mostly large, square-bodied bighorn sheep petroglyphs and a few Barrier Canyon style triangular bodied, big-eyed pictographs like the panel at the mouth of Courthouse Wash north of the Colorado River bridge. Mesa Verde Anasazi (1 A.D. - 1225 A.D.) petroglyphs are the most common in the area with many horned anthropomorphs, bighorn sheep, deer and geometric designs as representative. Hunting scenes with bow and arrow depicted are definitely Anasazi. Although no Fremont Culture (900-1100 A.D.) habitation sites are known near Moab, there are Fremont-like figures beside Utah 279 that have ear bobs, shields and form similar to larger petroglyphs found in the Uintah basin and identified as Fremont. Lastly a few petroglyphs identifiable, by the depiction of horses and riders, as having been made by the Ute Indians (1400 A.D. to now) can be found in the area. Pre-horse Ute petroglyphs are presently not identifiable.

Rock art in the Moab area is spread over the area in general, but there are good concentrations down the Colorado River from Moab on both sides. Some are marked with signs. Others, like the famed "Moab Mastodon" petroglyph, have to be searched out. There are also concentrations near the highway river bridge, up Kane Creek from the river and in the south fork of Mill Creek. There are scattered petroglyphs along the north side of Spanish Valley in favored locations on the south side of heavily patinated sandstone boulders and cliff faces. They are also found at the mouths of canyons, along obvious access trails and near open and cave habitation sites.

Lloyd M. Pierson, Curator
Moab Museum

Mill Creek Canyon.

250

Behind the Rocks.

Cane Creek Canyon.

Colorado River gorge.

251

Colorado River gorge.

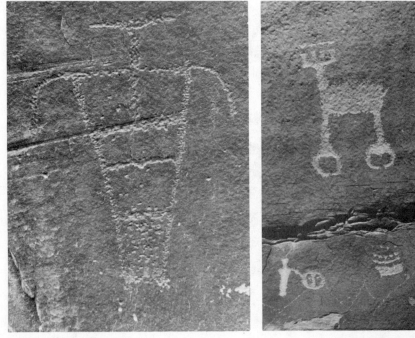

Colorado River gorge.

Behind the Rocks.

252

Colorado River gorge.

Colorado River gorge.

Cane Creek Canyon.

Colorado River gorge.

Colorado River gorge.

Cane Creek Canyon tributary.

Cane Creek Canyon tributary.

Cane Creek Canyon tributary.

Cane Creek Canyon tributary.

Colorado River gorge.

Spanish Valley.

Behind the Rocks.

Behind the Rocks.

Petrified Forest National Park

Much of the rock art of Petrified Forest National Park still waits to be recorded. Petroglyphs and some few pictographs are scattered throughout the park's 93,492 acres and neighboring lands, seen only by hardy hikers and occasional ranch hands on cattle roundups. Almost no interpretive research and little mapping has been done locating the rock art of the area. A handful of letters from visitors interpreting the petroglyphs as maps or equivalents of Nordic runes, join with a few reports comparing the petroglyphs with those in other areas and other countries.

The most noted petroglyphs are those at Newspaper Rock, just off the park road southwest of the Puerco Ruins. One hundred and twenty steps lead down a steep bluff face to the viewing area at Newspaper Rock. Those along the bluff at Puerco Ruins can be seen from two viewing areas along a short trail beside the ruins. The Rainbow Forest Museum in the south end of the park houses the cougar petroglyph removed from its original site at Blue Mesa during the 1940s.

Although many of the park's petroglyphs are located near ruins, no studies have been done to determine a direct association to the dwellings, some of which date prior to 500 A.D. Many other petroglyphs occur singly or in large panels near work or campsites. They range from rough outlines to very fine representations of animals, birds and heavenly bodies.

The Puerco Ruins, Newspaper Rock and the Painted Desert Petroglyphs are on the National Register of Historical Places. A topographical map and wilderness hiking are required to locate the Painted Desert site. Those on nearby lands are not accessible to the public.

Evidence of vandalism is as abundant as the rock art itself. Historical inscriptions left by European explorers and Civilian Conservation Corps workers, as well as recent graffiti, overlay the prehistoric markings. In some nearby areas, entire petroglyph panels have been removed.

The public's growing understanding of the importance of history to our present way of life and planning for the future has created a general interest in protecting archaeological resources, including the rock art. The Archaeological Resources Protection Act of 1979 has made it possible to prosecute those who would vandlize or remove these pages from our past, but only public and individual concern can truly protect these irreplaceable resources. They must be protected if they are to be incorporated into our knowledge of the past when better methods are available to study and understand them.

Susan J. Colclazer
Chief of Interpretation
Petrified Forest National Park

Rainbow Forest Museum.

NPS photo.

259

NPS photo.

Newspaper Rock area.

260

Newspaper Rock area.

San Juan River Gorge

Within a high-desert region a flowing river or stream is a source of life. In the Four Corners region, the San Juan River and its numerous tributaries have supported prehistoric Indian tribes for thousands of years, far back into the Desert Archaic cultural stage and earlier. For much of this time, the region's tribes had rock art traditions.

A majority of the rock art along the banks of this river system was created by various Anasazi sub-groups, their contemporaries and related historic tribes. Some of the most sophisticated Anasazi petroglyphs can be found beside the San Juan in the southwestern corner of Utah.

Rock graphics on the last 50 miles of the river above its confluence with the Colorado River are now drowned by Lake Powell, and the Navajo Reservoir has drowned great quantities of rock art beside the upper San Juan, but sites between Lake Powell and the town of Bluff can be reached by rubber raft, and Utah 262 parallels the river above Montezuma Creek, providing ready access to sites there. This easy access has led to considerable vandalism. In many locations, historic petroglyphs have been added to prehistoric panels.

Most of the San Juan's many perennial and seasonal tributaries contain rock art, a few in great quantity, but most of these tributaries are within the Navajo and Ute Indian Reservations and hence off-limits to hikers unless tribal permits are first obtained. One exception to this is the Grand Gulch Primitive Area. There, backcountry permits are also required, but the area is administered by the Bureau of Land Management.

Butler Wash.

Near Butler Wash.

Sand Island.

Butler Wash.

Near Butler Wash.

Butler Wash.

Sand Island.

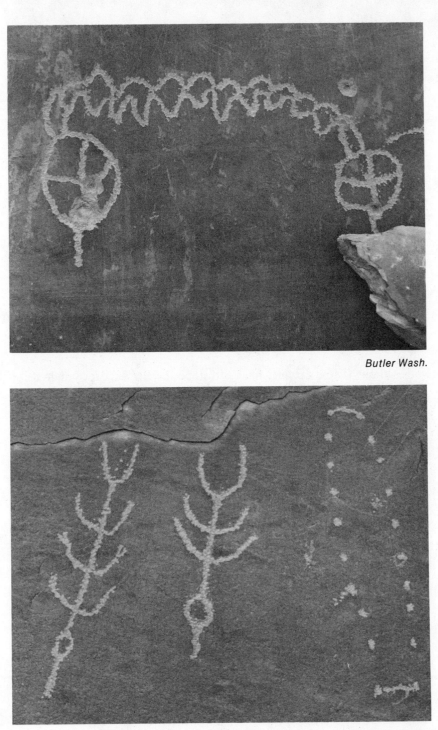

Butler Wash.

Butler Wash.

Three Rivers Area

Human populations first occupied the Tularosa Basin of southcentral New Mexico over 10,000 years ago. Around 900 A.D. their descendants, a people known as the Jornada Mogollon, established agricultural villages in the Three Rivers Drainage on the east side of the Basin and remained there until approximately 1400.

Today, while the latest innovations in military technology are being tested on the nearby White Sands Missile Range, the artwork of these people remains. A small ridge overlooking the Three Rivers Valley contains extensive carvings of masks, wildlife and geometric designs. Over 5,000 individual carvings have been found among the rock outcroppings, making this site one of the largest prehistoric petroglyph locations in the southwest.

Many of the designs are similar to the Mimbres style found throughout southwestern New Mexico. However, the Jornada Mogollon came into contact with many cultures, and the Anasazi influence is present in both the rock carvings and the pueblos constructed of masonry or masonry and coarsed adobe.

The meanings of the petroglyphs are as varied as their designs. Some have religious significance while others are sympathetic magic signs, where one wished for a good hunt by carving an arrow through the desired animal. Still others tell about previous hunts while the meaning of some remains unknown.

Although these carvings have withstood the elements for hundreds of years, many are being threatened by a more destructive force, man. Most of the carvings at Three Rivers have been well preserved; however, a disturbing number have been disfigured by those who insist on leaving their mark or on breaking off a souvenir. A caretaker watches over the site; however, even his presence does not completely deter those individuals who would thoughtlessly destroy an irreplaceable part of our heritage.

The ridge containing the densest concentration of petroglyphs is managed as a recreation site by the U. S. Bureau of Land Management. The recreation site lies within 30 miles north of Alamogordo, just east of Highway 54, and is open seven days a week. Picnic facilities have been installed and portions of a prehistoric village have been excavated and a pithouse and two other structures partially reconstructed.

Ben Fish
Outdoor Recreation Planner
U. S. Bureau of Land Management

All pictures in this section are Bureau of Land Management photos taken by Ben Fish at the Three Rivers Petroglyph Site, a BLM development.

Uintah Basin Area

The Uintah Basin in northeastern Utah is a major area for rock art and is the source for the well known "Classic Vernal" graphic style. While this style is attributed to the Fremont culture, other rock art in the broad basin and its many tributary canyons was created by cultures ranging from pre-Fremont Desert Archaic to historic Ute.

Typical Classic Vernal rock art figures are anthropomorphs that may be up to six feet tall, with trapezoidal bodies, simple arms and legs, and heads that are round, rectangular or bucket-shaped, often decorated with ornate headgear. The bodies may also be adorned with necklaces, kilts, sashes or breechclouts. A few of the petroglyph figures exhibit an elementary form of relief carving, and some still bear paint traces that have resisted centuries of weathering, indicating that the original images may have been very colorful and elaborate.

In addition to the human figures of the Classic Vernal style, other Uintah Basin rock art depicts deer, sheep, elk, birds, bear, scorpions, lizards and beetles, as well as bird and bear tracks. Birds shown are turkeys, eagles and owls. One site is believed to depict astronomical objects and what have been called "space helmeted figures." At many sites, geometric shapes are found among the naturalistic images. A few human figures appear to be performing actions, such as hunting or dancing.

While rock art is scattered throughout the Uintah Basin area, there are unusual concentrations at some locations. As with other regions, the cliffs along the Green River and its major tributaries bear rock art that can only be reached by boat. Many such sites are within Dinosaur National Monument. One rivergorge site that can also be reached by a backcountry road is at Little Rainbow Park. Here, the names of early trapper Denis Julien, trader Antoine Roubidoux and some of the soldiers from Fort Duchesne can be found among the prehistoric petroglyphs.

McKee Springs, in Dinosaur National Monument, east of Vernal, is considered to have some of the finest rock art in Utah. Exceptional rock art can also be found within Painted Canyon, which was named by members of the Dominguez-Escalante expedition in 1776, and within Dry Fork Canyon. In Dry Fork Canyon, most of the sites are on private land, but permission to view the rock art can sometimes be obtained from landowners.

Information about Uintah Basin rock art is available at the Dinosaur National Monument visitor center and at Utah's Dinosaur Natural History Museum in Vernal.

J. Curtiss Sinclear, Curator
Dinosaur Natural History Museum

A. G. Pratt, author
"Uintah Basin Rock Art"

Dry Fork Canyon.

Dry Fork Canyon.

Dry Fork Canyon.

Dry Fork Canyon.

Dry Fork Canyon.

Dry Fork Canyon.

Dry Fork Canyon.

Cub Creek, Dinosaur National Monument. Verne Huser photos.

Cub Creek, Dinosaur National Monument. A. G. Pratt photos.

273

Little Rainbow Park, Dinosaur National Monument. A. G. Pratt photos.

Jones Hole. A. G. Pratt photo.

274

Leland Bench. A. G. Pratt photo.

Near Ouray. A. G. Pratt photo.

Cockleburr Wash. A. G. Pratt photo.

Left, Ashley Creek. Right, Brush Creek. A. G. Pratt photos.

Left, Brush Creek. Right, Ashley Creek. A. G. Pratt photos.

McKee Springs, Dinosaur National Monument. A. G. Pratt photos. For more photographs of rock art in this region, refer to "Rock Art of the Uintah Basin" by A. G. Pratt.

West-Central Colorado Area

The rock art of west central Colorado is found chiefly along the drainages of the Dolores, Gunnison, Colorado and White Rivers. The region is one of plateaus and sandstone canyons, a terrain which has long sustained human occupation. Archaeologically the region reflects use by variations of the Desert Archaic Culture, the Fremont Culture, the Anasazi Culture, and the historic Ute. The Uncompahgre Plateau, located between the Dolores and the Gunnison Rivers, saw usage as early as about 8000 B.C., and a radiocarbon date of about 7000 B.C. has been obtained from the White River region to the north.

In the southern portion, most of the cultures that have been archaeologically identified in the region are represented in the rock art styles evident along the Dolores River. Several rock art sites exhibit the rectangular body shape of pre-A.D. 1050 Glen Canyon anthropomorphs and may be of Archaic origin. Similar figures are found along the Gunnison River as well, and elsewhere on the Uncompahgre Plateau. These figures vary from almost life-size along the Dolores River to less than a foot in the northern area of the Plateau. This rock art style may relate to the largely Archaic Uncompahgre Complex. One style within this Complex has been tentatively dated at being roughly contemporary with the development of the Fremont in Utah and the Anasazi in the northern Puebloan area. Anasazi influence is apparent in a rock art panel found along the San Miguel River above its confluence with the Dolores River. This site contains petroglyphs and a charcoal drawing executed in the style of the San Juan Basketmaker culture.

Farther north along the Dolores River is a petroglyph group of more than fifty small, linked anthropomorphs. Such figures are assigned to the Pueblo period, A.D. 700-1050, in the Navajo Reservoir District to the south of this area. Superimposed on the linked figures at the Dolores River site are Fremont-type anthropomorphs, obviously a later creation.

Examples of Fremont rock art styles such as the Classic Vernal and the Northern and Southern San Rafael Styles, are found in increasing numbers in the central and northern portions of the Uncompahgre Plateau. At the extreme northern end of the Plateau, near the Colorado River, are large petroglyphs of heroic anthropomorphs, probably a local variation of the Classic Vernal Style. Shield figures of the Southern San Rafael type are found nearby along the Colorado River in Colorado and Utah. One rock art site along the Colorado River at the base of the Uncompahgre Plateau displays large paintings of a "bear," a horned figure, and an indistinct figure capped with a Fremont-type headdress. The presence of elaborate owl images in Fremont rock art sites is regionally unique. At the northern end of the Uncompahgre Plateau and along the Colorado River are both paintings and petroglyphs of owls, some quite animated, others rather stiff. Some are naturalistic, others are depicted as wearing necklaces. Beautifully executed footprint petroglyphs are found on the Uncompahgre Plateau, as are painted and pecked heron images. Footprints and herons are associated with Fremont rock art in Utah.

The northern portion of west central Colorado, north of the Colorado River and the Uncompahgre Plateau, has numerous rock art sites. Many are concentrated north of the Bookcliffs, but south of Blue Mountain and Dinosaur National Monument, in the drainages of the White River. The earliest rock art styles represented in this area resemble the oldest Glen Canyon petroglyphs and the Barrier Canyon Style pictographs, both of which are associated with Archaic hunting and gathering cultures. Two panels south of the White River strongly resemble the Barrier Canyon Style panel above the Horseshoe Shelter in Barrier Canyon but contain elements found in other Barrier Canyon Style sites, such as dot crowns and hollowed-out eyes. Another panel bears a resemblance to a large Moab, Utah panel. Perhaps indicative of the continuing development of this style is the presence of a Barrier Canyon Style anthropomorph painted with clay and superimposed on earlier Barrier Canyon Style figures executed in polychrome pigments. Barrier Canyon Style rock art in this region appears as both rock paintings and petroglyphs.

A number of rock art sites in the White River region contain anthropomorphs, usually painted red, which may represent a separate rock art style reflecting a transition from Archaic styles to a Fremont style. This "Transitional Style" is found in both Colorado and neighboring Utah.

Archaeologically, there is evidence of continuous occupation of the area south of the White River from about 2700 B.C. to the end of the Fremont period, about 740 years ago. Fremont rock art styles, such as the Classic Vernal and the Northern and Southern San Rafael, are identifiable in both petroglyphs and rock paintings of the area. Combinations of painting and pecking are also found, attributed to both Archaic and Fremont manufacture. While superimpositions are relatively rare in the area, Fremont-related designs always appear over the Archaic-related designs when superimpositions of this type do occur.

North and east of the White River region, above the 8,000 foot elevation level and close to the Continental Divide, is a Fremont-related rock art site revealing polychrome paintings which closely resemble the "Transitional Style" anthropomorphs of the White River region. This interesting site is, at present, the easternmost Fremont-related rock art site in Colorado and the highest in elevation.

East of Dinosaur National Monument and north to the Wyoming state line are several major rock art sites, most of which exhibit a variant of the Classic Vernal Style. This area lies north and west of the White River rock art region.

Historic Ute rock art is found throughout west central Colorado, chiefly in the form of petroglyphs but also as scattered rock paintings. Especially fine examples are present on the east side of the Uncompahgre Plateau.

Sally J. Cole
Danni L. Langdon
Grand River Institute

All photographs in this section are by Sally J. Cole.

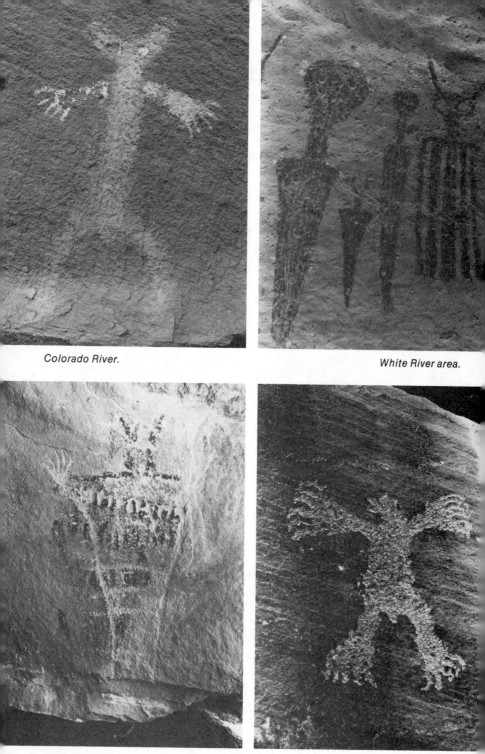

Colorado River.

White River area.

White River area.

Uncompahgre Plateau.

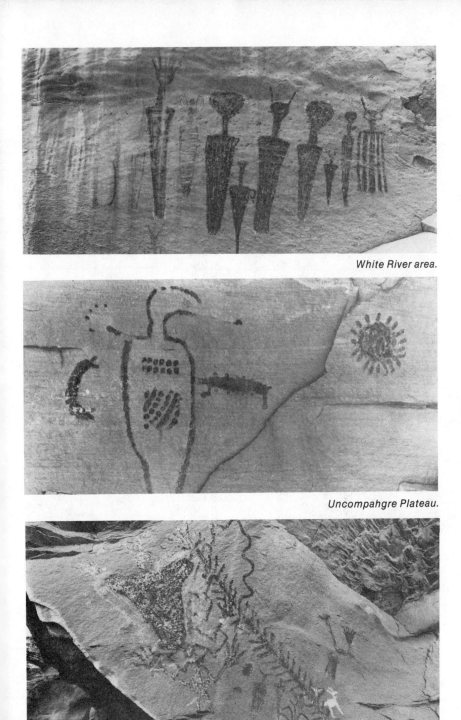

White River area.

Uncompahgre Plateau.

White River area.

281

White River area.

White River area.

Uncompahgre Plateau.

Gunnison River.

283

Zuñi-Cibola Area

The abundant prehistoric engravings and paintings on cliff faces and cave walls in this region represent a mixed Anasazi-Mogollon tradition that extends from prior to A.D. 400.

Perhaps the earliest rock art of this region is found in the Hardscrabble Wash district of Arizona. It is characterized by the use of pecked circles, lines and zigzags in a variety of configurations, including an interesting early mask complex.

The early culture of this area, especially Pueblo I through Pueblo III (A.D. 750-1300), appears to have been most closely related to that of the San Juan Anasazi to the north, and evidence exists of much interaction between the populations of Zuñi and the Chaco Canyon area. For example, archaeological excavations have shown that the ruins at the Village of the Great Kivas (A.D. 1000-1100) are strikingly similar to those of Chaco Canyon, and the site itself is designated as a "Chaco outlier." Much of the rock art above the ruins falls within the same time frame and is stylistically related to that of the Chaco Canyon area. Most of the figures of this time period are solidly pecked and grouped in panels. Human stick figures with slightly rectangular bodies and small heads are characteristic. Some are depicted with their arms held up or down, others with arms and legs bent in an attitude of motion. Hand-holding couples and rows of figures also occur. Mountain sheep, deer and long-bodied animals with tails bent over their backs are the most prevalent animal figures. The fluteplayer is also a common design element, occurring in human, animal or insect form. Human handprints and footprints, as well as animal and bird tracks, are frequent. Bird figures are not so common, but those which do appear often have the long legs characteristic of wading birds or several long tail feathers, perhaps indicative of the macaw. Other popular elements include lizard figures, snakes, insects, and frogs or toads. Complex geometric designs, as well as the more simple concentric circles, spirals, frets and wavy lines, are also characteristic of this rock art.

In the early Fourteenth Century (ca. A.D. 1325-1350), an extensive artistic and ceremonial complex originating with the Jornada Mogollon to the south, spread west from the Rio Grande drainage to Zuñi and Hopi. This new artistic tradition brought with it increasingly representational human and animal forms, as well as kachina figures, masks and shields. In contrast to the deeply pecked images of earlier periods, the predominant techniques of this time period are incising, abrading and drilling, with the retention of some lighter pecking.

The Pueblo of Zuñi has encouraged the recording, preservation and study of this rock art, for it forms an important part of the Zuñi cultural heritage. On the Zuñi Reservation, permission to visit rock art sites must be obtained from the Tribal Council. Off the reservation, permission must be obtained from private landowners.

M. Jane Young
Assistant Professor
Department of Anthropology
University of Texas

Hardscrabble Wash. M. Jane Young photo.

Petroglyph Canyon. Nancy L. Bartman photo.

285

Hardscrabble Wash. M. Jane Young photo.

Hardscrabble Wash. Robert H. Leibman photo.

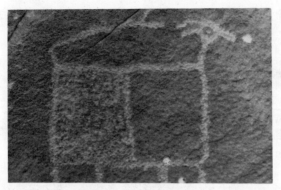

Lyman Lake area. Robert H. Leibman photo.

Hardscrabble Wash area. Robert H. Leibman photo.

Hardscrabble Wash. Robert H. Leibman photo.

Village of the Great Kivas. Nancy L. Bartman photo.

Village of the Great Kivas. M. Jane Young photo.

Hardscrabble Wash. Robert H. Leibman photo. For more photographs of rock art in this region refer to "Rock Art of the Zuni-Cibola Region" by M. Jane Young and Nancy L. Bartman.

Miscellaneous Areas

Forgotten Canyon, Glen Canyon National Recreation Area.

Fish Creek Canyon, Utah.

Clear Creek Canyon, Utah. Verne Huser photo.

Clear Creek Canyon, Utah. Verne Huser photo.

Parowan Gap, Utah. Verne Huser photo.

Parowan Gap, Utah. Verne Huser photo.

Parowan Gap, Utah. Verne Huser photo.

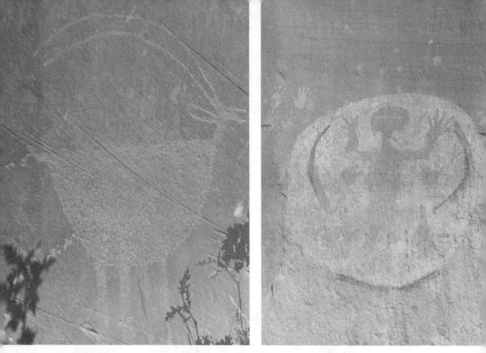

Betatakin Ruin, Navajo National Monument.

Left, Valley of Fire State Park, Nevada. Right, Valley of Fire State Park, Nevada. For more photographs of Anasazi and Fremont rock art refer to "Canyon Country Prehistoric Indians" by Barnes and Pendleton.

Anasazi Celestial Rock Art

Scholars investigate rock art for what it can tell them about the cultural groups that created the images on the canyon walls and field boulders of the Southwest. One of the most recent of these investigations studies the way in which the celestial realm is depicted in Anasazi rock art. Representations of the sun, moon and the stars are especially numerous in the rock art panels along the Rio Grande. They also appear in other regions, though with less frequency. The presence of these glyphs has led to a number of attempts to interpret their meaning. The representations of stars in the Rio Grande glyphs may be related to the Morning Star and Evening Star of historic Pueblo mythology. These powerful mythical beings, sons of the sun, were the helpers and the protectors of the Pueblo people during their emergence from the underworld. They were also the gods of war, and in the pictures that are painted on pottery or pecked on stone, they often possess claws.

Sometimes sun or moon glyphs exist in a context that suggests an interest in watching the sun or moon in order to set the calendar. For example, a panel of glyphs at Hovenweep National Monument, Utah, strongly indicates a sun-watching station. At sunrise on the summer solstice, the longest day of the year, a remarkable "sword of light" emerges to cross the pecked spirals on the left, while another sword of light creeps across a set of three concentric circles on the right. The latter symbol is the same one recognized by modern Pueblo groups as representing the sun. According to them, the central dot is the sun's umbilicus, from which his power emanates, and the three concentric circles are the rays of the sun. This striking appearance could have been used by the Anasazi who executed the glyphs to set the yearly calendar.

A particularly beautiful pictograph in Chaco Culture National Historical Park, New Mexico, has also been interpreted to mark a sunwatching station. From the cliffs directly above the glyph, the winter solstice sun would be seen to rise directly behind a break in the mesa across the canyon. Thus, here again, this time on the shortest day, the Anasazi who painted it would have had an essential mark in their yearly observations of the sun. At that time, the sun appears to halt its slow daily motion south and pause, as if making up its mind whether to return north again. It must have been an important part of Anasazi life to assure themselves that the sun would indeed turn north to warm the earth once again.

Another, more speculative, suggestion has been made for this set of pictographs. It might be a record of the explosion of a distant star in A.D. 1054. On July 4, 1054, Chinese astronomers noted a very bright new star (supernova). It stayed visible in the daytime sky for almost a month and only disappeared from the night sky after nearly two years! The explosion led to a large expanding gas cloud in the constellation Taurus that is now called the Crab Nebula. Astronomers calculate that when it appeared over Chaco Canyon, and indeed throughout the Southwest and West, the bright star appeared near the waning crescent moon — a striking visual appearance indeed, since it was brighter than any other star or planet for several days. The Chaco Canyon pictograph is a highly accurate representation of what the occurrence would have looked like to a native observer in 1054. The Anasazi culture of Chaco Canyon was flourishing at the time, and it is possible that the inhabitants of the canyon were sufficiently interested in the stellar interloper to have recorded its appearance. In all, some eighteen rock art examples of this kind are known in the western United States. When better dating techniques become available, it may be possible to know with certainty whether some of these glyphs could be records of the supernova.

Dr. Ray A. Williamson
Center for Archaeoastronomy
University of Maryland

Petroglyphs pecked on the sandstone wall of a narrow natural corridor near Holly Ruin in Hovenweep National Monument. On the left are two spirals, one partly obliterated by water seepage. On the right is the traditional Pueblo sun symbol — three concentric circles with a central dot. The outer circle is about a foot in diameter. Below and to the left of the sun symbol is a faint twin-like figure that may represent the "Twins" of Pueblo mythology, Morning Star and Evening Star. A serpent-like figure is barely visible along the right hand edge of the picture. National Park Service photo by R. L. Trick. All captions and all other photos in this section are by R. A. Williamson.

This sequence of photographs illustrates the movement of light on the Hovenweep celestial calendar on and near the summer solstice. About an hour after local sunrise, sunlight begins to penetrate the narrow corridor containing the petroglyphs. A small point of light appears first to the left of the spirals. About the time that the sword of light crosses the second spiral from the left, a second sword of light appears to the right of the sun symbol and begins to move toward the first one. After about seven minutes, the two swords meet between the spirals and the sun symbol. The pattern of sunlight then moves down the face of the boulder and illuminates the "Twin" figure and the lower part of the serpent 'glyph.

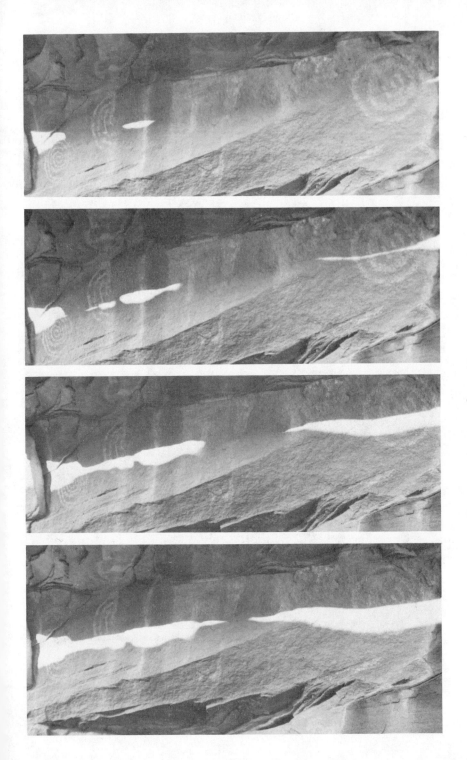

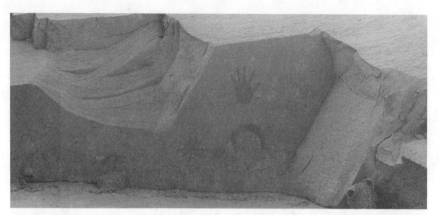

Pictographs in Chaco Culture National Historical Park. The hand, crescent and star-like figures were painted with a red pigment that is probably hematite, on a horizontal surface about fifteen feet above ground level. Note the intact swallow's nest and remnants of others. The hand is adult sized. Below the red figures, on the vertical surface, are three concentric circles with a central dot. This sun symbol was also painted in red pigment but is now barely visible. From about seventy-five feet above this site on the canyon edge there is a clear view of the eastern horizon. The horizon is broken at convenient places for marking a solar calendar, especially the winter solstice.

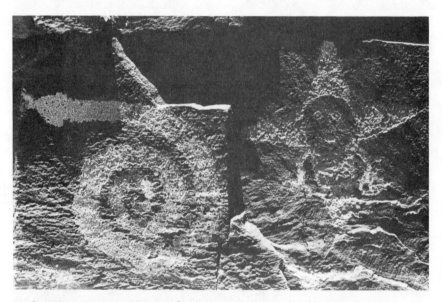

Coiled snake and "Morning Star" petroglyphs in the Abo district south of Albuquerque. Note the face and claws on the Morning Star figure. The snake is partly covered with lichens. For more photographs and information about prehistoric celestial rock art refer to "Archaeoastronomy in the Americas" edited by R. A. Williamson.

298

BIBLIOGRAPHY

Following is a partial list of the books, scientific papers and other literature used for research during the writing of this book:

Aikens, C. M., *Indian Petroglyphs from White Pine County, Nevada,* Anthropological Paper No. 19, University of Utah, 1978.

Appleton, LeRoy, *American Indian Design and Decoration,* 1950, Dover reprint, 1971.

Barnes & Pendelton, *Canyon Country Prehistoric Indians,* Wasatch Publishers, 1979.

Bartlett, J. R., *Personal Narrative of Explorations and Incidents in Texas, New Mexico, California, Sonora and Chihuahua, 1850-1853,* 1854, Rio Grande Press reprint, 1965.

Bartless, R. A., *Great Surveys of the American West,* University of Oklahoma Press, 1962.

Beck & Haase, *Historical Atlas of New Mexico,* University of Oklahoma Press, 1969.

Berry, M. S., *An Archaeological Survey of the Northeast Portion of Arches National Park,* Antiquities Section Selected Papers Vol. 1, No. 3, Utah State Historical Society, 1975.

Boas, Franz, *Primitive Art,* Harvard University Press 1928, Dover reprint, 1955.

Bolton, H. E., *Pageant in the Wilderness,* Utah State Historical Society, 1972.

Bolton, H. E., *Coronado on the Turquoise Trail,* University of New Mexico Press, 1949.

Brandt & Williamson, *The 1054 Supernova and Native American Rock Art,* Archaeoastronomy No. 1, supplement to Journal for the History of Astronomy, Vol. 10, 1979.

Brandt, J. C., *Pictographs and Petroglyphs of the Southwest Indians,* Technology Review, December, 1977.

Busby, Fleming, Hayes & Nissen, *The Manufacture of Petroglyphs: Additional Replicative Experiments from the Western Great Basin,* North American Rock Art No. 1, Ballena Press, 1978.

Castleton, K. B., *Petroglyphs and Pictographs of Utah,* Utah Museum of Natural History, two volumes, 1978 and 1979.

Cole, S. J., *The History of the Sacred and Fantastic: Image and Symbol in Early and Primitive Art,* Department of Art, Mesa College, Colorado, 1981.

Cressman, L. S., *Prehistory of the Far West,* University of Utah Press, 1977.

Day & Dibble, *Archaeological Survey of the Flaming Gorge Reservoir Area, Wyoming-Utah,* Anthropological Paper No. 65, Department of Anthropology, University of Utah, 1963.

Dellenbaugh, F. S., *The Romance of the Colorado River,* 1904, Rio Grande Press reprint, 1965.

Dodge, B. S., *The Story of Inscription Rock,* Phoenix Publishing, 1975.

Dorman, J. E., *The Archaeology of Eastern Utah,* College of Eastern Utah Prehistoric Museum, 1980.

Driver, H. E., *Indians of North America,* University of Chicago Press, 1961.

Evans, T., *A Heritage of Prehistoric Art,* from Our Public Lands, a BLM publication, Fall 1973 edition.

Ferg, A., *Petroglyphs of the Silver Creek/Fivemile Draw Confluence, Snowflake, Arizona,* University of Arizona Undergraduate Archaeological Field School, 1974.

Fewkes, J. W., *Sikyatki and its Pottery,* 1898, Dover reprint, 1973.

Fewkes, J. W., *Designs on Prehistoric Hopi Pottery,* 1919, Dover reprint, 1973.

Frazier, K., *The Anasazi Sun Dagger,* Science 80, November/December 1979 edition.

Garvin, G., *Shamans and Rock Art Symbols,* North American Rock Art No. 1, Ballena Press, 1978.

Gibson & Singer, *Ven-195: Treasure House of Prehistoric Cave Art,* North American Rock Art No. 1, Ballena Press, 1978.

Gillin, J., *Archaeological Investigations in Nine Mile Canyon, Utah: A Republication,* Anthropological Paper No. 21, Department of Anthropology, University of Utah, 1955.

Grant, C., *Rock Art of the American Indian,* 1967, Outbooks reprint, 1981.

Grant, C., *Canyon de Chelly, Its People and Rock Art,* University of Arizona Press, 1978.

Gunnerson, J. H., *The Fremont Culture: A Study in Cultural Dynamics on the Northern Anasazi Frontier,* Papers of the Peabody Museum of Archaeology and Ethnology, Vol. 59, No. 2, Harvard University, 1969.

deHaan, P. A., *An Archaeological Survey of Lower Montezuma Canyon, Southeastern Utah,* Department of Anthropology and Archaeology, Brigham Young University, 1972, unpublished.

Hunger, K. F. H., *Ritual Coition in Pre-Columbian Rock Art,* University of Dusseldorf, 1981.

Heizer & Hester, *Two Petroglyph Sites in Lincoln County, Nevada,* North American Rock Art No. 1, Ballena Press, 1978.

Hibben, F. C., *Kiva Art of the Anasazis,* KC Publications, 1975.

Hobler & Hobler, *An Archeological Survey of Upper White Canyon Area, Southeastern Utah,* Antiquities Section Selected Papers, Vol. 5, No. 13, Utah State Historical Society, 1978.

Hurst & Louthan, *Survey of Rock Art in the Central Portion of Nine Mile Canyon, Eastern Utah,* Brigham Young University Printing Service, 1979.

Ives, J. C., *Report Upon the Colorado River of the West,* 1861, Da Capo Press reprint, 1969.

James, Janetsky & Vlasich, *Prehistory, Ethnohistory and History of Eastern Nevada,* BLM Cultural Resource Series No. 3, 1981.

Jennings, J. D., *Glen Canyon: A Summary,* Department of Anthropology, University of Utah, 1966.

Jennings, J. D., *Prehistory of Utah and the Eastern Great Basin,* Anthropological Paper No. 98, University of Utah Press, 1978.

Koenig, S. H., *Stars, Crescents and Supernovae in Southwestern Indian Art,* Archaeoastronomy No. 1, 1979.

Lindsay, L. W., *Big Westwater Ruin,* Utah BLM Cultural Series No. 9, 1981.

Lucius. W. A. et al. *Archaeological Investigations in the Maze District, Canyonlands National Park, Utah,* Antiquities Section Selected Papers Vol. 3, No. 11, Utah State Historical Society, 1976.

Mallery G., *Picture Writing of the American Indians,* Bureau of American Ethnology, 1889, Dover reprint, 1972.

Manning, S. J., *A Hypothesis for a Pueblo IV Date for the Barrier Canyon Style,* ARARA Symposium Paper, 1981.

Martineau, LaVan, *The Rocks Begin to Speak,* KC Publications, 1973.

Mayer, D., *Miller's Hypothesis: Some California and Nevada Evidence,* Archaeoastronomy No. 1, 1979.

McKern, W. C., *Western Colorado Petroglyphs,* BLM Cultural Resources Series, written 1922, published 1978.

Mera, H. P., *Pueblo Designs — The Rainbird,* Laboratory of Anthropology, 1938, Dover reprint, 1970.

Mertz, H., *Pale Ink,* Swallow Press, 1972.

Minor, R., *The Pit-And-Groove Petroglyph Style in Southern California,* Ethnic Technology Notes No. 15, San Diego Museum of Man, 1975.

Morss, N., *The Ancient Culture of the Fremont River in Utah, Report on the Explorations under the Claflin-Emerson Fund, 1928-29,* Papers of the Peabody Museum of American Archaeology and Ethnology, Harvard University, 1931, Kraus reprint, 1978.

Newberry, J. S., *Report of the Expedition from Santa Fe, New Mexico, to the Junction of the Grand and Green Rivers of the Great Colorado River of the West, in 1859, under command of Captain J. N. Macomb, Corps of Topographical Engineers, U. S. Army,* U. S. Government Printing Office, 1876.

Nordenskiold, G. E. A., *The Cliff Dwellers of the Mesa Verde,* 1893, Rio Grande Press reprint, 1979.

Oppelt, N. T., *Prehistoric Ruins of the Southwest,* Pruett Publishing, 1981.

Pike & Muench, *Anasazi,* American West Publishing, 1974.

Powell, J. W., *The Exploration of the Colorado River and its Canyons,* 1895, Dover reprint, 1961.

Pratt, A. G., *Rock Art of the Unitah Basin,* 1972.

Schaafsma, P., *Rock Art in the Navajo Reservoir District,* Museum of New Mexico Press, Papers in Anthropology, No. 7, 1963.

Schaafsma, P., *A Survey of Tsegi Canyon Rock Art,* National Park Service, about 1966, unpublished.

Schaafsma, P., *Rock Art in the Cochiti Reservoir District,* Museum of New Mexico Press, Papers in Anthropology, No. 16, 1967.

Schaafsma, P., *The Rock Art of Utah,* Peabody Museum, Harvard University, 1971.

Schaafsma, P., *Rock Art of New Mexico,* University of New Mexico Press, 1975.

Schaafsma, P., *Rock Art and Ideology of the Mimbres and Jornado Mogollon,* The Artifact, Vol. 13, No. 3, El Paso Archaeological Society, 1975.

Schaafsma, P., *Indian Rock Art of the Southwest,* University of New Mexico Press, 1980.

Sharrock, F. W., *An Archaeological Survey of Canyonlands National Park,* Department of Anthropology, University of Utah, 1966.

Shutler & Shutler, *Archaeological Survey in Southern Nevada,* Nevada State Museum, Anthropological Papers, No. 7, 1962.

Siegrist, R., *Prehistoric Petroglyphs and Pictographs in Utah,* Utah Museum of Fine Arts, 1972.

Steed Jr., P. P., *Rock Art in Chaco Canyon,* El Paso Archaeological Society, 1980.

Steward, J. H., *Petroglyphs of the United States,* Smithsonian Institution Annual Report, 1936, Shorey reprint, 1972.

Stokes & Stokes, *Messages on Stone,* Starstone Publishing, 1980.

Sutherland, K., *Petroglyphs at Three Rivers, New Mexico,* The Artifact, Vol. 16, No. 2, El Paso Archaeological Society, 1978.

Swartz Jr., B. K., *Aluminum Powder: A Technique for Photographically Recording Petroglyphs,* American Antiquity, Vol. 28, No. 3, 1963.

Swartz Jr., B. K., *Klamath Basin Petroglyphs,* Ballena Press Anthropological Papers, No. 12, 1978.

Turner II, C. G., *Petroglyphs of the Glen Canyon Region,* Glen Canyon Series No. 4, Museum of Northern Arizona Bulletin No. 38, 1963.

Walker & Bufkin, *Historical Atlas of Arizona,* University of Oklahoma Press, 1979.

Wellmann, K. F., *Kokopelli of Indian Paleology,* Journal of the American Medical Association, Vol. 212, June 8, 1970.

Wellmann, K. F., *Ancient Designs and Modern Man in North America,* The Artifact, Vol. 13, No. 4, El Paso Archaeological Society, 1975.

Wellmann, K. F., *An Astronomical Petroglyph in Capitol Reef National Park,* from Southwest Lore, 1976.

Wellmann, K. F., *A Survey of Style Designations in North American Indian Rock Art,* The Artifact, Vol. 17, No. 1, El Paso Archaeological Society, 1979.

Wellmann, K. F., *Further Remarks on an Astronomical Petroglyph in Capitol Reef National Park, Utah,* Archeoastronomy No. 1, 1979.

Wellmann, K. F., *North American Indian Rock Art,* Akademische Druck — u. Verlagsanstalt, Graz, Austria, 1979.

Williamson, R. A., *Native Americans were Continent's First Astronomers,* Smithsonian, October, 1978.

Young & Bartman, *Rock Art of the Zuñi-Cibola Region,* 1981.

Zwinger, A., *Wind in the Rock*, Harper & Row, 1978.

American Indian Rock Art, Volumes I through VII, American Rock Art Research Association, published 1975 through 1982.

Archaeoastronomy in the Americas, edited by R. A. Williamson, Ballena Press/Center for Archaeoastronomy, 1981.

Artificial Colouring of Sandstone and Concrete, National Parks & Wildlife Service and Department of Main Roads, N. S. W., Australia, letter dated 5 July 1968.

Canyon Graphics & Graffiti, Utah Museum of Natural History, undated.

Fremont Perspectives, edited by D. B. Madsen, Antiquities Section Selected Papers Vol. VII, No. 16, Utah State Historical Society, 1980.

Prehistoric Indian Rock Art: Issues and Concerns, edited by Tilberg & Meighan, Monograph XIX, University of California at Los Angeles, Institute of Archaeology, 1981.

Seven Rock Art Sites in Baja California, edited by Meighan & Pontoni, Ballena Press, 1978.

The Care and Repair of Petrolglyphs, BLM Technical Note 6231 (D-370), 1969.

Hardscrabble Wash area, Arizona. R. H. Leibman photo.

OTHER
CANYON COUNTRY
PUBLICATIONS

The above guidebooks and maps can be purchased from retail outlets throughout canyon country or ordered directly from Wasatch Publishers. Please send for the current price list.

Wasatch Publishers, Inc.
4647 Idlewild Road
Salt Lake City, Utah 84124